FOOTBALL CLUB
ORIGINS AND NICKNAMES

FOOTBALL CLUB
ORIGINS AND NICKNAMES

MICHAEL HEATLEY

Ian Allan
PUBLISHING

Photo
The author would like to thank all the clubs that co-operated by supplying photographs, especially AFC Wimbledon, FC United of Manchester, Sheffield FC, Fulham FC and Walsall FC.

Thanks also to Drew Heatley (ground photos), EMI Records and Dennis Turner (vintage programmes and cigarette cards).

All other photos/memorabilia are from the author's collection or The Footballer library.

First published 2008
Reprinted 2008

ISBN (10) 0 7110 3271 8
ISBN (13) 978 0 7110 3271 2

Published by Ian Allan Publishing, Riverdene Business Park, Hersham, Surrey, KT12 4RG
Printed in England by Ian Allan Printing Ltd, Hersham, Surrey, KT12 4RG

Code: 0810/A

Visit the Ian Allan Publishing website at www.ianallanpublishing.com

Contents

Appendices

Timeline

1862	Notts County formed.
1863	Stoke City formed as Stoke Ramblers.
1865	Nottingham Forest formed.
1866	Chesterfield formed.
1867	Sheffield Wednesday formed as The Wednesday Cricket & Football Club.
1871	Reading formed.
1872	Wrexham formed.
1873	Glasgow Rangers officially formed.
1874	Aston Villa formed; Bolton Wanderers formed as Christ Church FC.
1875	Birmingham City and Blackburn Rovers formed.
1876	Middlesbrough and Port Vale formed.
1877	Crewe Alexandra formed; Rotherham formed as Thornhill United.
1878	Everton and Ipswich Town formed; Manchester United formed as Newton Heath LYR, Grimsby Town formed as Grimsby Pelham, West Bromwich Albion formed as West Bromwich Strollers.
1879	Doncaster Rovers and Fulham formed; Sunderland formed as Sunderland and District Teachers' AFC, Wolverhampton Wanderers created from the merger of St. Luke's FC and Wanderers FC.
1880	Preston North End committed themselves to association football having dabbled in the past with other sports.
1881	Preston North End formed (as football club), Swindon Town formed; Leyton Orient formed as Glyn Cricket and Football Club, Newcastle United formed as Stanley, Watford formed as Watford Rovers.

1882	Burnley formed; Tottenham formed as Hotspur Football Club.
1883	Darlington formed; Bristol Rovers formed as Black Arabs, Coventry City formed as Singers FC, Stockport County formed as Heaton Norris Rovers.
1884	Derby County, Lincoln City and Workington Town formed; Leicester City formed as Leicester Fosse, Tranmere Rovers formed as Belmont AFC.
1885	Bury, Luton Town and Chester City formed; Millwall formed as Millwall Rovers, Queens Park Rangers formed as St Jude's, Southampton formed as Southampton St Mary's.
1886	Shrewsbury Town and Kidderminster Harriers formed; Arsenal formed as Royal Arsenal, Plymouth Argyle formed as Argyle Athletic Club.
1887	Barnsley, Blackpool and Wycombe Wanderers formed; Manchester City formed as Ardwick FC.
1888	Football League founded by 12 clubs: Accrington, Aston Villa, Blackburn Rovers, Bolton Wanderers, Burnley, Derby County, Everton, Notts County, Preston North End, Stoke, West Bromwich Albion and Wolverhampton Wanderers. Barnet founded; Walsall founded as Walsall Town Swifts.
1889	Brentford and Sheffield United formed, Wimbledon formed under the name of Wimbledon Old Centrals.
1890	AFC Bournemouth formed as Boscombe St John's; Sunderland join League.
1892	Cheltenham Town, Liverpool and Leeds United formed. The new

	Division 2 of the Football League is formed. Birmingham City, Crewe Alexandra and Sheffield United attain league status.
1893	Gillingham formed as New Brompton, Oxford United formed as Headington United. Arsenal and Newcastle United attain league status.
1894	Bristol City formed as Bristol South End. Northwich Victoria leave league; Bury attain league status.
1895	Yeovil formed; Oldham Athletic formed as Pine Villa, West Ham formed as Thames Ironworks.
1896	Blackpool attain league status.
1897	Mansfield Town formed as Mansfield Wesleyans. Burton Wanderers leave league; Luton Town join.
1898	Portsmouth formed. Barnsley attain league status.
1899	Scunthorpe United formed; Cardiff City formed as Riverside FC, Torquay formed as Torquay Town. Blackpool lose League status (regained 1900); Middlesborough gain it.
1900	Thames Ironworks is wound up and reformed under the name of West Ham United. Loughborough leave league; Stockport County join league.
1901	Brighton and Hove Albion formed. Bristol City join league.
1902	Norwich City formed.
1903	Bradford City formed and attain league status; Carlisle United formed as Shaddongate United.
1904	Hull City formed. Stockport County leave league.
1905	Charlton Athletic, Chelsea and Crystal Palace formed. Stockport County rejoin league, Leyton Orient also join.
1906	Southend United formed.
1907	Rochdale formed. Burton United are replaced in League by Fulham.
1908	Huddersfield Town formed; Hartlepool United formed as
	Hartlepools United, Riverside FC becomes Cardiff City. Tottenham Hotspur join league.
1909	Dundee United formed as Dundee Hibernian.
1910	Mansfield Wesley renamed Mansfield Town; the club previously named Millwall Rovers then Millwall Athletic become Millwall. Huddersfield Town join league.
1911	Halifax Town formed.
1912	Newport County formed; Swansea formed as Swansea Town.
1919	Leeds United formed; Cambridge United are formed under the name of Abbey United. Port Vale join League after Leeds City are ejected, West Ham United join league, South Shields, the name under which Gateshead were formed, join league.
1920	Division Three formed with the members being: Brentford, Brighton, Bristol Rovers, Crystal Palace, Exeter, Gillingham, Luton, Merthyr Town, Millwall, Grimsby Town, Newport County, Northampton Town, Norwich City, Plymouth Argyle, Portsmouth, Queens Park Rangers, Reading, Southampton, Southend, Swansea, Swindon, Watford. Cardiff attain league status.
1921	Football League takes on a new face and now consists of four divisions: Division 1, Division 2, Division 3 (North) and Division 3 (South). Charlton Athletic join league.
1923	Bournemouth & Boscombe Athletic attain League status. Wembley stages its first F.A. Cup Final.
1924	Hereford United formed.
1927	Torquay United join league, Aberdare Athletic leave league.
1928	Carlisle United attain league status.
1929	Sheffield Wednesday becomes the official new name for the Wednesday Cricket & Football Club.

1930	South Shields become Gateshead FC. Merthyr Town leave league.
1931	Newport County leave league.
1932	Wigan Athletic formed. Newport rejoin league.
1934	Boston United and Peterborough United formed.
1937	Colchester United formed.
1950	Scunthorpe United, Colchester United and Shrewsbury Town join league.
1951	Workington Town join league, Abbey United change their name to Cambridge United.
1958	Division Three (North) and Division Three (South) revamped into Divisions 3 and 4.
1960	The League Cup introduced into the English game. Gateshead leave league, Peterborough join league.
1962	Oxford United join the league.
1965	Five days after his fiftieth birthday, Sir Stanley Matthews retires from professional football.
1967	Celtic beat Inter Milan 2–1 in Lisbon to become the first British club to win the European Cup.
1968	Manchester United become the first English club to win the European cup when they beat Benfica 4–1 at Wembley Stadium.
1970	Bradford Park Avenue leave league, Cambridge United join league.
1972	In frustration at not finding a place in the English Football League, Wigan Athletic apply to join the

Sir Stanley Matthews who, having continued to play until the age of 50, holds the record as the oldest player ever to play in England's top flight. Here Sir Stanley proudly displays his 'magic boots' at a guest appearance some years later.

CLUB FACTS

Of the Football League's twelve founder members, Preston North End are the only club still playing on the same ground as they did all those years ago. Although they were still a cricket club at the time, Preston North End first took a lease on Deepdale on January 21st 1875, with the first football match under Association rules taking place on October 5th 1878. By contrast, Queens Park Rangers have led a nomadic existence, playing on no less than 13 different grounds since their formation in 1886. Perhaps Queens Park Rovers might have been a more appropriate name...

Scottish League to no avail. Bournemouth & Boscombe Athletic change their name to AFC Bournemouth. Barrow leave league and Hereford United join.

1977   Workington leave league, Wimbledon join league.

1978   Southport fail to be re-elected to the Football League, Wigan Athletic join.

1983   Chester FC change their name to Chester City.

1986   Middlesbrough re-formed after liquidation.

1987   Lincoln City leave league, Scarborough join.

1988   Newport County leave league, Lincoln City join.

1989   Darlington leave league, Maidstone United join.

1990   Darlington rejoin league, Colchester leave league.

1991   Barnet join League.

1992   FA Premier League formed. Founder members: Arsenal, Aston Villa, Blackburn Rovers, Chelsea, Coventry City, Crystal Palace, Everton, Ipswich, Leeds, Liverpool, Manchester City, Manchester United, Middlesborough, Norwich, Nottingham Forest, Oldham, Queens Park Rangers, Sheffield United, Sheffield Wednesday, Southampton, Tottenham Hotspur, Wimbledon. Colchester United join league. Troubled Aldershot resign from league as do Maidstone United.

1993   Halifax Town leave league, Wycombe Wanderers join.

1996   Macclesfield Town fail to join league due to their ground not being up to scratch.

1997   Hereford United leave league, Macclesfield Town make it into the League.

1998   Doncaster Rovers leave league, Halifax Town join.

1999   Scarborough leave league, Cheltenham Town join league.

2000   Chester City leave league, Kidderminster Harriers join.

2001   Barnet leave league, Rushden & Diamonds join.

2002   Halifax Town leave league, Boston United join.

2003   Exeter City and Shrewsbury leave league, Yeovil Town and Doncaster Rovers join.

2004   Carlisle United and York City leave league, Chester City and Shrewsbury Town join. Wimbledon become Milton Keynes Dons.

2005   Barnet and Carlisle United join league, Kidderminster and Cambridge United leave.

2006   Accrington Stanley and Hereford United join league, Rushden & Diamonds and Oxford United leave.

2007   Boston United and Torquay exit league, Dagenham & Redbridge and Morecambe join.

Introduction

"And they'll be dancing in the streets of Raith tonight . . . "

Ironically the famous quote from the 1960s – attributed to BBC sports broadcaster David Coleman but actually said by his Scots colleague Sam Leitch – has rung down the years. The club in question is located in Kirkcaldy, Fife – a fact Sky Sports' Jeff Stelling is well aware of, and one he played on whenever Welsh team Total Network Solutions (now The New Saints FC) won a game.

This in turn inspired the song 'Dancing In The Streets Of TNS' (Stelling's catchphrase) by the band Project Valkyrie which was performed at half-time when the club was drawn against Liverpool in the 2005 Champions League. The cyclical nature of football fact and folklore has surely never been so graphically demonstrated...

TNS are perhaps the best example of how sponsorship, or football's need/greed for money, has changed the face of the game. At a slightly lesser level, Arsenal, Bolton, Stoke and Huddersfield are just four clubs playing in stadia to whom the 'naming rights' have been sold.

The changing nature of football has undoubtedly been accelerated by three forces – the Premiership, which formalised the divide between the top clubs and the rest, Sky

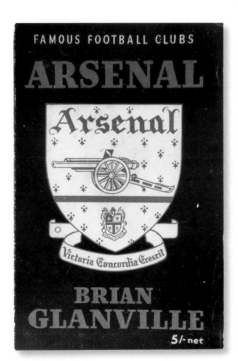

FAMOUS FOOTBALL CLUBS

ARSENAL

Arsenal

Victoria Concordia Crescit

BRIAN
GLANVILLE

5/- net

television, whose money has confirmed and exaggerated it, and the gentrification of the game which followed the Taylor Report. As grounds became all-seated, so ticket prices increased and the game lost its working-class tag to become a game for the monied fan and corporate client.

Not everybody is in favour of this, of course. Roy Keane expressed his contempt for the 'prawn sandwich brigade' when at Manchester United, but the fact that such a small percentage of true fans were able to get tickets for the first FA Cup Final at the 'new Wembley' in 2007 showed a certain contempt. The FA retained 40,000 of the 90,000 total for themselves, their representatives and Club Wembley, the 'prawn sandwich brigade' whose money helps finance its running.

Worse, when Liverpool went to Athens the same month to attempt to reclaim the Champions League trophy, they had only 11,000 tickets for regular supporters to service an estimated 50,000 travelling fans. Little wonder there was trouble, UEFA then attempting to blame the fans to avoid facing up to their own failings.

In times like these it is even more important for supporters to know all they can about the origins of their football club. They may find that, as it rises up the footballing 'pyramid' towards the summit, much is gained but an equal amount of priceless history and tradition is, if not lost, at least forgotten. The arrival of foreign owners, allied to the large number of overseas-born players in our game, suggests that awareness of history may quickly be fading.

So much goes to make up the nature of the football club. The soul that cannot be bought or sold…until they compound their move from the time-honoured old ground by flogging the naming rights of the new one! The badge that has graced the shirt since time immemorial? They've brought in an ad agency to redesign it! The club colours worn by so many legends? Changed…

The historical details in this book will, sooner or later, become outdated, but at the time of writing they are worth your consideration. Clubs have disappeared and will continue to do so in the face of commercial pressure. There can only be so many winners, but the losers now have further to fall – and with increasing risks being taken to maintain or improve status, there will be many more Leeds Uniteds in seasons to come.

Chelsea and Fulham must hope Messrs Abramovich and Fayed look both ways before crossing the road, as must supporters of all clubs being run beyond their means. But the prestige of the Premiership will ensure that, for those clubs at least, there will never be a shortage of would-be investors from all corners of the world. It's just unfortunate that more of the wealth does not trickle down to those waiting for crumbs off their table.

It is interesting to note that, two decades ago, it was widely forecast that clubs in the lower two English divisions would go part-time and play in regionalised leagues. Instead, the non-league game has a sizeable fully professional segment, the stakes upped by relegated league clubs anxious to 'bounce back'.

Enjoy this pot pourri of football history, trivia, folklore and tradition.

Michael Heatley

The author would like to acknowledge the assistance of Peter Gamble, Alan Kinsman Dennis Turner and Chris Mason in the preparation of this book.

An understanding of a club's history has long been important to many football fans, as amply demonstrated by these publications (both) from Tottenham Hotspur (and arch-rivals Arsenal). Such publications are designed to commemorate the club's history but does this admiration of the past remain in today's big-money game?

FAMOUS FOOTBALL CLUBS

1/-

OFFICIAL HISTORY OF TOTTENHAM HOT-SPURS

THE EXCITING STORY OF TOTTENHAM HOTSPURS. SIXTY-SIX YEARS OF FOOTBALL THRILLS . . . GREAT GAMES AND GREAT PLAYERS OF THE PAST AND PRESENT

by FRED WARD

SPURS

Julian Holland

The Complete Official Story of Tottenham Hotspur F. C.

PART I: Origins

Chapter 1

Sheffield FC

At the end of the 2006–07 season, as Sheffield United suffered the misery of relegation from the Premiership, another famous Sheffield club was celebrating promotion. No, not Wednesday (although Owls fans had plenty to shout about after a splendid run-in left them 9th in the Championship). It was Sheffield FC, officially the oldest football club in the world, who topped the Northern Counties East League to secure a place in the Unibond League First Division, a brilliant way to mark this proud old club's 150th anniversary.

Sheffield FC's anniversary was also marked with a friendly against Inter Milan, a match attended by Pele, perhaps the most famous footballer of all time. The club also have links with the mighty Real Madrid, these two being the only clubs in the world to have been awarded the FIFA Order of Merit. The awards were made at a special ceremony in Paris in 2004, when Sheffield FC's chairman, Richard Tims, stood proudly shoulder to shoulder with the legendary Alfredo Di Stefano and Emilio Butragueno. Real Madrid received the award for being the most successful club in Europe during the preceding 100 years. Sheffield FC received their citation in recognition of their historical importance to the world's most popular sport, and for their contribution to its development into the game we love today.

Football had been played in various forms in England since the Middle Ages, and by the end of the 18th century, most of the country's public schools played football in some manner. The working classes also played the game, sometimes in small groups on local common land, sometimes in noisy crowds through the streets of villages and towns, and occasionally whole communities would compete against each other over 'pitches' several miles in length with 'goals' in each of the opposing towns or villages. This kind of football sometimes posed a threat to public order, and there are several recorded instances of the army being called out to quell riots resulting from overzealous participation in the rough and tumble. No, there were football clubs in existence before Sheffield FC, but Sheffield's importance lies in their constant re-evaluation of the rules of the game, and in introducing and refining several of the important features of the sport as we know it today.

Back in the middle of the 19th century, behind the walls of England's top educational establishments, football was seen as a way of building character, and instilling a sense of teamwork and discipline in the pupils. The Victorians made a strong link between a healthy body and a healthy mind, and football was seen as one of the ways this balance could be achieved. The problem was that each school played the game according to its own set of rules, and this clearly stopped any of them playing against any of the others. Things were no different in the country at large, and competition was limited to local teams who played by the same rules. Sides could include

The earliest known team picture of Sheffield FC, dating from 1857.

as many as twenty players, games were of unspecified lengths, and there were no standard rules about handling the ball, or what constituted unacceptable physical contact.

The Cambridge Rules

Even within a single town, not every team played to the same code. In Cambridge, a large open space known as Parker's Piece was used for football by a number of local sides, and in 1848 the idea of assembling a definitive set of rules to broaden competition and settle the frequent disputes that arose was put forward by a group of Cambridge players. Soon afterwards, representatives of several major public schools – Eton, Harrow, Marlborough, Rugby, Shrewsbury and Westminster – got together at Cambridge University to formulate what soon became known as the Cambridge Rules, the first attempt to create a unified

code under which the different sides could play each other. Copies of the new code were attached to trees around Parker's Piece, and slowly gained acceptance among the teams that played there. In the years that followed, the Cambridge Rules were gradually adopted by teams in the surrounding countryside, and they are now acknowledged as the oldest set of rules governing the game of football in existence.

Under the 1848 rules, goals were awarded for balls kicked between the flagposts (or uprights) and beneath a string stretched between them. Players were forbidden to catch the ball and run with it, but were allowed to catch the ball directly from a kick, provided they, in turn, kicked it immediately. Only the goalkeeper was allowed to hold the ball, and he could also punch it from anywhere in his own half of the field, a privilege that goalkeepers retained as late as 1912!

There were rules regarding restarting play after the ball had left the field, including goal kicks and throw-ins, and even an offside rule:

'If the ball has passed a player, and has come from the direction of his own goal, he may not touch it till the other side have kicked it, unless there are more than three of the other side before him. No player is allowed to loiter between the ball and the adversaries' goal.'

Surprisingly, given their origins in the often violent public school game, the Cambridge Rules placed severe restrictions on physical contact, both 'pushing with the hands' and 'tripping' being expressly forbidden.

The Sheffield Rules

Football was gaining in popularity across the nation by this time, and many cricket clubs began to see the game as a way for their players to maintain fitness levels during the long winter months. It wasn't only cricketers who were taking up football – in Sheffield, members of a fencing club in Clarkehouse Road are recorded as playing the game as early as 1852. Two years later a new cricket club was formed in the city, choosing the name Sheffield United, thought to be the first sports club in the world to use the name 'United'. By the end of the year, Sheffield United CC had taken a 99-year lease on some land next to Bramall Lane, and by April 1855, the first game of cricket on the new pitch had been played. It wasn't long before some of the cricket club members were organising informal games of football and, by May 1857, these kick-abouts were sufficiently well-established for the idea of a separate football club to be proposed.

The men responsible were two Old Harrovians: Nathaniel Creswick, a solicitor and chairman of a silver plate company, and William Prest, a local wine merchant. From their initial, informal discussion in the late spring came the idea of Sheffield FC, which officially came into being at a meeting on 24th October 1857. At this historic meeting, Creswick was elected the club's first Secretary and Captain, and the club's headquarters were set up in makeshift premises in a greenhouse and a potting shed in the garden of Park House at the end of East Bank Road.

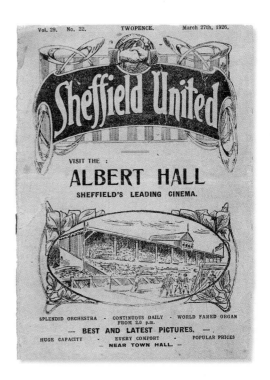

Even before the club officially came into existence, Creswick and Prest had been giving some thought to a set of rules for the club to play by. They had experience of the game from their days at Harrow, but wanted to see if the other public schools had variations in the rules that might improve the game, so they wrote to a number of them requesting copies of the codes they used. From these, they drew up a new code that became known as the Sheffield Rules. They were as follows:

- The kick from the middle must be a place kick.
- Kick Out must not be more than 25 yards out of goal.
- Fair Catch is a catch from any player provided the ball has not touched the ground or has not been thrown from touch and is entitled to a free-kick.
- Charging is fair in case of a place kick (with the exception of a kick off as soon as a player offers to kick) but he may always draw back unless he has actually touched the ball with his foot.

- Pushing with the hands is allowed but no hacking or tripping up is fair under any circumstances whatever.
- No player may be held or pulled over.
- It is not lawful to take the ball off the ground (except in touch) for any purpose whatever.
- The ball may be pushed or hit with the hand, but holding the ball except in the case of a free kick is altogether disallowed.
- A goal must be kicked but not from touch nor by a free kick from a catch.
- A ball in touch is dead, consequently the side that touches it down must bring it to the edge of the touch and throw it straight out from touch.
- Each player must provide himself with a red and dark blue flannel cap, one colour to be worn by each side.

Under Sheffield Rules, football was a more physical sport than it had been under Cambridge Rules, and allowed for more pushing, shoving and shoulder charging, although tripping and hacking were still frowned upon. The rules also allowed players to catch the ball in order to earn a free kick, and the best idea of what a game under Sheffield Rules might have looked like can probably be gained from watching Aussie rules football, which started in 1858, and was based closely on the Sheffield game.

For the first few years, Sheffield FC members seem to have played games organised from within their own ranks. Teams would be drawn up in some arbitrary fashion – members whose surnames started with the letters A to M would play those with surnames beginning N to Z, married members would play unmarried members, those drawn from the professional classes would play those from trades, and so on. If there were any other clubs to play in the city, Sheffield FC appear not to have played them, but all this changed on Boxing Day 1860, when a game against a new local side, Hallam FC, was played at Hallam's ground in Sandygate Road. This historic game was not only the world's first derby match, but also the first of what has become the longest-running derby in the world, since Sheffield and Hallam still play each other every year in what has become known as the Sheffield or Rules Derby.

Hallam FC claim to be the second oldest football club still in existence, although this is disputed by Cray Wanderers, also formed in 1860. What isn't in doubt is Hallam's claim to have the oldest football ground in the world – almost 150 years after that first historic game against Sheffield FC, Hallam still play at Sandygate Road, an achievement recognised by the Guinness Book of World Records.

The Sheffield Rules were under constant revision, and in 1861, the idea of 'rouges' was introduced. Rouges were flags placed four yards either side of the goal, which was now reduced in width from eight yards to four yards. If the ball was kicked over the line between the rouge and the goalpost and subsequently touched down, the team scored a 'rouge'. In the event of each side scoring an equal number of goals, the team scoring the most rouges would be declared the winners.

By 1862, the game had grown in popularity to such an extent in Sheffield that there were now 15 football clubs in the city, all playing by the Sheffield Rules. The first published version of the rule book appeared, although its existence doesn't seem to have prevented some violent disagreements on the field of play. The first football match at Bramall Lane was played in December 1862, and was, fittingly, the Sheffield Derby. On this occasion, it was played to raise money for the Lancashire Distress Fund, making it the world's first charity match, but the players themselves seem to have been less than charitable towards each other. A local newspaper report described it as 'The Battle of Bramall Lane' (a name which would, incidentally, also be given to the events of a 2002 match between Sheffield United and West Bromwich Albion) and went on to say that 'Creswick was being held by two players and accidentally punched one of them (Waterfall). A general riot ensued after which Waterfall was sent to guard the goal as punishment.'

Sheffield FC spreading the gospel of football in Africa.

The FA Rules

Until now, football had developed in a rather haphazard manner in various parts of the country, but the idea of a governing body which would formalise a set of rules and oversee the development of the game wasn't long in coming. In 1863, members of the country's leading clubs and public schools met in the Freemason's Tavern in Great Queen Street in London to discuss the formation of what would become known as the Football Association. Represented that day were Barnes, Blackheath, Crusaders, Crystal Palace, Forest (of Leytonstone, later to become The Wanderers), Kensington School, No Names (Kilburn), Perceval House School, Surbiton and War Office.

Prior to the historic meeting in London, Ebenezer Cobb Morley, a leading light in the formation of the FA, and its first Honorary Secretary, had drawn up a list of 23 rules for consideration by the committee. The earlier Cambridge Rules formed the backbone of Morley's list, although he re-introduced some of the more physical elements of the game retained in the rules still being used in the public schools.

Recommending his version of the Cambridge Rules to the committee, Morley said 'they embrace the true principles of the game, with the greatest simplicity', while committee member JF Alcock agreed 'the Cambridge Rules appear to be the most desirable for the Association to adopt.'

There were dissenters – some felt that the draft rules allowed too much physical contact, and would make the game 'uncivilised', while FW Campbell, the Blackheath representative, was adamant that hacking, charging and kicking were essential to developing what he described as 'masculine toughness' and maintained that 'hacking is the true football'. His stand marked the parting of the ways between Association Football and Rugby Football; Campbell resigned from the FA when the vote on the issue went against him, and subsequently formed the Rugby Football Union.

The rules approved by the newly-formed FA were as follows:

- The maximum length of the ground shall be 200 yards, the maximum breadth shall be 100 yards, the length and breadth shall be marked off with flags; and the goal shall be defined by two upright posts, eight yards apart, without any tape or bar across them.

- A toss for goals shall take place, and the game shall be commenced by a place kick from the centre of the ground by the side losing the toss for goals; the other side shall not approach within 10 yards of the ball until it is kicked off.
- After a goal is won, the losing side shall be entitled to kick off, and the two sides shall change goals after each goal is won.
- A goal shall be won when the ball passes between the goal-posts or over the space between the goal-posts (at whatever height), not being thrown, knocked on, or carried.
- When the ball is in touch, the first player who touches it shall throw it from the point on the boundary line where it left the ground in a direction at right angles with the boundary line, and the ball shall not be in play until it has touched the ground.
- When a player has kicked the ball, any one of the same side who is nearer to the opponent's goal line is out of play, and may not touch the ball himself, nor in any way whatever prevent any other player from doing so, until he is in play; but no player is out of play when the ball is kicked off from behind the goal line.
- In case the ball goes behind the goal line, if a player on the side to whom the goal belongs first touches the ball, one of his side shall he entitled to a free kick from the goal line at the point opposite the place where the ball shall be touched. If a player of the opposite side first touches the ball, one of his side shall be entitled to a free kick at the goal only from a point 15 yards outside the goal line, opposite the place where the ball is touched, the opposing side standing within their goal line until he has had his kick.
- If a player makes a fair catch, he shall be entitled to a free kick, providing he claims it by making a mark with his heel at once; and in order to take such kick he may go back as far as he pleases, and no player on the opposite side shall advance beyond his mark until he has kicked.
- No player shall run with the ball.
- Neither tripping nor hacking shall be

Sheffield's current ground, the Bright Finance Stadium – Stadium of Bright to fans.

allowed, and no player shall use his hands to hold or push his adversary.

- A player shall not be allowed to throw the ball or pass it to another with his hands.
- No player shall be allowed to take the ball from the ground with his hands under any pretence whatever while it is in play.
- No player shall be allowed to wear projecting nails, iron plates, or gutta-percha on the soles or heels of his boots.

It's interesting to note that, even though the size of the pitch and certain aspects of the players' boots were stipulated, there's no rule governing the size of the ball to be used.

Sheffield FC became founder members of the FA, but the FA's members were not initially required to adopt the new rules. Indeed, the minutes of the FA's AGM in February 1866 note that only three clubs – Barnes, Crystal Palace and No Names – appeared to be playing by the FA code. For now, all of the Sheffield clubs continued to play by the Sheffield Rules, although these were constantly being updated to include new ideas and improvements. Immediately after the formation of the FA, for example, officials at Sheffield FC took time out to assess the new FA rules to see whether anything in them could be used to improve the club's own code. By the end of the year, according to a letter from Sheffield officials to the FA, they seem to have adopted a version of the FA's offside rule, a concept missing from the 1857 Sheffield code.

In March 1866, Sheffield FC travelled to London to play a side representing all the London clubs. Played under the FA's version of the rules, the game was significant for two reasons – it was the first time that the length of a game was fixed at 90 minutes, and it was also the first time that the size of the ball was specified, a 'Lillywhite's No. 5' being stipulated. Sheffield FC were once again involved in promoting ideas that found their way into the rules of the game – when the FA introduced the world-famous Challenge Cup competition in 1872, the Harrow Chequers club suggested that a standard ball should be used for all games played in the competition. The Lillywhite's No. 5 was again chosen, although later the rule was altered to allow any

ball with a circumference between 27 and 28 inches. By 1883, the rule had been applied to all games, and six years later a standard weight was also introduced.

The Sheffield FA

In 1867, the Sheffield clubs formed their own association, known, logically enough, as the Sheffield FA. The newly-formed body wasted no time in organising the world's first cup competition, 12 of the Sheffield clubs competing for the Youdan Cup. The final was played at Bramall Lane, and winners were Sheffield's arch-rivals Hallam.

The same year saw Sheffield FC introduce the corner kick, while rouges were abandoned in 1868. In the years that followed, Sheffield were responsible for bringing the crossbar into use in place of the earlier tape or rope, for pioneering the idea of the free kick to restart a game after a player has been fouled, and for introducing the concept of heading the ball, a practice unknown in the south until Sheffield travelled to the Oval to play a London side in 1875.

In 1877, the remaining Sheffield clubs, now 26 in number, joined Sheffield FC as members of the FA. Sheffield Rules were abandoned the following year, although several of the city's footballing innovations had already found their way into the FA code. Sheffield FC continued to help bring new developments into the game – on October 14th 1878, the club's Bramall Lane ground hosted the world's first-ever floodlit football match, although Sheffield FC themselves were not playing. Instead, two sides picked by the Sheffield FA, the Reds and the Blues, played out a friendly game under four arc lamps in front of 20,000 curious spectators. By all accounts, it wasn't a huge success, both crowd and players having problems seeing what was happening, but it was an idea way ahead of its time. By the time floodlit Football League matches became the norm, we'd had two World Wars and rock n' roll was sweeping the nation.

In 1882, the FA adopted the crossbar, probably the last of Sheffield FC's innovations to be absorbed into the rules of the game. By now, the club's days at the forefront of the development of the game were numbered.

The rise of professionalism in the mid-1880s meant that amateur clubs found it increasingly difficult to retain their best players. Sheffield FC remained staunchly amateur, and paid a heavy price, losing ground to the professionals, and slipping into decline. In 1885, Sheffield FC played games against Aston Villa, Nottingham Forest and Notts County, three professional clubs, and lost heavily to all of them.

Sheffield Clubs

As the 1880s drew to a close, Sheffield FC was no longer a force in the national game, or even in the city of Sheffield, where The Wednesday had taken over as undisputed top dogs. The idea of forming a professional club to play in the impressive Bramall Lane stadium was floated, and in 1889 Sheffield United FC was born. Sheffield FC was instrumental in bringing the new club into existence, providing some of its initial squad of players, and providing sides for the new team to train against.

The formation of Sheffield United did, however, mean that Sheffield FC could no longer use Bramall Lane as its home ground, and they had to look for an alternative. It turned out to be a long search. In the century that followed, Sheffield FC played at a succession of grounds, including East Bank, Newhall Road, the Old Forge and Ecclesall Road before a period of relative stability at Abbeydale Park. Later, they were forced to move again, and played at Hillsborough Park, Owlerton Stadium and Don Valley Stadium, with some games being staged at Sheffield Wednesday's training ground at Middlewood Road. Finally, in 2000, the club was able to purchase a ground of its own, its first ever, adjacent to the Coach and Horses pub in Dronfield on the outskirts of Sheffield. The ground was initially known rather prosaically as The Coach and Horses Ground, but a sponsorship deal has seen it renamed the Bright Finance Stadium, a 1500-capacity venue known affectionately to fans as the Stadium of Bright.

For most of this time, Sheffield FC led a quiet, unspectacular existence, the only real highlights coming in the amateur cup competition that Sheffield themselves suggested to the FA in the early 1890s. Professional teams were dominating the FA Cup competition, so the FA introduced the FA Amateur Cup in 1893, and eleven years later, Sheffield FC beat Ealing 3–1 at Bradford's Valley Parade to win the trophy. More than 80 years would pass before they had another shot at the Amateur Cup, by which time it had been replaced by the FA Vase. In the 1977 final, Sheffield FC held Billericay to a 1–1 draw at Wembley, but lost the replay at the City Ground, Nottingham, 2–1.

Sheffield FC have survived against all the odds, kept alive by loyal fans who realise the special place the club holds in football history, and through the patronage of some of sport's biggest names – the club can count such luminaries as Sven-Göran Eriksson, Sepp Blatter and fellow Sheffielder Michael Vaughan amongst its members. It's a club with a strong community spirit, and today boasts two senior teams, nine junior teams, a women's team and a disability team. Promotion at the end of the 2006–07 season means that things are indeed looking good for the team from the Stadium of Bright.

A 150th anniversary exhibition at Sheffield's Millennium Galleries saw the FA Cup on display as well as a copy of the club's original rules of the game, a winner's medal from their 1904 Amateur Cup win and a replica of the 1966 World Cup as won by England. Celebrations on the pitch included games against Sheffield United and Inter Milan, the latter attended by Pele, himself made an honorary member of Sheffield FC.

Whatever the future holds for Sheffield FC, the club can look back on their contribution to the national game with pride. It's fair to say that the game we know and love today would have been very different without the pioneering spirit of those early Sheffield FC players. Here's to the next 150 years!

Chapter 2

How Your Club Was Formed

The Victorians were really quite remarkable people. Not only did they invent all sorts of machines and develop all kinds of industries, but they also created thousands of sports clubs of all kinds. Cricket, rugby, tennis and – later on – cycling were all increasingly popular, and interest in them caused clubs to spring up all over the place. Football grew in popularity amongst the urban poor in the latter half of the nineteenth century, and it soon became clear, especially to those in Northern parts of the country, that a professionally organised game could prove very entertaining for the masses, as well as being a pretty good money spinner.

The late Victorian period was therefore the heyday of the formation of football clubs, many of which started off as amateur organisations, before later turning professional. Football clubs were often offshoots of other clubs, notably those involved with rugby or cricket, and sometimes they came about as the result of work colleagues, who originally got together for a kick-about. Churches and chapels, and their ministers, also tended to get in on the act. Perhaps football was thought of as a good way of keeping youngsters off the streets or out of the pubs and drinking palaces. Mind you, where churches and chapels were not involved, and even occasionally when they were, it was quite often the case that a football club was founded as a result of a meeting in a hotel or other hostelry.

Clubs of the English Football League

There follows, in alphabetical order, a very brief account of the foundation of each of the 92 clubs featured in the Premiership and Football League during the 2007–08 season.

Accrington Stanley

A club called Accrington was founded in 1876. Its team played in the original Football League in 1888, but the club resigned after just five years. In 1891, Stanley Villa was formed, and this club renamed itself Accrington Stanley in 1893. Accrington Stanley was re-formed after The Great War, and in 1921 was invited to join the newly formed League Division Three North. Life was always a struggle for the Lancashire club, and in 1962 it got into severe financial difficulties and resigned from the League. In 1968 a meeting to revive the club once more was held in the local public library and in 1970 Accrington Stanley was formed as a new club with a new ground, The Crown Ground, now known as the Fraser Eagle Stadium. Having progressed through the leagues, Accrington Stanley became a Football League club again, when it entered League Two in 2006.

Arsenal

Arsenal Football Club was founded in 1886 by workers at the Royal Arsenal, Woolwich. The club was originally called Dial Square, but its players turned professional in 1891 under the name of Royal Arsenal. Following election to the Football League Division Two in 1893, Royal Arsenal became Woolwich Arsenal, this being shortened simply to Arsenal around 1913, when the club moved from Plumstead to Highbury, where it remained until the recent transfer to the Emirates Stadium.

Aston Villa

Aston Villa was founded in 1874 by cricketers from the Villa Cross Wesleyan Chapel, Handsworth, Birmingham. The first ground was in Wellington Road, Perry Barr. In 1888, Villa were founder members of the Football League: The League's founder, William McGregor, was an official of the club. Aston Villa moved to Aston Lower Grounds, later to be known as Villa Park, in 1897.

Barnet

A Barnet Football Club was founded in 1888. As an amateur side, this Barnet played at a ground in Queens Road, until the club was disbanded in

1901. The present Barnet FC came about via various name changes and mergers, and was a stalwart of the Athenian League from 1912 until 1965. Conference champions in 1991, Barnet then entered League Division Four. The side was out of League football from 2001 until 2005, but returned for the 2005–06 season. Underhill has been Barnet's slightly sloping home since 1907.

Barnsley

Barnsley is another club which was formed by church members. It came into being in 1887 at the instigation of Rev. T. Preedy, curate of St. Peter's Church in Barnsley. The club was called Barnsley St. Peter's until it was admitted to Division Two in 1897, when 'St. Peter's' was dropped. Barnsley still play at their now much improved Oakwell Stadium.

Birmingham City

In the latter part of the nineteenth century, there was not a lot of association football played in the Birmingham area. It was a group of cricketers who formed Birmingham City, then known as Small Heath Alliance. The club was founded by the cricketing members of Trinity Church, Bordesley, and played initially on waste ground in Arthur Street. Original members of Division Two in 1892, Small Heath's name was changed to Birmingham in 1905, and to Birmingham City in 1945. Small Heath was reputedly the first football club to become a limited company (1888). Birmingham have been at St. Andrews since 1906.

Blackburn Rovers

Old Boys from Blackburn Grammar School founded Blackburn Rovers in 1875, and their club was to become a founder member of the Football League in 1888. One John Lewis, who was a noted referee and vice president of both the Football League and the Football Association, is credited as being the prime mover in Rovers' establishment. The club played at several grounds, moving to Ewood Park in 1890.

Blackpool

In 1887 some old boys from St. John's School met in the Stanley Arms Hotel, Blackpool, and formed a football club called Blackpool FC. The team played initially at the Athletic

Grounds, Stanley Park and at Raikes Hall Gardens. There was then a merger with a club called South Shore and they moved to Gamble's Field, later to be known as Bloomfield Road. Blackpool were accepted into Division Two in 1896.

CLUB FACTS

Blackburn Rovers' first ground was located at Oozehead, hardly an inspiring name for a football ground, and hardly an ideal venue for practitioners of the beautiful game – there was a long-established watering hole close to the centre circle, which was covered by a Heath-Robinson arrangement of timber planks overlaid with turf during games. This bizarre situation lasted only a short time before the club moved to a more suitable location at the nearby Pleasington Cricket ground. Rovers would ply their trade at two more venues before moving to their current home at Ewood Park in 1890.

Bolton Wanderers

Christ Church Sunday School, Blackburn Street, Bolton, saw the beginnings of what was to become Bolton Wanderers Football Club. Thomas Ogden founded the club in 1874 but three years later, with some members of the congregation unhappy about the use of church premises for football, it severed its links with Christ Church. Bolton were founder members of the Football League and played for 102 years at Burnden Park, before moving to the Reebok Stadium in 1997.

AFC Bournemouth

Founded in 1890 as Boscombe St. John's, and later known as both Bournemouth United and Bournemouth & Boscombe Athletic, Bournemouth were elected to Division Three South in 1923. They were renamed AFC Bournemouth in 1971, while their Dean Court ground is currently known as the Fitness First Stadium.

Bradford City

Bradford City arose in 1903, when rugby club Manningham decided that, due to financial difficulties, they would abandon oval balls in favour of round ones. Manningham had played at Valley Parade, and the newly formed association football club continued to play there. Entering Division Two in the year of their formation, Bradford remain at their Valley Parade ground to this day.

Brentford

Founded in 1889 so the local rowing club would have a winter pastime, Brentford enjoyed much footballing success at local level, being champions of the West London Alliance in 1893. They then entered the Southern League and, in 1920, became one of the founder members of Division Three of the Football League. Brentford have been at their Griffin Park ground since 1904, but are currently seeking to move.

Brighton & Hove Albion

There were several earlier Brighton sides, before Brighton & Hove Albion was formed following a meeting at the Seven Stars pub on Ship Street in 1901. A club called Brighton Rangers had folded, so the new club took its place in the Southern League, eventually joining Division Three of the Football League in 1920. Brighton played at the Goldstone Ground, Hove, for many decades, before groundsharing with Gillingham and then moving into the Withdean Stadium, Brighton. They seek a further move, but it's taking an awful long time.

Bristol City

Bristol South End was formed in 1894, and three years later this club was renamed Bristol City. The newly named club's first manager was Sam Hollis, from Woolwich Arsenal, who was given the princely sum of £40 with which to buy players. In consequence, Bristol City were elected to Division Two in 1901. They have been at their Ashton Gate ground since 1904.

Bristol Rovers

Bristol Rovers, founded in 1883, originally wore black shirts and were known as the Black Arabs. They then became known as Eastville Rovers, before adopting their present name in 1898, a year or so after becoming

fully professional. Rovers became founder members of the Third Division in 1920. They played at the Eastville Stadium for 89 years, before sharing Bath City's Twerton Park ground for a decade. In 1996 they moved to the Memorial Stadium, Horfield, Bristol.

Burnley

Burnley were founded in 1881 when Burnley Rovers Rugby Club merged with a local soccer club. Rugby continued to be played for a while, but Burnley were soon successful on the soccer front, and they were to be original members of the football League in 1888. Turf Moor remains home.

Bury

In 1885, the representatives of two football clubs, Bury Weslyans and Bury Unitarians, met at the Old White Horse Hotel in Fleet Street, Bury, to enlist support for the founding of a new club. Nine years later, Bury were elected to the Second Division of the Football League. In 1885 a lease was taken out on the Gigg Lane ground, and Bury are still there.

Cardiff City

South Wales is of course a rugby stronghold, but cricket is played there too and Cardiff City Football Club was formed there by members of the Riverside Cricket Club in 1899. The new club was called Riverside until after Cardiff achieved city status, whereupon it was re-named Cardiff City. After a few seasons in the Southern League, Cardiff were elected to the League Division Two. This was quite an achievement, as the club by-passed the newly formed Third Division. Cardiff City have plans to move from their Ninian Park home in the near future.

Carlisle United

Carlisle United was created from the amalgamation of Shaddongate United and Carlisle Red Rose in 1903. The side played in the Lancashire Combination and was eventually elected to the League Division Three North in 1928. Playing initially at Millhome Bank, the club moved to Devonshire Park in 1905. It later moved to Brunton Park, its present home.

Charlton Athletic

Charlton came about in 1905, when a group of lads from local youth clubs decided they should form a football club. The club did so well that it raced through local leagues, going on to join the Kent League and then, in 1920, the Southern League. A year later Charlton Athletic was ready for admittance to the Third Division South. The club had a number of grounds in its early days, before its move to the vast terracing of The Valley. It is still there, despite having had to move out and ground-share with Crystal Palace in 1985, an exile which lasted for seven years.

Chelsea

Chelsea FC was formed because Fulham declined the opportunity to rent the Stamford Bridge ground, preferring to remain at the far prettier Craven Cottage. The Great Western Railway wanted the Stamford Bridge site but its owner, one H.A. Mears, decided he wanted a football ground and club. Thus, in 1905, Chelsea FC came into being. The club was denied admittance to the then prestigious Southern League, but was immediately allowed to join Division Two of the Football League.

Cheltenham Town

Cheltenham Town FC appears to have been founded in 1892, although a Cheltenham club was in existence several years earlier. A non-league club for most of its life, Cheltenham finally achieved Football League status in 1999. Having once played matches at a local cricket ground, the club has been at its Whaddon Lane home since 1901.

Chester City

Chester City was founded in 1884, through the amalgamation of Chester Rovers and King's School Old Boys. For many years in the shadow of Northwich Victoria and Crewe Alexandra, Chester were eventually elected to Division Three North in 1931. In 1990, the club's ground was sold for development and for two years they shared Macclesfield's ground while their new Deva Stadium was built.

Chesterfield

One of the country's oldest clubs, Chesterfield were playing friendlies way back in 1866. By 1871, membership of the club cost two shillings (10p). Having achieved success in a

Chelsea began life not as a club looking for a stadium, but as a stadium looking for a club! Chelsea have remained at their Stamford Bridge home ever since, now a truly world-class stadium.

number of cup competitions in their early days, Chesterfield were elected to the Second Division in 1899. For a while they were known as Chesterfield Town, and then, from 1909 until 1920, as Chesterfield Municipal. The club's ground is known both as the Recreation Ground and, more usually, as Saltergate. Like so many other football clubs, Chesterfield plan to move to a new stadium in the not too distant future.

Colchester United

In 1909, amateur side Colchester Town moved into the Layer Road stadium. It was not until 1937 that some members of the club decided that it was time to form a limited liability company and to call the team Colchester United. The new club entered the Southern League and in 1950 was elected to Division Three South. Layer Road is still Colchester's home but not for much longer, as a move to a newly built stadium at Cuckoo Farm is due in 2008.

Coventry City

Coventry City was originally called Singers FC – not because its players were members of a local choir, but because they all worked at Singers bicycle factory. Fifteen years after their formation in 1883, Singers FC became Coventry City. The club entered the Southern League in 1908, and in 1919 Coventry were elected to the Second Division of the Football League. Highfield Road was Coventry's home from 1899 until 2005, and during the 1980s this became Britain's first all-seater stadium. Jimmy Hill was to blame. Coventry City now play at the Ricoh Arena.

Crewe Alexandra

Crewe Alexandra was formed in 1877. It seems uncertain whether the club was named Alexandra after Princess Alexandra, or after a pub of that name where the founders first met. Either way, Crewe went on to play in a number of local leagues before becoming founder members of Division Two in 1892. They returned to non-league status after just five seasons, but became members of Division Three North in 1921. They remain at their Gresty Road home.

Crystal Palace

The current Crystal Palace Football Club was formed in 1905, although there was a club of the same name way back in 1861. Palace played initially at the Crystal Palace Stadium in Sydenham, on the site of the Crystal Palace which was erected for the Great Exhibition. In 1915 they moved to Herne Hill, and three years later they were again on the move, this time to a ground called The Nest. Having at first played in the Southern League, Palace gained Football League status when they were admitted to Division Three in 1920. Four years after that they moved to Selhurst Park, and have been there ever since.

Dagenham & Redbridge

The League's newest club can trace its origins back to four famous amateur clubs: Ilford (formed 1881), Leytonstone (1886), Walthamstow Avenue (1900) and Dagenham (1949). All enjoyed success, particularly Leytonstone who won the FA Amateur Cup three times and the Isthmian League title nine times. Ilford and Leytonstone merged in 1979, to become Leytonstone/Ilford, and in 1988 absorbed the struggling Walthamstow Avenue to become Redbridge Forest. Redbridge moved in at Dagenham's Victoria Road ground, and achieved promotion to the Football Conference in 1991. Finally, landlord and host merged in 1992 to form Dagenham & Redbridge. Fifteen years later League status was attained.

Darlington

The present Darlington FC was founded in 1883. For many years the club was one of the most successful amateur outfits in the north-east of England, and it turned professional in 1908. Darlington were founder members of Division Three North in 1921. They played for many years at Feethams, a ground very close to the town centre. In 2003 the then chairman, George Reynolds, who had great ambition for his club, moved it into a new stadium. Having undergone one or two name changes, this ground is now known as the 96.6 TFM Arena – perhaps one of the more ludicrous names engendered by sponsorship.

Derby County

Derby County was formed as an adjunct to Derbyshire County Cricket Club, in the hope that football income would bolster the finances of Derbyshire CC. The football club made something of a habit of using grounds named for other sports. They started off playing, along with the cricket club, at the Racecourse Ground and then, in 1895, they moved to the Baseball Ground – so named because baseball had for a time been played there. Derby County were founder members of the Football League in 1888. They moved from the Baseball Ground to Pride Park in 1997.

Doncaster Rovers

One Albert Jenkins, a fitter at the local railway works, is credited with having been the prime mover in the foundation of Doncaster Rovers in 1879. The club was first elected to Division Two of the Football League in 1901. In its early years, it was twice voted out of the League, but the Rovers returned. They left the League once more in 1998, but were back five years later. Belle Vue was Doncaster's home from 1922 to 2006, when the club moved to the newly constructed and delightfully named Keepmoat Stadium.

Everton

The young gentlemen of St. Domingo's Methodist Sunday School in Liverpool decided, in 1878, to form a football team. Originally called St. Domingo, the name was soon changed to Everton as people from the local area became interested in the club. The team played in a corner of Stanley Park before moving to Anfield (later the home of Liverpool FC). After a dispute over rent in 1892, they moved to Goodison Park, where they currently remain. Everton were original members of the Football League in 1888.

CLUB FACTS

Of the current 92 League clubs, 35 have never enjoyed top-flight football, and a further five – Barnsley, Carlisle, Leyton Orient, Northampton and Swindon – have tasted the high life for a single season.

Fulham

Fulham was another club founded by members of a church. It first saw the light of day as Fulham St. Andrews Church Sunday School FC in 1879. Soon to be known simply as Fulham, the club turned professional in 1898. The team played in the Southern League from 1903 until 1907, before being elected to League Division Two. Fulham moved to their Craven Cottage ground in 1896 and, with the exception of a couple of seasons of ground-sharing with Queens Park Rangers at Loftus Road so that the Cottage could be brought up to Premier League standards, they have been there ever since.

Gillingham

In 1893, a group of chaps met in a pub called the Napier Arms and decided to form a football club called New Brompton, incorporating some players from another club called Chatham Excelsior. A piece of land was then purchased, and this later became the Priestfield Stadium. New Brompton joined the Second Division of the newly formed Southern League a year later, and turned professional. The club, which was renamed Gillingham FC in 1912, for many years had little success on the field, but even so, Gillingham were elected to the new League Division Three in 1920. They lost their League place again in 1938, but regained it in 1950.

Grimsby Town

Pubs were full of aspiring footballers in the latter part of the nineteenth century. Grimsby Pelham came about as a result of a meeting of cricketers in 1878, in the Wellington Arms, Freeman Street. The name Pelham, which was the surname of local landowners, the Earls of Yarborough, was later dropped. Grimsby Town were elected to Division Two in 1892. They have been at their Blundell Park ground in Cleethorpes, since 1899.

Hartlepool United

Hartlepools United, as Hartlepool were then known, were formed in 1908, although a club called West Hartlepool had been in existence since 1881. Hartlepools were to become founder members of Division Three North in 1921 – earlier applications having been refused because there were already several teams from the Durham area in the League. Their Victoria Park ground is very near the coast.

Hereford United

Hereford United came into being with the merger of two amateur clubs – St. Martin's and RAOC – in 1924. For a time the new club ground-shared at Edgar Street (where United still play) with amateur rivals Hereford City. In 1971 Hereford United were elected to the League Division Four, and enjoyed great success in their early years. They were however relegated back to the Conference in 1997, regaining league status nine years later.

Huddersfield Town

A meeting was held in the Imperial Hotel in 1906, to try to establish whether or not a football club was likely to succeed in the rugby stronghold of Huddersfield. It seems no decision was reached at the time but, a couple of years later, a meeting in another hotel – The Albert – came to the conclusion that a football team was indeed a viable proposition. Thanks to the enthusiasm and money of one Hilton Crowther, Huddersfield Town was born, and was elected to the Second Division two years later. Leeds Road was the club's home until 1994, when Huddersfield moved to what is now called the Galpharm Stadium.

Hull City

Hull City came into being in 1904, and the new club managed to persuade the local Rugby League club to rent their ground, The Boulevard, to them under a three-year agreement. Later, the Rugby League forbade the use of any of their grounds by the upstart association football clubs, but by this time Hull City were well established. They were elected to Division Two in 1905. Hull spent fifty-six years at the Boothferry Road ground but in December 2002, not long after being in severe financial difficulties, they moved to the impressive Kingston Communications Stadium.

Ipswich Town

Considering the club was founded during a meeting at Ipswich Town Hall in 1878, it is perhaps a little surprising that Ipswich did not make it into the League for another 60 years, two years after the club turned professional in 1936. In 1938, Ipswich were voted into Division Three South. In the succeeding years, the team from Portman Road has won the league title once, in 1962, and supplied two England national managers.

Leeds United

A club known as Leeds City was founded in 1904, and was elected to Division Two a year later. The Football Association closed Leeds City down in 1919, following accusations of illegal payments to players but a local solicitor, one Alf Masser, almost immediately formed a new club: Leeds United. United played initially in the Midland League, almost merged with hard-up Huddersfield, and were then elected to the Second Division. Leeds United still occupy their Elland Road ground, although the club no longer owns it. The ground was originally called The Old Peacock Ground, after a pub called the Old Peacock, and was once the home of Holbeck Rugby Club.

Leicester City

In 1884 a group of young men, mainly old boys from Wyggeston School, met in a house on the old Roman road called Fosse Way, and founded Leicester Fosse Football Club. Leicester Fosse were elected to the League Division Two ten years later, having moved to a ground at Filbert Street in 1891. After the war, the club was wound up, but a new club, Leicester City, was formed immediately to take its place. It remained at Filbert Street until the move to the Walkers Stadium in 2002.

Leyton Orient

The club now known as Leyton Orient was founded, in 1881, by members of Glyn Cricket Club, in east London. It has undergone a number of name changes over the years, including Eagle FC (1886) and Clapton Orient (1898). The word 'Orient' is thought to have been appended because some employees of the Orient Shipping Line were involved with the club. Having turned professional in 1901, Clapton Orient were elected to Division Two in 1905. A move to Brisbane Road, Leyton, in 1937, saw the club change its name once more – this time to Leyton Orient. It has been Leyton Orient ever since, except for a period between 1966 and 1987, when the club was known simply as Orient.

Lincoln City

Lincoln City was formed in 1883. The club was a founder member of the Midland League in 1889, and finished in top spot at the end of the first season. Lincoln became one of the original members of Division Two in 1892, but over the years were on several occasions forced to seek re-election – often without success – to the Football League. They had turned professional in 1891, and moved to their Sincil Bank ground in 1895.

Liverpool

Had it not been for Everton's argument over the rent at the Anfield Road ground, Liverpool Football Club might not have come into existence. As it was, Everton people who wished to remain at Anfield formed a new club in 1892. Liverpool were elected to the new Division Two immediately, and have of course been Football League members ever since. The club remains at Anfield, but plans are afoot to move to a brand new stadium, complete with some sort of a 'Kop End', in the not too distant future.

Luton Town

In April 1885, a meeting at Luton Town Hall confirmed the amalgamation of Luton Wanderers with Luton Excelsior, to form a new club: Luton Town. Luton became the first club in the south of England to employ professional players. After a short period in the Southern League, the club was elected to the League Division Two in 1897. Luton have been at their Kenilworth Road ground since 1905, but it is very cramped and they would like to move.

Macclesfield Town

Macclesfield originally played rugby, converting to Football Association rules in 1874. The club underwent a series of name changes before, just after World War Two, it finally became Macclesfield Town. The team then played in the Cheshire County League, before moving on to the Northern Premier League and then to the Conference. They topped the table and qualified for admittance to the Football League in 1995, but the Moss Rose ground, where they had played since 1891, was deemed not up to standard. Macclesfield Town won the Conference title again in 1997, and this time were promoted to the League Division Three.

Manchester City

In 1880, some parishioners of St. Mark's Church, West Gorton, decided to take up football as well as cricket. Seven years later West Gorton joined with Gorton Athletic to form Ardwick, which became one of the founder members of Division Two in 1892. A couple of years later a limited company came into existence and Manchester City was born. A fire in a stand at City's Hyde Road ground in 1920 caused a move, three years later, to a purpose built stadium at Maine Road, Moss Side. A further move took place when the club moved to the City of Manchester Stadium (for a time known as Eastlands) in 2003.

Manchester United

It may now be one of the biggest clubs in the world, with an alleged 50 million supporters around the globe but, like many others, Manchester United had humble beginnings. In 1878, the dining room committee of the local works belonging to the Lancashire and Yorkshire Railway Company formed a cricket and football club to be called Newton Heath. This club gained admittance to the Football League Division One in 1892, having severed links with the rail depot in 1890. It adopted the name Manchester United in 1902, and moved to Old Trafford in 1910. Old Trafford was bombed during World War Two and for a while Manchester City graciously allowed United to play at Maine Road.

Mansfield Town

Mansfield Town was founded as Mansfield Wesleyans in 1897. The club became Mansfield Wesley in 1906 but by 1910 the Chapel trustees asked the club to change its name, as it no longer had anything to do with either the chapel or its school. Mansfield Town had several goes at gaining admittance to the League, and finally made it in 1931, when they were voted into Division Three South.

In 1995 they opted to re-develop their Field Mill ground – reputedly one of the oldest in the country, with football having been played there as early as 1861 – rather than to seek a stadium elsewhere.

Middlesbrough

It used to be believed that Middlesbrough Football Club was founded at a tripe supper, but apparently this is not so. What a pity. It was in fact the Middlesbrough Cricket Club which met in the gymnasium of the Albert Park Hotel during 1875, in order to create the football club. Middlesbrough soon turned professional. They then tried, but failed, to amalgamate with Middlesbrough Ironopolis, before reverting to amateur status and winning the Amateur Cup in both 1895 and 1898. They then turned professional again and entered the League Division Two in 1899. Middlesbrough's first ground was in Linthorpe Road, and the club moved to Ayresome Park in 1903. The move to the Riverside Stadium took place some 92 years later.

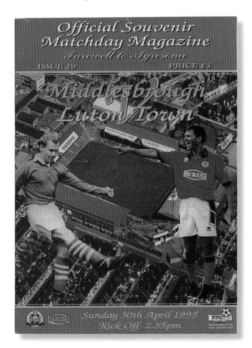

A commemorative programme for the game against Luton Town in 1995 marks Middlesbrough's last ever game at Ayresome Park, home to the club since 1903.

In 1989, Wimbledon celebrated their centenary season – 14 years later the club would be no more after relocation to Milton Keynes and an attendant change of name to MK Dons.

Milton Keynes Dons

The club known as MK Dons was born on June 21st 2004, nine months after its predecessor, Wimbledon Football Club, relocated to the National Hockey Stadium at Milton Keynes. Whilst initially MK Dons were seen as the legal continuation of Wimbledon FC, all club history and honours (including the 1988 FA Cup win) were reverted back to AFC Wimbledon; the MK Dons became a separate identity beginning August 2004. In summer 2007, the club relocated to a new 22,000-capacity stadium:mk (to expand to 32,000) at nearby Denbigh, under a new manager in ex-England international Paul Ince. The 2007-2008 campaign saw them challenging at the top of League Two and win their first club honours beating Grimsby 2-0 at Wembley Stadium in March 2008.

Millwall

Millwall Rovers came into being in 1885, when the mainly Scottish employees of Morton and Company, an East End of London canning and food processing firm, decided to form a football club. The new club's headquarters was at first a pub called The Islanders, in Millwall. As Millwall Athletic, the club took a leading part in forming the Southern League, and were members of this league from 1894 until 1920. They were elected to the new Football League Division Three in 1920, and in 1925 dropped the 'Athletic' to become known simply as Millwall FC. Having attracted consistently large crowds at several home grounds, the club played at The Den, New Cross, from 1910 until 1993, when it moved to the New Den in Bermondsey.

Morecambe

Formed in May 1920 after a meeting at the West View Hotel, Morecambe joined the Lancashire Combination. Within five years they were champions, while their ground was renamed Christie Park after JB Christie donated the land to the club. In season 1937–38 the club reached the first round of the FA Cup for the first time, losing 0–1 at South Liverpool. 1961–62 was the Shrimps' greatest season, being both League champions and Lancashire Junior Cup winners, triumphing 3–1 over rivals Wigan Athletic in front of 8,000 spectators at Deepdale. They also reached the third round of the FA Cup, winning at Chester in the previous round before losing to Weymouth at Christie Park in front of a record 9,234. 1974 found them at Wembley, beating Dartford 2–1 in the FA Trophy final in front of 19,000.

Graduating to the Conference in 1995 under manager Jim Harvey, they came close to securing League football twice in succession before making it third time lucky and finally triumphing in the play-offs over Exeter in 2007. Seasoned boss Sammy McIlroy had repeated his success with Macclesfield in 1997.

Newcastle United

A football club called Stanley was formed in South Byker, Newcastle, during 1881, and this was renamed Newcastle East End in October 1882. At about the same time, Newcastle West End came into being. East met West in the early 1890s, when the West End club went out of business and its remaining committee members asked East End if they would care to move to their home at St. James' Park, which West End had occupied since 1886. Having sorted all that out, Newcastle United came into being during 1892. The team was elected to the Second Division in 1893, and still plays at a much modified St James' Park.

Northampton Town

Northampton Town was founded in 1897 by schoolteachers who were members of the local Elementary Schools Association, in conjunction with one AJ Darnell, a local solicitor. The club survived severe financial difficulties in its early days, losing a then massive £675 in its first year. However, Northampton first joined the Midland League and, by 1901, were members of the Southern League. Election to the newly formed League Division Three followed in 1920. From its early days the club played its home matches at the Northamptonshire County Cricket Ground, but the team was not originally allowed to play there between May and September. Northampton Town were at the County Ground for 93 years, before moving to the Sixfields Stadium in 1997.

CLUB FACTS

The lowest official attendance figure for a first-class match in England is nil – this distinction goes to Norwich City's FA Cup Third Round second replay in the 1914-15 season, played on neutral territory at Lincoln City's Sincil Bank ground. The authorities decided that football would be too much of a distraction for local munitions workers, engaged as they were in the war effort, so the match was played behind closed doors. In the end, the large crowds gathered outside the gates of the ground posed such a threat to public order that the decision was taken to admit them.

Norwich City

Two more local school teachers were responsible for the formation of Norwich City. They met to create the club, which they considered to be amateur, in 1902 and were very upset when a Football Association commission decided they were in fact professional, and threw them out of the FA Amateur Cup (1904). A professional club was soon legally formed, and it entered the Southern League in 1905. In 1920, Norwich became one of the founder members of the League Division Three. Having moved to a disused chalk pit in Rosary Road, which became known as The Nest, Norwich City survived bankruptcy in 1913 and, in 1935, moved to the Carrow Road ground.

CLUB FACTS

The unusually named Fisher Athletic with its headquarters in London's docklands was formed in 1908 by Michael Culliton, Headmaster of Dockhead School, and The John Fisher Catholic Society. The original crest which was reintroduced from the start of the 2001–02 season featured a fish and a cross to represent Catholic Bishop John Fisher who became a Saint in 1935.

Nottingham Forest

Nottingham Forest is one of the world's oldest football clubs, although the team originally played shinney, or bandy, which was a kind of hockey. The Forest Football Club was founded at a meeting in the Clinton Arms in 1865. The founding fathers immediately decided to buy a set of red caps for the players to wear during the match. Most fetching. The club also loaned a set of red shirts to Arsenal to help out the London club in its early days. Forest were elected to the League Division One in 1892. Their City Ground is on the south side of the River Trent.

Notts County

There is some debate regarding the official year of Notts County's foundation, as the club came into being either at a meeting held in Cremorne Gardens in 1862, or at the George Hotel in December 1864. At all events, County is regarded as the oldest league club in the world. It turned professional in 1885, and became one of the original members of the Football League in 1888. The club moved to its Meadow Lane ground in 1910 and has

been there, on the north side of the Trent and opposite Nottingham Forest's ground, ever since. Notts County are credited with inventing the offside trap.

Oldham Athletic

One John Garland, landlord of the Featherstall and Junction Hotel, Oldham, decided to form a football club in 1895. He called it Pine Villa FC, and at first the team played in the Oldham Junior League. Four years later a professional club – Oldham County – ceased to exist, and the liquidators persuaded Pine Villa to take over their Boundary Park ground in Sheepfoot Lane. Renamed Oldham Athletic, the club was elected to Division Two in 1907 and was soon promoted to the top division.

Peterborough United

Peterborough and Fletton United came about in 1923 as the result of the merger of two other football clubs from the area. This club was disbanded in 1933, but a year or so later a new club called Peterborough United arose and was soon competing in the Midland League. Peterborough remained in that league until 1960, before being elected to the League Division Four. The side from London Road scored a record 134 goals in its first League season.

Plymouth Argyle

The Argyle Football Club was founded in 1886 by a group of young gentlemen who wished to continue playing football after they left school. They met in a coffee house to get things organised. How very sedate. The origin of the name 'Argyle' is uncertain, but it may have had something to do with Queen Victoria and her love of Scotland. The club became known as Plymouth Argyle in 1903, when it turned professional and was admitted to the Southern League. Football League membership came about with Plymouth's election to the newly formed Third Division in 1920. The club's Home Park ground was severely damaged during the Second World War, and had to be rebuilt. It has been largely rebuilt again in recent years.

Portsmouth

A local solicitor, one Alderman J. E. Pink, together with a group of like-minded business men and professional persons, met in 1898 to form a football club. They also agreed to buy some land for £4,950, on which they would build Fratton Park stadium. Portsmouth FC was thus born, some professional players were signed, and admittance to the Southern League was gained almost at once. In 1920, Portsmouth became founder members of the Third Division, and they still play at Fratton Park.

Port Vale

Port Vale came into being in 1876, but the club was renamed Burslem Port Vale in 1884 when it moved to Burslem, one of Stoke's five towns. The club transferred from the Midland League to the newly formed League Division Two in 1892, and the team from Vale Park dropped the Burslem prefix in 1909. Life was not easy for Port Vale in the early years. On a couple of occasions they failed to gain re-election to the League, and were forced back to temporary non-league status.

Preston North End

North End Cricket and Rugby Club was founded in Preston during 1863. In 1879, football was added to the club's sports, and within two years the other games were dropped. Preston North End became founder members of the Football League in 1888, and they were league champions for the first two

seasons. In 1888–89, they were undefeated in both the League and the FA Cup. In the League, they won 18 and drew four matches. Dubbed 'Invincibles', they lost no league games and conceded no cup goals.

Queen's Park Rangers

Around 1882, or perhaps a little later, St. Jude's Institute FC merged with Christchurch Rangers, to form what was to become Queen's Park Rangers. Rangers' name came about because most of the players came from the Queen's Park area of London. The side played in the Southern League from 1899, until elected into the League Division Three in 1920. Q.P.R. played at a remarkable number of 14 home grounds before more or less settling at Loftus Road in 1917. They are still there, but they did experiment with moves to the White City in 1931 and again in 1962.

Reading

In 1871, a public meeting was held in the Bridge Street Rooms in Reading, and a football club was founded. Reading later amalgamated with both Reading Hornets and Earley Football Club. The FA Cup competition was first entered in 1877, and Reading FC joined the Southern League in 1894. In 1920, they became one of the original members of the League Division Three. The club played at a number of venues, including a couple of cricket grounds, prior to the move to a purpose built stadium at Elm Park in 1896. One hundred and two years later, Reading moved to the new Madejski Stadium.

For many clubs, particularly those for whom genuine success may be infrequent, age is a pedigree worthy of veneration, as here at Portsmouth's Fratton Park where the year of the club's founding is proudly displayed to visitors.

Rochdale

Rochdale is largely rugby country, and early attempts to form an association football club in the town were doomed to failure. One of them, Rochdale Town was formed in 1900, but this club went out of business in 1907. In the same year, the present Rochdale club was formed. Playing initially in the Manchester League, Rochdale moved in time to the Lancashire Combination. Entry to the Football League was gained in 1921, when the club was admitted to the newly formed Division Three North. Rochdale still play at their Spotland ground.

Rotherham United

Rotherham United underwent some name changes in the early days. A club called Rotherham was founded in 1870, adopting the name Rotherham Town some years later. Meanwhile, a club called Thornhill United was formed in 1877, and changed its name to Rotherham County in 1905. Rotherham Town entered the League Division Two 1893, but were voted out again in 1896. Rotherham County were elected to Division Two in 1919, after the Great War. There was deemed to be insufficient support to maintain two major football teams in the area, so Town amalgamated with County in 1925 to form Rotherham United. Rotherham's Millmoor is noted as having been the first football ground in the country to sell Pukka Pies.

Scunthorpe United

In the early part of the twentieth century, a club known as Brumby Hall FC, which had been founded in 1899 and which played its home games at the Old Showground, amalgamated with several other clubs and became Scunthorpe United. Not long afterwards, in 1910, Scunthorpe amalgamated with North Lindsey United. For many years the new club was called Scunthorpe & Lindsey United, and it was still called that in 1950, when it was admitted to Division Three North. In 1988 Scunthorpe became the first English football club to build a new stadium in more than 30 years, when it moved from the Old Showground to a new ground at Glanford Park.

Sir Charles Clegg, an important figure in the founding of Sheffield United and later FA President.

Sheffield United

Charles Stokes, a member of Yorkshire County Cricket Club, was instrumental in the foundation of Sheffield United FC. He had watched an FA Cup semi-final between Preston North End and West Bromwich Albion, and this had convinced him that it would be a good idea to have a new professional football team playing on the ground Yorkshire used at Bramall Lane. In 1889 therefore, he persuaded others to join him in the creation of Sheffield United FC, and three years later the side was invited to join the newly created League Division Two. Bramall Lane remained a 'three-sided' football ground (the fourth side being left open to allow for the ground's use as a cricket ground) until the 1970s.

Sheffield Wednesday

The city of Sheffield was a popular place for football from the early days. In 1867 the Sheffield Wednesday Cricket Club, which had

Opposite: **Known today as Sheffield Wednesday, the club would not in fact adopt the Steel City's name until 1929, being known simply as The Wednesday Football Club until that point, as can be seen from this photo, where the name is clearly visible on the sign atop the main stand's roof!**

been founded four decades earlier, gave birth to Sheffield Wednesday FC, which was known simply as The Wednesday until 1929. Meetings were held on Wednesday afternoons, traditionally the day on which local steel workers took a half-day in order to play sports.

Interestingly, the original committee numbered amongst its members one Charles Stokes – who was later to play a major role in the foundation of Sheffield United. The Wednesday were elected to the League Division One in 1892. More than one ground, including Bramall Lane, was used in the early years but eventually some land was purchased outside the city limits, in a village called Owlerton, and in 1899 The Wednesday adopted it as their home. It later became known as Hillsborough.

Shrewsbury Town

There was a football club in Shrewsbury in 1876, but the present Shrewsbury Town was founded ten years later. The lads from Shrewsbury seem to have decided that they were Welsh and they knew they were as, in 1891, they won the Welsh FA Cup. The side played in the Shropshire District League, the Birmingham League and the Midland League before, along with Scunthorpe, it was elected to a slightly enlarged Division Three North in 1950. The club's Gay Meadow ground is by the River Severn, and is very picturesque. Whenever it dropped into the river, a man called Fred Davies used to retrieve the match ball in his coracle. The football field itself is rather inclined to be waterlogged, and Shrewsbury moved to a new, and drier, Meadow in 2007.

Southampton

A club called St Mary's Young Men's Association FC was founded in 1885. It was connected to St Mary's Church, Southampton, and many of its first players had previously played for a club called Deanery FC; the first club chairman of St. Mary's was the church's curate. The club changed its name to Southampton St. Mary's in 1894, but 'St Mary's' was dropped in 1897. Southampton played in the Southern League from 1894 until 1920, when the side entered the League Division Three. They had moved to The Dell in 1898 and they moved again, after 103 years, to St. Mary's Stadium. St Mary had been selected once more.

Southend United

An amateur club called Southend Athletic was founded around 1890, but this had little or nothing to do with the professional club, Southend United, which was formed after a meeting at the Blue Boar pub in 1906. The club went immediately into Division Two of the Southern League, before moving into the League Division Three in 1920. Southend played at The Kursaal from 1919 until a move to Roots Hall as late as 1955. The Roots Hall ground is now owned by property developers, and the club is planning to move to a new ground in the very near future.

Stockport County

The Stockport area is non-conformist country and, in 1883, the Wycliffe Congregational Chapel was responsible for the formation of Stockport County FC, at first known as Heaton Norris Rovers. In 1890 the club's name was changed in honour of Stockport having become a County Borough and, having played in the Lancashire League, Stockport County entered the League Division Two in 1900. The team did not do well for the first few seasons, and failed to gain re-election at the end of 1903–04. It was however, back in the League by 1905–06. Stockport played at a number of venues prior to 1902, when the club moved to Edgeley Park. This was the home of Stockport Rugby League Club, but the Rugby club folded a few years later. County have been at Edgeley Park ever since.

Stoke City

The origins of Stoke City can be traced back to a group of old boys from Charterhouse School who were, unlikely as it may seem, apprenticed to the North Staffordshire Railway Works. The exact date of formation is a little unclear, but it was no later than 1868 and possibly as early as 1863, which makes Stoke one of the league's oldest clubs. Originally called Stoke Ramblers, the club was then called simply Stoke, until 'City' was added in 1924. Stoke were members of the original Football League in 1888, but did have a couple of spells out of the League (1890–91 and from 1908 until after World War One). The club left its Victoria Ground in 1997, and moved to the new Britannia Stadium.

Sunderland

James Allan, a Glaswegian schoolmaster, led a group of fellow professionals in the formation of Sunderland and District Teachers' Association FC in 1879. It soon became clear that a team of teachers was not really a viable project if the club was to grow. Non-teachers were therefore admitted to the club a year or so later, and it was renamed Sunderland AFC. The club did then grow, and in 1890 it was elected into the Football League at the expense of Stoke. More success followed,

and for a time late in the nineteenth century the side was known as 'the team of all talents'. Sunderland moved to The Stadium of Light in 1997, after 99 years at Roker Park.

Swansea City

There was little association football played in South Wales until late in the nineteenth century. There were a few clubs, including one from Swansea, but Swansea City (then Swansea Town) was not founded until 1912. Swansea played in the Southern League, being elected to the new League Division Three in 1920. The club moved from its city centre Vetch Field home in 2005, to the farther-flung Liberty Stadium. Many supporters don't like the name of the new ground, and tend to call it either The Morfa or Whiterock Stadium.

Swindon Town

Swindon Town Football Club started off in 1881 as 'Spartans', and was an offshoot of a cricket club. The name was changed to Swindon Town in 1883 when its captain, the Rev. William Pitt, engineered an amalgamation with St. Mark's Young Men's Friendly Society. The new club turned professional in 1894, and entered the Southern League in the same year. Election to the League Division Three followed in 1920, with Swindon's first match

The decision to move to a new stadium can be a difficult one. Before moving to the brand new Stadium of Light, Sunderland offered supporters a range of options in a fans' referendum.

Walsall Football Club. Fellows Park.

ending in a magnificent 9–1 victory over Luton Town. The club's first pitch was adjacent to a quarry, but when a young supporter fell into said quarry, it decided to move. A couple of home venues later, Swindon settled at the County Ground in 1893, and has been there ever since.

Tottenham Hotspur

The Hotspur, as Spurs were then called, came into being as yet another offshoot of a cricket club in 1882. Most of its founding members were old boys from St. John's Presbyterian School and Tottenham Grammar School, and they initially adopted the local YMCA as their meeting place. The club turned professional in 1895, and joined the Southern League. Football League status was gained in 1908, with election to Division Two. A year later the team was promoted to the First Division. Tottenham moved to their White Hart Lane ground, the site of a former market garden, in 1899.

Tranmere Rovers

Founded in 1884 as Belmont, Tranmere Rovers changed their name a year later and in 1889 joined the West Lancashire League, and

also won the Wirral Challenge Cup. Ten years later the club almost went out of existence, when most of its players left to join another club. Tranmere entered Division Three North from the Central League in 1921. The club played at several grounds in its early days, but has been at the present Prenton Park ground since 1912.

Walsall

The Walsall area had a couple of sizeable clubs in the 1880s – Walsall Swifts, formed in 1877, and Walsall Town, founded two years later. These clubs amalgamated as Walsall Town Swifts in 1888, the new club becoming just Walsall in 1895. Election to Division Two occurred in 1892. Walsall was the smallest of the Black Country clubs, and there were a couple of failures to gain re-election in the early years, the second of these occurring in 1901. The club was back in the League (Division Three North) in 1921. A move from Fellows Park to a new ground, the Bescot Stadium, occurred in 1990, a supermarket having since been built on the Fellows Park site.

Watford

Watford Rovers were founded in 1881, but changed their name to West Hertfordshire twelve years later. With the absorption of rivals Watford St. Mary's in 1898, the club was renamed Watford. Entry into the Southern League was gained in 1900, and in 1920 Watford joined 21 other clubs in the newly formed League Division Three. A ground in Cassio Road was Watford's home for many years, but the club moved to Vicarage Road in 1922, and is still there.

West Bromwich Albion

Poverty is a terrible thing, and it seems that the young men of West Bromwich were particularly affected by it. When some employees of Salters Spring Works decided they wanted to start a football club in 1878, they found that nobody possessed a football, so they had to send someone over to Wednesbury to buy one. Then they founded their club, called it West Bromwich Strollers, and charged everyone tuppence (2p) a week to belong to it. West Brom became members of the original League in 1888, having just won the FA Cup. The club had several grounds in the early days, but moved to the Hawthorns in 1900.

West Ham United

The employees of a shipbuilding yard founded a club called Thames Ironworks in 1895. In 1899 the club was elected to the Southern League, but it soon got into financial difficulties. It was wound up in 1900, but re-formed, as West Ham United, within weeks. West Ham were eventually elected to League Division Two in 1919. As Thames Ironworks, the club played at Hermit Road in Canning Town and Browning Road in East Ham, before moving to the Memorial Grounds, Plaistow, in 1897. The final move, to The Boleyn Ground, Upton Park, took place in 1904.

Wigan Athletic

There were several early attempts to create a major association football club in Wigan, but Wigan Athletic was founded in 1931 following the demise of Wigan Borough. The latter had resigned from the League Division Three North in October of that year, having entered the Football League in 1921. Athletic hoped to gain early admission to the league, but in the event it took them until 1978, when they finally made it into the Fourth Division. Earlier, in 1972, so desperate were they for league football, that they tried to get into the Scottish Second Division. Wigan Athletic had taken over the Springfield Park ground from the defunct Borough, and had paid £2,850 for it. They were to move to the £30 million JJB Stadium in time for the 1999–2000 season.

Wolverhampton Wanderers

John Baynton and John Brodie together founded a club called St Luke's in 1877. Two years later, St. Luke's merged with a local football and cricket club called The Wanderers, and thus Wolverhampton Wanderers FC was born. The club at first made use of a couple of fields which were put at its disposal, and later played at a ground in Dudley Road. The move to Molineux took place in 1889. Wolves were members of the original Football League in 1888. In their first season they finished in third place, a point behind Aston Villa, and 12 points behind Preston North End.

Wrexham

Wrexham FC was founded in 1872, and is certainly one of the oldest football clubs in Wales. It was formed by some cricket club members who wanted something to do in the winter, and they met to get things started at the Turf Hotel. The club was one of the founder members of what was to become the Football Association of Wales. Entry to the League Division Three North was gained in 1921. A rebuilt Turf Hotel still stands at one corner of Wrexham's home, the Racecourse Ground.

Wycombe Wanderers

In 1887, a group of workers from the local furniture manufacturing industry met at a pub called The Steam Engine to form a football club. They may have adopted the name 'Wanderers' after a visit from The Wanderers club some years earlier. Wycombe entered the Southern League in 1896. They finally became a league team after winning promotion in 1993. Their home ground was for many years at Loakes Park, but they moved to a new stadium at Adams Park in 1990.

Yeovil Town

Founded in 1890 as Yeovil FC, Yeovil became Yeovil Casuals in 1895 and Yeovil Town in 1907. Then, following an amalgamation, the club was known as Yeovil & Petters United until 1946, when it reverted once more to Yeovil Town. For many years, Yeovil were famous as FA Cup giant-killers, but they finally achieved league status in 2003, when they won the Conference championship without losing at home. Yeovil's old Huish ground was noted for its side to side slope. The new Huish Park, to which the club moved in 1990, does not have this nice little aberration.

Clubs of the Scottish Football League

There follows, in alphabetical order, a very brief account of the foundation of each of the 42 clubs featured in the Scottish Premier League and Scottish Football League during the 2007–08 season.

Aberdeen

Aberdeen FC was born when three teams – Aberdeen, Victoria United, and Orion – merged in 1903. Within a year the club was elected to the Scottish Second Division and although they finished 7th out of 12 teams, Aberdeen were promoted to an expanded First Division after just one season. In later years their manager, one Donald Coleman, was credited with the invention of the dug-out. Aberdeen still play at their Pittodrie ground.

Airdrie United

Airdrie United came into existence in May 2002, following the bankruptcy of Airdrieonians. The original club had been formed in 1878, and had entered the Scottish League Division Two in 1894. Airdreonians were replaced in the League by Gretna, but Jim Ballantyne bought the near bankrupt Clydebank FC, changed its name to Airdrie United, and moved it to the town of Airdrie. Admission to the League was thereby gained. United play at the Excelsior Stadium, but this is known to the fans as 'New Broomfield', in honour of Airdreonians' old ground.

Albion Rovers

A merger of two Coatbridge clubs – Albion and Rovers – saw the creation of Albion Rovers in Lanarkshire during 1882. The resulting club was admitted to the Second Division in 1903. Having played at several grounds, Albion Rovers moved to their Cliftonhill Stadium on Christmas Day 1919. A group of expatriates formed a club of the same name in South Wales, and this Albion Rovers currently plays in the Gwent County League.

Alloa Athletic

The foundation of Alloa Athletic took place around 1878, or perhaps a bit later. At all events it was many years before the club found its way into the Scottish League. In 1921 however, league status was achieved, and the team went on to win the Second Division title in its first season. Promotion followed, but this was sadly followed by relegation a year later. Alloa still play at their Recreation Park ground on Clackmannan Road.

Arbroath

Arbroath FC came into being in 1878 and, rather like Alloa and a number of other Scottish clubs, spent many decades outside the Scottish League. They finally made it into Division Two in 1921, where they struggled quite a lot for a few seasons. Arbroath are famous for beating Bon Accord 36–0 in a Scottish Cup game in 1885. Their Gayfield Park ground is in a very exposed position, right by the sea and with a small funfair next door.

Ayr United

In 1910, Ayr Parkhouse and Ayr FC merged to form Ayr United. Ayr FC had been elected to the Scottish Second Division in 1898, and the new club continued in that division. Their Somerset Park stadium has survived in relatively unchanged condition, having one stand and three terraces. Moves are however afoot to sell Somerset Park to Barratt Homes, and to move to a new, albeit lower capacity, stadium in the Heathfield area of town.

Berwick Rangers

Over the centuries, the border town of Berwick has many times changed hands between

England and Scotland. However, it has been in England now for quite a while, even though its football team, Berwick Rangers, plays in the Scottish League. Founded around 1881, or possibly a little later, Berwick played for many years in the Scottish Border League. They were however elected to the Second Division of the Scottish League in 1955. They had moved to their Shielfield Park ground a year or so earlier, having played at a number of previous locations.

Brechin City

Brechin City was founded when two junior clubs – Brechin Harp and Brechin Hearts – decided upon amalgamation in 1906. The club from one of Scotland's smaller cities was elected to the Second Division in 1929. Brechin formerly played at Nursery Park but their current home, Glebe Park, is noted for a rather fine hedge which runs down one side of the pitch.

CLUB FACTS

The Isles of Scilly host the smallest league not only in Britain but in the world, with just two clubs, the Garrison Gunners and the Woolpack Wanderers. They play at the Garrison football ground on St Mary's, the largest of the islands just 28 miles off the Cornish coast.

They play 13 league games as well as two cup competitions, though the path to the final is an undemanding one. Occasionally they go on 'international' duty, hopping over to the mainland once a year to take on a team in Newlyn and a team from Truro.

Celtic

During the latter part of the nineteenth century, Glasgow had a large population of Roman Catholic Irish immigrants. Under the direction of one Brother Walfrid, these workers created Celtic Football Club, and even built up the ground behind a necropolis (graveyard) in the east end of the city during 1888. Parkhead, currently known as Celtic Park, is still Celtic's home and is now one of the largest stadiums in the United Kingdom. Along

with their great rivals, Rangers, Celtic were founder members of the Scottish League in 1890, and have done rather well ever since.

Clyde

It is likely that members of a rowing club got Clyde under way in 1877. The club's first home was Barrowfield Park, close to the River Clyde, but there was a move to the Shawfield Stadium in 1896. Clyde joined the Scottish League in 1891, but often struggled to get decent gates, due to the close proximity of Celtic and Rangers. In 1986 they were evicted from Shawfield and so were forced to groundshare with both Partick Thistle and Hamilton Accademical. Since 1994 Clyde have played at the Broadwood Stadium, Cumbernauld.

Cowdenbeath

Cowdenbeath FC was founded in 1882 when Cowdenbeath Rangers and a club called Raith Rovers merged. This Raith Rovers was unconnected with the present Raith Rovers. Cowdenbeath were elected to the Second Division in 1905, and they are the oldest surviving football club in Fife. Their early home was at North End Park, but in 1917 they moved to their current Central Park ground. The small stadium is noted for a tarmac track, which is used for banger racing and other forms of motor sport.

Dumbarton

One of the older Scottish sides, Dumbarton was formed in 1872. The club was a founder member of the Scottish Football Association a year later. Having joined the Scottish League for its first season in 1890–91, Dumbarton finished joint top with Rangers. The club had been at its Boghead Park ground since 1879, but a hundred and more years later it was extremely dilapidated. There were plans to renovate it, but eventually a decision was taken to sell the ground for housing development, and to move to new home. The transfer to the Strathclyde Homes Stadium took place in November 2000.

Dundee

Dundee FC came into being in 1893 when two local sides, rejoicing in the names of Our Boys and East End, merged to form a new club. The team enjoyed little success in its early years, but it was admitted to the Scottish First Division in 1893. At that time Dundee played at a ground called Carolina Port, but they were to move to Dens Park, their current location, in 1899. Rivals Dundee United were later to move to a ground just down the road. Dundee have experienced severe financial difficulties in recent years.

Dundee United

In 1909 a group of Roman Catholics, inspired by the examples of Hibernian in Edinburgh and Celtic in Glasgow, decided to form a football club in their own city and call it Dundee Hibernian. The new club played its home games at Clepington Park, later to be re-named Tannadice Park, and entered the Scottish League Division Two in 1910. A few years later, financial difficulties caused a group of businessmen to decide to widen the appeal of the club and, in 1923, Dundee Hibs became Dundee United. The side still plays at Tannadice.

Dunfermline Athletic

Dunfermline was formed after a meeting in a pub called the Old Inn during 1885. Scottish League status was not however achieved until 1921, when the team gained entry into the Second Division. Dunfermline Athletic's original East End Park ground was very close to the one at which they still play.

East Fife

Located in the town of Methil, East Fife FC was founded in 1903. The team played in various local leagues, before joining the Central League and then the Scottish League Division Two in 1921. In 1998 East Fife moved to the New Bayview Stadium, relocating from their old Bayview Stadium across town. The new Bayview is near the River Forth and is overlooked by the derelict Methil Power Station. Everyone in the ground is accommodated in the 2,000-seater stand, as the other three sides are simply surrounded by a wall.

East Stirlingshire

East Stirlingshire FC is based in Falkirk. Formed in 1891, the club was known originally as Bainsford Britannia – Bainsford being a district of Falkirk. East Stirlingshire entered

the Second Division in 1900. In 1964 the club moved to Clydebank and played under the name of East Stirlingshire Clydebank. This arrangement however lasted for just one season, after which they returned to their Firs Park ground and became East Stirlingshire once more. Firs Park, East Stirlingshire's home since 1921, is somewhat dilapidated and once more moves are afoot to relocate the club.

Elgin City

Elgin Rovers and Vale of Lossie amalgamated in 1893 to form Elgin City FC. The North of Scotland club has spent much of its time playing in the Highland League, which it joined in 1895. Entry to the Scottish League was gained in 2000, when two additional clubs were added – Elgin and Peterhead, both of which went into Division Three. Elgin have been at their Borough Briggs ground since 1921. Their previous home, Station Park, had been ploughed up during the Great War.

Falkirk

Falkirk Football Club came into being around 1876, and entered the Scottish Second Division in 1902. The team first played at a ground called Randyford (1876–81) before moving to the wonderfully named Blinkbonny Grounds in 1881. A couple of years later Falkirk moved to Brockville Park, where the team played until 2003. Eventually, Brockville Park was considered not to be up to standard, and the team now plays at the Falkirk Stadium, which has an official capacity of just 8,000.

Forfar Athletic

During 1885, Angus Athletic's reserve team broke away to form a new club called Forfar Athletic. Entry into the new Scottish Second Division was finally gained in 1921. In common with but a few Scottish League clubs, Forfar have remained at their original ground – in this case another Station Park, where they have been for more than 120 years.

Gretna

Gretna Football Club was founded in 1946. Being on the Scotland/England border, they decided to play initially in English football, and joined the Carlisle and District League. Gretna later graduated to the Northern Premier

League and after that decided they would go for Scottish League football. In 2002 they achieved their objective and have since been remarkably successful. Much of this success is due to the money put into the club by multi-millionaire chairman Brooks Mileson. Gretna play at Raydale Park.

Hamilton Academical

Hamilton Academical came into existence in 1874, when the rector and pupils of Hamilton Academy decided to form a football club. Scottish Second Division status was achieved in 1897, when the club replaced Renton. Douglas Park was home to Hamilton from 1888 until 1994. Then for seven years they had to ground-share with both Albion Rovers and Partick Thistle. Hamilton finally moved in to New Douglas Park (which is very close to the old one) in 2001.

Heart of Midlothian

Reputedly named after a dance hall which in turn took its name from the title of Sir Walter Scott's novel, Heart of Midlothian Football Club came into existence in 1874. Hearts were founder members of the Scottish League in 1890–91, the campaign which saw them lift the Scottish Cup for the first time. Although Heart of Midlothian was initially a Protestant club, the sectarian rivalry with fellow Edinburgh club Hibernian was never as passionate as it was between Celtic and Rangers in Glasgow. Their patron was Lord Rosebury.

Hibernian

Founded by members of St. Patrick's Roman Catholic Church, Edinburgh, in 1875, Hibernian was the first of the major Scottish clubs to be founded by members of the Catholic Irish immigrant community. Hibs were elected to the Scottish Second Division in 1893, and were champions in their first season. The club had several grounds during its early years originally playing, along with other teams, on The Meadows, to the south of Edinburgh, before moving to the Leith area of the city and a ground called Hibernia Park. Easter Road has been the home of Hibernian since 1891.

Inverness Caledonian Thistle

Formed in 1994 as the result of a merger between Caledonian FC and Inverness Thistle, both of which were members of the Highland League, Inverness Caledonian Thistle have enjoyed remarkable success in their short history. Having entered the Scottish League just after the formation of the club, Caley Thistle earned promotion to the Scottish Premier League in 2004. They had to ground-share at Aberdeen for a season, while their Caledonian Stadium was brought up to SPL standards, but they are now back at their picturesque home overlooking the Moray Firth.

Kilmarnock

The oldest professional club in Scotland, Kilmarnock was founded in 1869 by a group of cricketers in search of a winter pastime. Rugby football was the club's original choice, but with the increasing popularity of the round ball game, the club soon adopted soccer rules. Kilmarnock joined the Scottish Second Division in 1895, and soon achieved considerable success, winning the Second Division championship in 1897–98 and in 1898–99, before being promoted to Division One. The club has been at its present stadium, the aptly named Rugby Park, since 1899.

Livingston

The new town of Livingston got a Scottish League team when Meadowbank Thistle moved from Edinburgh and changed its name to Livingstone in 1995. Meadowbank had been a League side since 1974, when it ceased to be known as Ferranti Thistle. Ferranti Thistle was a works side founded in 1943, which had played in the East of Scotland League. Livingston FC won the Third Division championship at the end of their first season and continued to make good progress until fairly recently. They play at the Almondvale Stadium.

Montrose

Montrose is probably one of Scotland's least successful professional football clubs, although it did enjoy a certain amount of success in the 1970s. Founded in 1879, the club joined the Second Division in 1929, at the same time as Brechin City. The team continues to play at its long term home of Links Park.

Morton

Morton Football Club was founded as long ago as 1874, and entry to the Scottish Second Division was gained in 1893. After one or two previous grounds, the club settled at its present home – Cappielow Park – around 1883. It was renamed Greenock Morton in 1994, but encountered severe financial difficulties in the first few years of the twenty-first century. The Greenock prefix, indicating the club's home district, has now been dropped.

Motherwell

After combining for a game against a Glasgow select eleven, Motherwell Glencairn FC and Alpha FC decided in 1886 to amalgamate and to form a club called Motherwell. Alpha's old ground was used at first, before the new club moved to a pitch in the Airbles district of the town. In 1893 Motherwell became founder members of the new Scottish Second Division, and five years later moved to their current ground at Fir Park, the land having been granted to the club from the estate of Baron Hamilton of Dalzell.

Partick Thistle

Partick Thistle FC was founded in the Burgh of Partick, now a part of Glasgow, during 1876. In 1893 the club gained entry into the Second Division. It went on to become one of Scotland's major clubs, although recent years have seen something of a decline. The team originally played at a ground near to the River Kelvin, and went on to have several more homes, including one on a site which is now the Kelvingrove Art Gallery and Museum. Partick Thistle's current ground is the Firhill Stadium, Maryhill, Glasgow, which is not actually in Partick. The club has been there since 1909.

Peterhead

The year 1890 saw the formation of Peterhead FC, whose team was to play for many years in the Highland League. Finally, Peterhead were brought into the Third Division, along with Elgin City, in 2000–01. Having played at their Recreation Park ground for 106 years, Peterhead moved to a new stadium called Balmoor in 1997. This was not without its problems however, as the new ground was not ready on time, and the side had to play early fixtures away from home in the 1997–98 season.

Queen of the South

Queen of the South – the only football team whose name can be found in the Bible (Luke 11: 31) – was founded in 1919 following a meeting in Dumfries Town Hall. It was there decided that three clubs – Dumfries FC, Maxweltown Volunteers FC and a works side called Arrol-Johnston – would merge to form the new club. A poll was held to decide on the name, and for some reason the poetic sounding Queen of the South was chosen. The team entered the Scottish League Division Two in 1925. Palmerston Park has always been home.

Queen's Park

Queen's Park FC was founded in Glasgow on July 6th 1867, and it is Scotland's oldest club. It was founded as an amateur club and it has remained an amateur club ever since – the only one in the Scottish League. In 1890, Queen's Park refused to join the new league, fearing that it would lead to the demise of smaller clubs, but the committee finally bowed to pressure and joined in 1900. The club has been at the present Hampden Park Stadium, which it shares with the Scottish national side, since 1903. The stadium once had the largest capacity in the world, and was famous for its 'Hampden roar'. Its home club, which was once the most important in Scotland, now attracts crowds of only a few hundred spectators to its games. But it's still there.

Raith Rovers

Raith Rovers came into being in 1883 in Kirkaldy, Fife, and joined the Second Division in 1902. The club has always been well supported, and Prime Minister Gordon Brown is a passionate fan. Raith have been at their Stark's Park Stadium, which currently has seating for more than 10,000 spectators, since 1891.

Rangers

Named after an English rugby union club, Rangers were founded in 1873 and went on to become probably the most successful of all football clubs, having won more than 50 Scottish League titles to date. They were founder members of the Scottish League in 1890–91, when they finished joint top of the table, along with Dumbarton. Rangers were traditionally supported by Protestants and from the beginning there was great rivalry with Catholic-supported Celtic. The rivalry led to the term The Old Firm, reputedly coined in 1904 by a journalist from *The Scottish Referee*. A preview of an upcoming derby game contained a cartoon of a man carrying a sandwich board bearing the legend 'Patronise the Old Firm – Rangers, Celtic Ltd'. The suggestion was that the rivalry between the teams was good for business – and that continues to be the case over a century later. Having occupied a variety of grounds in the early days, during 1887 Rangers settled at Ibrox Park in the Govan area of Glasgow.

Ross County

Founded in 1929 in Dingwall, Ross & Cromarty, in the north of Scotland, Ross County went on to become Highland League champions in 1967, 1991 and 1992. The club joined the Scottish Third Division in 1994, having beaten several league clubs in the Scottish Cup over the years, and plays at Victoria Park.

St Johnstone

St. John's Toun (St. John's Town) is the ancient name for the city of Perth, and St. Johnstone FC was founded in that city by a group of cricketers, around 1885. The club joined the Second Division in 1911. Its first home was Craigie Haugh, later known as the Recreation Grounds, but in 1924 St Johnstone moved to a ground known as Muirton Park. They remained there until a move to a purpose built stadium at McDiarmid Park in 1989.

St Mirren

St Mirren was originally a gentlemen's club, with members playing cricket and rugby.

By 1877, however, football was king. The side played at Shortroods, before moving to Thistle Park in 1879. Westmarch was home from 1883 until 1894, after which the club moved to St Mirren Park, Love Street. St Mirren were founder members of the Scottish League in 1890.

Stenhousemuir

Founded in 1884, Stenhousemuir has enjoyed little success on the field. The club joined Division Two in 1921 and has been in the lower divisions ever since. Stenhousemuir attract considerable support from Norway, with Norwegians owning 5% of the club's shares. Ochilview Park has been home since 1890, and now has a Norway Stand in honour of its overseas support.

Stirling Albion

A local businessman called Thomas Ferguson formed Stirling Albion in 1945. The club replaced King's Park FC, which had not survived the Second World War, partly because the only bomb to fall on the small city of Stirling fell on King's Park's pitch. Stirling entered the Second Division (Division 'B') in 1947. The club's first home was called Annfield, but Stirling Albion were never likely to rival Liverpool. In 1992 the club moved to its present home, the Forthbank Stadium, which is further away from the city centre than was Annfield.

Stranraer

Stranraer Football Club was formed in 1870, and is the third oldest of the country's current league clubs. Due to its comparative isolation in the south west of Scotland, Stranraer did not enter the Second Division (Division 'B') of the Scottish League until 1955. The club had previously played in, amongst other competitions, the South of Scotland League. Stranraer is currently semi-professional, its home ground being Stair Park.

Works Teams

There are many football clubs that started life as teams of workmates. And while most now have associations with sponsors rather than employers, there's still a tale to be told of football teams who worked and played together. Note: we have omitted Total Network Solutions who, though bearing a company name, did so for reasons of sponsorship.

Leigh RMI

Leigh Railway Mechanics Institute Football Club, usually known as Leigh RMI, are based in Leigh, Greater Manchester. The club was founded in 1896 and was known as Horwich RMI FC until 1995 when it relocated from Horwich to Hilton Park, home of rugby league club Leigh Centurions. Ten years later, they were planning to move again, this time to a new purpose-built stadium to again be shared with Leigh Centurions.

Traditionally, rugby league dominated the town, leading to low attendances. This led to discussions of a merger with FC United of Manchester, but United fans voted to keep their separate identity. Leigh's finest hour was an FA Cup draw with Fulham in 1998 when the London club were managed by Kevin Keegan. Leigh were in the Conference North in 2006–07.

Vauxhall Motors

Vauxhall Motors FC was founded in 1963, in Ellesmere Port, Cheshire, in the wake of a new car plant opening. By 1970 the club had achieved several promotions and played on the company-owned Hooton Park, but for the past 20 years they have played at Rivacre Park, opened in 1987 by England manager Bobby Robson.

The Motormen have enjoyed considerable FA Cup success in the last few years, even defeating Queens Park Rangers in a 1st Round replay at Loftus Road on penalties in 2002.

Ferranti Thistle

Scottish football club Ferranti Thistle was formed in 1943 as a works side of the Ferranti engineering firm, playing in the East of Scotland League. On their election to the Scottish Football League for the 1973–74 season, the club moved to the Meadowbank Stadium in Edinburgh and renamed itself Meadowbank Thistle but moved again at the start of the 1995–96 season, this time to the new town of Livingston.

In the 1986–87 season, Meadowbank won the Scottish Division Two championship and

won promotion to Division One. They finished runners-up the following season but were denied promotion to the Premier Division due to a reduction in the size of the division.

The club suffered from the restructuring of the Scottish Football League in the 1995 season; having finished mid-table in Division One, it was relegated to Division Two because the league was scrapping its format of two 12-club and one 14-club divisions in favour of four divisions of 10 clubs. Meadowbank suffered a second successive relegation in 1994–95.

The club bounced back and, after finishing champions of Division One in 2000–01, gained promotion to the Scottish Premier League after just six seasons in existence. The club's first SPL campaign, 2001–02 (with the club by now known as Livingston), brought more success as they finished third and qualified for the UEFA Cup. They won their first national trophy in 2004 by winning the Scottish League Cup, a 2–0 win secured over Hibernian at Hampden Park, but financial administration and relegation followed two years later.

Airbus UK

When promoted to the League of Wales for the first time in 2004, Airbus UK FC followed in the footsteps of TNS in becoming the league's second team to bear the name of their sponsor. Based in Broughton, North Wales, they are the works team of the Airbus aerospace factory where the wings of the European Airbus airliner are produced, and are consequently nicknamed The Wingmakers or The Planemakers. The club shared Conwy United FC's ground before their own, the Airfield (capacity 2,100), had its pitch brought up to League of Wales standard. The Airfield is adjacent to an operational runway and so has unusual retracting floodlights.

Formed in 1946 as Vickers-Armstrong, the club has since borne the names of several factory owners including de Havilland, Hawker Siddeley, British Aerospace and BAE Systems.

Metropolitan Police FC

The club was formed in 1919, 90 years after the law enforcement body from which it took its name. The Blues, as they were inevitably dubbed, joined the Spartan League in 1928, and they remained in that competition until

1960. They currently play in the Ryman League Division One

In 1984, when in the Isthmian League, the Met reached the first round proper of the FA Cup and were drawn at home to Dartford, a tie that was subsequently featured on BBC television's Match of the Day programme. Their home ground at Imber Court, East Molesey in Surrey is about one and a half miles from the historic Hampton Court and was acquired by the force for use as a sports ground in 1919.

The rules of eligibility, which can be changed at the club's AGM and do get altered from time to time, state that 75 per cent of the playing staff must be employees of the Metropolitan Police (not necessarily police officers). This is a condition of the club's use of the Imber Court facilities. The football club don't deny that they would like more freedom to sign non-police players, but it just isn't allowed.

The other 25 per cent are required to be 'persons of good character'. Having a relative in the police is no longer essential, although it still helps. But if the football management attempted to sign a player with more than the most petty of criminal records, the committee wouldn't allow it. Furthermore, any police officer who is sent off while playing for Met Police runs the risk of disciplinary proceedings at work.

Ford United

The works team of the car giant's Dagenham, Essex plant was the stepping stone for at least one professional footballer in Fulham and Gillingham keeper Jim Stannard. When he came back to manage the club in the early 2000s, it had changed its identity to Redbridge despite objections from Dagenham & Redbridge. They are currently in the Ryman League Division One North.

Edinburgh City

There has been more than one Edinburgh City FC. The current club that plays at Meadowbank Athletics Stadium were originally Postal United – so named because most of the players worked for the Royal Mail – and adopted the historic name in 1986. It is said that they traced the one director of the original club still alive and 'paid' him a bottle of whisky for the rights to the name!

Cammell Laird

Cammell Laird started life as the works team for the famous Merseyside shipyard that bore the name. The yard is sadly now gone but Lairds carried on to celebrate their centenary in 2007. There have been suggestions that they should change their name to Birkenhead Town in order to create an identity with the town, but die-hards felt it would be sad to lose the link to the history of the club. They currently play in the UniBond League Division One Midlands.

Formed by Fans

With money pulling the strings, fans up and down the country have attempted to take back control of the game they love. Whether by forming new clubs, trying to take over old ones, starting again from the bottom when their club has gone bust or forming a supporters trust as a lifebelt in case the worst should happen, their efforts are to be commended.

This list of clubs and a potted history of their founder/owners' motives is accompanied by details of Supporters Direct, the government-funded agency helping supporters set up trusts, and MyFootballClub.com, a 2007 attempt to gather together enough fans to buy a club via the internet. Also of note is the fact that Charlton Athletic and Millwall have a supporter director on their board.

AFC Telford United

The name of Telford United was first registered when Wellington Town (formed 1879) changed its name in 1969 and the side achieved a fair degree of non-league success including some spectacular 1980s FA Cup runs. In 2000 the club's players went full-time and a new stadium was constructed but, at the back end of the 2003–04 season, which on the pitch had been a good one, the club were forced into liquidation despite the fans raising thousands of pounds in a vain attempt to stave off the inevitable. The business of their main benefactor had got into trouble, and the club came down with it. Total oblivion was avoided by a supporters trust which became owners of a newly formed club, AFC Telford United.

Taking a place in the Unibond Northern Premier Division 1, having a secure ground lease on their Bucks Head stadium and a degree of financial stability plus a new manager in Bernard McNally, success came instantly. The new outfit made it into the play-offs and secured a place in the Unibond Northern Premier League Premier Division. After only two seasons, they defeated Witton Albion in the play-off final of 2006–07 to take another step up the ladder into the Blue Square Northern League (Conference North in old money). They were now just one rung below where they had been at liquidation, and two from the League.

FC United of Manchester

FC United associations are perhaps obvious; the club sprang out of objections by Manchester United fans to the takeover at Old Trafford by American magnate Malcolm Glazer and his family. Like the residents of Old Trafford they can justifiably claim support all over the world.

From its infancy in 2005, the club have had a great deal of success, winning the second division of the North West Counties Football

League in their first season and bagging the first division title in 2006–07. This meant elevation to the Northern Premier League First Division, surely beyond everybody's wildest expectations in such a short space of time.

Games are played at Bury's Gigg Lane ground, boasting a capacity of close to 12,000. Pulling in healthy crowds for non-league football, this democratically-run club has many ambitions for the forthcoming years, including elevation to Conference North, the building of a new stadium in the Greater Manchester area and the formation of a women's team.

AFC Wimbledon

AFC Wimbledon was formed by disillusioned Wimbledon FC supporters who objected strongly to the move of the existing club from south London to far off Milton Keynes. The fans felt the new club, which found itself ground-sharing with Kingstonian at Kingsmeadow just outside the borough of Merton, was the true upholder of all things associated with the original club and regarded the Milton Keynes Dons as having no tangible links to Southwest London.

FC United of Manchester were a success story on and off the pitch.

From foundation in 2002, the non-leaguers soon made their mark, climbing out of the Combined Counties League after a couple of seasons, took the Isthmian League First Division title in an unbeaten first season and made the play-offs in the Isthmian Premier League in 2005–06. Over a period of three seasons they went a total of seventy-eight games unbeaten. Not bad for a side that had been initially put together after trials on Wimbledon Common. Although there are many difficulties with such a plan, many supporters still hanker after a return to the original club's heartland from their current Surrey base.

AFC Wimbledon's first game against Sutton United in July 2002 drew a crowd of 4,500.

Fan Takeovers

Brentford

In January 2006, the supporters' trust Bees United became the major shareholders in Brentford Football Club, appointing Greg Dyke as club chairman. The 100% commitment to the Brentford cause is admirable and substantial funds have been raised to help the club keep afloat as they struggle in the lower reaches of the Football League. Unfortunately, the Trust's faith in the future of the club was not rewarded in 2006–07 when the West London side were relegated to League 2.

Rushden & Diamonds

Rushden & Diamonds were formed in 1992, when Max Griggs, the owner of both Rushden Town and Irthlingborough Diamonds merged

the two clubs. Success came quickly enough for R&D and by 1996 they were in the Vauxhall Conference having been successful in the Beazer Homes Southern League Division 1 and Beazer Homes Premier League. In 2001 they were promoted to the Football League Division 3 and took the league title in 2003, which was when the club's problems really started. Things started to slide on the pitch with immediate relegation in 2003–04 and further demotion only narrowly avoided the following season.

In 2005 Griggs, who had become vulnerable at the helm, passed the running of the club over to a supporters' trust, which was unable to halt the slide and by the end of the 2005–06 season R&D were back in the Conference. By November 2006, the fans' short-lived takeover came to an end as Keith Cousins became owner of the club.

York

In March 2003, the York City Supporters Trust completed a bailing out operation for their ailing club under the name of York City Football Club Limited. Just over a year later the lease on the club's Bootham Crescent ground was due to run out and after a £2 million loan from the Football Stadia Development Fund the supporters were able to ensure that York City would be able to continue playing at their home of seventy years.

In 2005 naming rights were taken up by local company Nestle and the ground took on the new name of KitKat Crescent. By the middle of 2006 the Trust opted for a restructuring of ownership, relinquishing three-quarters of their share to JM Packaging Ltd.

Supporters Trusts

Supporters Trusts have become a valuable part of football life in the last few years and can mean the difference between a club's continued existence or descent into oblivion. The status of the club is no barrier to the involvement of such Trusts. The government backed Supporters Direct was set up to assist supporters in the act of seeking ownership of their club and should always be consulted when fans seek to take matters into their own hands via a Trust. A growing number of clubs have Supporters Direct to thank for their current state of good health.

Charlton Athletic

Charlton were one of the first clubs in English Football to introduce an elected supporters director. For the first 10 years of the scheme, the voting was open to supporters who had contributed to the Valley Investment Plan (VIP). When this came to an end in 2001, the election was opened up to the wider supporter base, with one vote being allocated to each adult season ticket holder. In the most recent election in 2006, Ben Hayes was elected supporters director until 2008.

CLUB FACTS

Nottingham Forest are the only club to have been drawn to play FA Cup ties in all four home countries. In the early days of the competition, clubs from Scotland and Ireland could, and did, enter. In 1885, after a drawn semi-final tie against Glasgow's Queen's Park at Derby, Forest ventured north of the border for the replay in Edinburgh. This proved to be the only FA Cup semi-final ever contested outside England. Four years later, Forest were drawn against Irish club Linfield in the first round – after a 2–2 draw in Nottingham, a replay was scheduled in Ireland, but Linfield scratched before the game was played. Within a couple of years, both the Scottish and Irish Football Associations had banned their clubs from entering, so Forest's record will remain unique.

Myfootballclub.co.uk

A website was launched in 2007 with the revolutionary aim of recruiting 50,000 fans to take over a football club. The idea was for people to pay £35 in a bid to raise £1.4m to buy a team, with each member an equal partner. Members would have a vote on transfers as well as player selection and all major decisions affecting the club.

'I've created a vehicle that will pool fans' opinions, passion and wealth and turn fantasy football into reality,' said creator Will Brooks, a former football journalist. 'I've always had the notion of a group of fans putting money into a club and not taking it out – it is a potent force for good as most owners look at clubs as a way of making money.'

Brooks acknowledged the scheme could encounter teething problems, particularly as regards to members picking the team. 'Before members voted on team selection the head coach would provide a briefing on the previous week's game, the next opponents and potential players and formations,' he suggests. 'Then the owners would vote and the head coach would have to follow their decision, although I think the owners would probably follow the head coach's advice.'

> ### 'The head coach would know that this is a club with a difference – where the owners have their say – and, in many ways, the pressure will be taken off him because of this.'

If the website is successful in taking control of a club, Brooks expects the day-to-day running of the business to go on normally, with members only voting on the most important decisions. As of November 2007, the site reports that a deal has been agreed in principle to purchase Ebbsfleet United of the Blue Square Premier (formerly the Football Conference). The specifics of the deal, and the future success of such an arrangement, remain to be seen.

Two Into One Will (Sometimes) Go

Joining forces is a controversial idea and one often fraught with problems. Local rivalries have to be buried, often for the sake of economic survival, and matters such as club colours, badge and even the songs sung from the terraces can acquire importance out of all proportion to reality.

Amalgamations made with the intention of increasing a club's size and chances of rising up the football pyramid are most often done outside of the Football League itself, but as the success of Rushden & Diamonds and, more recently, Dagenham & Redbridge, shows, such visions can prove more solid than mere mirages. Rushden & Diamonds have since returned to the Conference, but there's little doubt that neither constituent club would have tasted league football had Max Griggs not got them together.

So while you may not have heard of some of the new clubs formed by joining forces, that may well change in the future. We also list some projected amalgamations that got no further than the drawing board – the reasons why are fascinating in themselves!

Successful Amalgamations

Corinthian Casuals

Corinthian Casuals was formed when two leading amateur sides came together in 1939, both having histories stretching far back into the 19th century. The Corinthians (formed 1882) carried a famous name signifying their position as honest, upstanding purveyors of early association football. They can claim to have inspired the formation of a top Brazilian side, a Swedish cup competition and the colour of Real Madrid's shirts. They merged with Casuals, formed in 1883.

Many more people have heard of Corinthian Casuals than know where they play (Tolworth, Surrey). Their President is Jimmy Hill OBE and their stated aim is 'to promote fair play and sportsmanship, to play competitive football at the highest level possible whilst remaining strictly amateur and retaining the ideals of the Corinthian and the Casuals Football Clubs.'

Dagenham & Redbridge

D&R started life as two separate clubs – Redbridge Forest and Dagenham – before merging in 1992 (the situation is confused as 12 years later Ford United adopted the name Redbridge). Leading amateurs Walthamstow Avenue had been part of the creation of Redbridge Forest just four years earlier when they'd joined forces with Leytonstone/Ilford.

The new club had a very successful first season, finishing third in the GM Vauxhall Conference and reaching the first round proper of the FA Cup, where they were defeated 5–4 in a thrilling game against Leyton Orient. But they then fell out of the Conference and only returned in 2000.

The club should have gained league status in 2003 had it not been for the illegal activities of Boston United who secured elevation from the Conference in their place. First manager John Still who returned to take them up in 2007 believes Dagenham & Redbridge's historic Nationwide Conference National championship victory has 'righted the wrong'. He dedicated the side's historic achievement to the memory of his late father Len – a devoted Daggers' fan: 'It does mean more to me because my Dad was a fan. He brought me to Dagenham years ago. It would have been his birthday on Tuesday, as well, so it's funny how it has happened.'

Havant & Waterlooville

Havant & Waterlooville was formed in 1998 by the amalgamation of the two non-league clubs of those names situated just outside Portsmouth. Waterlooville's ground was sold and Havant's West Leigh Park redeveloped.

Havant FC's history dated back to 1883. The team plied their trade in the Portsmouth Football League and in the 1950s produced Chelsea and England forward Bobby Tambling. In 1969 the club merged with Leigh Park FC, formed in 1958 and that season's winners of the FA Sunday Cup.

The amalgamated team, still known as Havant, became founder members of the Wessex League in 1986, and were runners up three times before finally clinching the title and promotion to the Southern League in 1991. Waterlooville FC, founded 1905, had arrived in the Southern League twenty years earlier but ran into money problems.

While Havant & Waterlooville (the Hawks) have suffered by their proximity to Portsmouth – now enjoying Premier League status – they have gained by allowing their neighbours to play reserve matches at their ground – a valuable income stream for the Conference South club which would be very much at home in the Conference National.

Westleigh Park, home of Havant & Waterlooville, one of the growing number of clubs formed by mergers. The stadium is also home to Portsmouth's reserve team matches.

Rushden & Diamonds

The formation of Rushden & Diamonds in 1992 was the brainchild of one Max Griggs, the boss of boot manufacturers Dr Martens. He persuaded two neighbouring Northamptonshire non-league clubs, Rushden Town and Irthlingborough Diamonds, that they would enjoy a brighter future pulling together than competing for custom.

History proved him right. Rushden Town had been compulsorily relegated from the Southern League Premier Division at the end of the 1990–91 season as their ground was deemed unfit for that level of football, while the Diamonds, whose Nene Park ground was revamped to accommodate the new team, were in the United Counties League. Nine years and several million pounds of investment later, Rushden & Diamonds was a league club. While a Conference club (they left as Champions in 2001) they drew Leeds United in the Third Round of the FA Cup. The game, played in January 1999, took them within 10 of Nene Park's official maximum attendance of 6,431. In 2002,

they pulled in record receipts of £46,592 when playing in the Division Three play-offs against Rochdale. Though unsuccessful, they made no mistake the following season when they topped the division under manager Brian Talbot.

Unfortunately the fairytale turned sour in 2006. Rushden & Diamonds' five-year league tenure ended with relegation, and their first season in the Conference saw them flirting with another drop. Griggs had left the club in the hands of a fans' trust, but he was reportedly displeased when they took the course of action of ceding control to an individual, Keith Cousins.

Solihull Moors

In January 2007, it was announced that Moor Green had applied to the FA for permission to merge with local rivals Solihull Borough. Moor Green FC was formed in 1901 by players from the Moseley Ashfield Cricket Club but did not play competitive football until 1922, when they joined the Birmingham AFA.

In 2003–04, they secured a place in the newly-formed Conference North but a 2005

CLUB FACTS

Huddersfield Town played at Leeds Road for over eighty years, from the club's formation in 1908, until the move to the new Galpharm Stadium in 1994. But things could have been rather different, if newspaper reports from the closing months of 1919 are to be believed. With the club in deep financial difficulties, a move to Elland Road, home of Leeds City until their expulsion from the league just a month earlier, was proposed. Leeds Road would be sold off for redevelopment, and Town would start afresh more than 15 miles away. Not surprisingly, this proved unpopular with the Huddersfield faithful, and fans raised the money needed to rescue their club and its ground. We can only guess what they would think if they could see the site today, buried under a retail park with only a brass plaque in the tarmac to show where the centre circle once lay.

arson attack on the Moorlands stadium, their home since 1930, rendered the ground unusable. The merger with the club whose ground they have shared since the attack meant Solihull Moors would play its games at Damson Park, Solihull, and start 2007–08 in the Conference North.

Hayes & Yeading United

The merger of Hayes FC and Yeading FC, West London's senior semi-professional football clubs, in 2007 was intended to raise the profile of non-league football in an area that traditionally struggles for crowds against local Premiership and Football League sides. Though Yeading pulled 11,000-plus to Loftus Road for an FA Cup game against Newcastle United in 2004, their next home crowd increased by just 15.

With both clubs punching above their weight to stay in the Conference South division, Hayes having stayed up on a technicality, the hope was that the integration would create a side and facilities to meet Conference National requirements and, in the longer term, a club capable of promotion into the Football League. Their new name was arrived at alphabetically, the United added at the request of fans, and the club would play at Hayes' ground prior to a new one being built.

Hayes were originally formed as the Botwell Mission in 1909, taking the name of Hayes Football Club in season 1928–29 and have unearthed such talents as Robin Friday, Cyrille Regis, Les Ferdinand and Jason Roberts. Yeading began life more recently, formed as Yeading Youth Club in 1960. Famous old-boys include Andrew Impey, Charlie Oatway and DJ Campbell.

Unsuccessful Amalgamations

Fulham Park Rangers

The concept of Fulham Park Rangers was mooted in 1987 when Fulham FC was sold by then chairman Ernie Clay to property developers Marler Estates. Their motivation to combine the two west London clubs was the value of Fulham's Thames-side ground, Craven Cottage, which would be ripe for redevelopment as flats. The concept was, however, presented as a way of increasing the clubs' status by joining forces. In the end, the outcry from both sets of supporters against the merger ensured their continuing separate existence. QPR did, however, make off with Fulham's best players in Dean Coney and future England international Paul Parker.

CLUB FACTS

London added its 14th senior club in 2007 when Dagenham & Redbridge attained Football League status. They joined Arsenal, Barnet, Brentford, Charlton, Chelsea, Crystal Palace, Fulham, Leyton Orient, Millwall, QPR, Tottenham Hotspur, Watford and West Ham.

Thames Valley Royals

This grandly named club was the intended result of a merger proposed in 1983 by newspaper tycoon Robert Maxwell. Maxwell, who then owned Oxford United, wanted to merge his club with then-struggling Reading to form the Didcot-based Thames Valley Royals. The revenue from the sale of the Manor Ground and Elm Park would be the financial basis of the new club. This inspired fans of both clubs to protest. Former United captain and then Manchester United manager Ron Atkinson commented: 'Mr. Maxwell obviously believes that if you add 6,000 United fans to 6,000 Reading fans you'll get 12,000 supporters for the new club. You won't'.

Maxwell's intention was to acquire Reading FC by purchasing the whole of the issued share capital (73,000 shares). Reading's chairman Frank Waller, who recommended it to the Reading shareholders, did not in fact have a controlling number of shares, and when rebel director Roy Tranter served him an injunction forbidding transfer of shares until early in May the merger was scuppered as there was insufficient time to make plans for the following season. A change of ownership at Reading was accompanied by dramatic improvements on the field. Looking at the respective positions of the clubs in 2007, Reading in the top half of the Premier League and Oxford in non-league oblivion, it's not hard to see who would have gained.

Lymington & New Milton

Lymington & New Milton (the Linnets) was formed in 1998 when the old Wessex League club AFC Lymington merged with New Milton Town, then a Hampshire League side. As the senior club, AFC Lymington had the proud record of winning the Wessex League title three times during the 1990s. But the new club made their home at New Milton's Fawcett's Field where the first part of their name caused friction with their council landlords. 'I can understand why the council get upset,' said manager Ian Robinson. 'Fifty per cent of the budget for the upkeep of pitches in the area is spent on our pitch – and yet we're called Lymington.'

Acting chairman Ian Snook agreed: 'The council spend a lot of money doing a very good job for us and the change of name would be a way of us giving something back to them.' Lymington & New Milton became New Milton Town, but withdrew from the Southern League to return to the Wessex League in summer 2007 amid board-level dissent and a management walkout.

West London United?

In January 1967, QPR made an unsuccessful bid to take over west London neighbours Brentford, while in 2001 *The Sun* newspaper reported a move to merge QPR with then nomadic Wimbledon. As with the Fulham Park Rangers proposal in 1987 these proposals were successfully opposed by the fans.

Other amalgamations to have made column inches if nothing else included a idea of uniting rivals Crystal Palace (the Eagles) and Brighton (the Seagulls) in a super stadium somewhere near Gatwick Airport (i.e. equidistant between their current location). It is hard to see what this would do apart from enrage the respective supporters' groups.

More recently, plans were mooted for up and coming FC United of Manchester to absorb struggling Leigh RMI, then two rungs above them in Conference North. These plans fell through as United fans wanted to keep their separate identity, but the two clubs remain on cordial terms and a merger could still be on the table in the future.

Geographically Challenged

Not all clubs have remained where they began, sometimes moving such vast distances as to constitute the formation for what is essentially a new club. Others have endured short spells away from home – several clubs, including Charlton, Brighton and, at the time of writing, Bristol Rovers, have moved out of their original grounds for various pressing reasons – before returning. Charlton returned in triumph, Brighton eventually found lodgings in a local athletics stadium while Rovers will return to a modernised Memorial Ground after their spell with Cheltenham.

For others, though, there is more of a geographical gap between where they originated or were named after and where they currently play. We also highlight some anomalies where clubs from one country play in the league of another.

CLUB FACTS

Brentford have been at their Griffin Park ground for more than 100 years. It's hardly surprising – the ground has a pub on each corner, one of them owned by the football club itself.

Arsenal

Arsenal moved to Highbury in 1913 but their history lay in Southeast London, having been founded by a group of workers from the Woolwich Arsenal Armament Factory. Prior to the relocation, they had played under the names of Dial Square, Royal Arsenal and finally Woolwich Arsenal.

Derry City

Derry City from Northern Ireland played in the Football League of Ireland from 1985 to 2006. From 2007 they continue to play in southern Ireland, in the FAI National League.

Grimsby Town

The club's Blundell Park ground is actually situated in nearby Cleethorpes. For some time a move to pastures new has been proposed and by the 2009–10 season Grimsby Town should be playing at the Conoco Stadium which is to be constructed in Great Coates… west of Grimsby!

Port Vale

Port Vale is only named as such due to the club's inaugural meeting being held at 'Port Vale House' situated in the environs of Stoke-on-Trent. The club played under the name of Burslem Port Vale for a number of years due to the location of their ground but dropped the prefix early in the twentieth century when they located elsewhere. Their ground for the last 50-odd years, Vale Park, has a Burslem address.

Wimbledon

After Wimbledon relocated to Milton Keynes in 2003 amidst much controversy, the only connection to the club's past existed in the new name of Milton Keynes Dons. The spin-off club AFC Wimbledon, formed by disillusioned fans of the former Southwest London club, also had location problems as all home games are played some miles away in Kingston, Surrey.

Temporary Moves

Brighton & Hove Albion

Brighton came close to extinction after the Goldstone Ground, their home since 1902, was closed in 1997. A ground-share with Gillingham some 70 miles away proved unpopular, and they returned to the locality to lodge at the three-sided Withdean athletics track with a 7,000 capacity. A new 22,000-capacity ground on the outskirts of the town at Falmer was proposed, and Brighton are still hoping to move there in time for the start of the 2009–10 season.

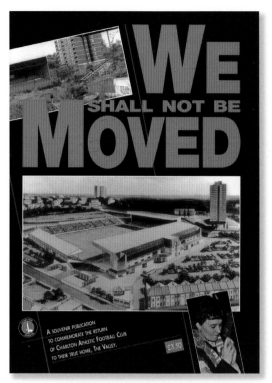

'We Shall Not Be Moved', a souvenir publication issued to commemorate Charlton's long overdue return to their the Valley ground. A picture in the top left corner of the cover clearly shows the dilapidated and overgrown state in which the stadium was left for many years while planned refurbishment was repeatedly delayed.

Bristol Rovers

Having previously spent a ten-year spell up to 1996 at Bath City's Twerton Park, Bristol Rovers will groundshare with Cheltenham Town when their Memorial Ground shuts down for redevelopment for the 2008–09 season at the least. They expect to spend 18 months without a permanent home. Fan enmity made sharing with neighbours Bristol City an impossibility. Rovers ground-shared with Bristol Rugby Club until their landlords hit money troubles and sold them half the ground for £2.3 million. In 1998 the Rugby Club called in the receivers, and Rovers acquired the ground completely due to a contract clause.

Charlton Athletic

Against the odds, the Addicks managed to gain promotion to the top flight during their time away from the Valley. This included the period 1985–91 at Selhurst Park and a single season at Upton Park. Their campaign to return included putting up supporters as candidates in local elections.

Fulham

The Thames-side club left Craven Cottage, the riverside site they'd occupied since 1896, in 2002 for a spell at QPR's Loftus Road ground, some four miles distant. The club's plans to redevelop the ground they'd vacated into a 28,000 stadium proved beyond Fulham's means so they returned in 2004 after standing terraces had been seated.

Gretna

The club's unexpected and rapid ascent to the Scottish Premier League led to them having to lodge with Motherwell for six months while necessary upgrades were made to their Raydale Park ground. The border club's ground-sharing agreement represents a departure by the SPL from their insistence in previous years that Falkirk could not be admitted to the top division because they wished to rent premises from a fellow member until the old Brockville could be replaced.

Inverness Caledonian Thistle

Caley ground-shared with Aberdeen, over 150 km (100 miles) away, for half a season in 2004. They were able to return early after a change in Scottish Premier League rules during the 2004–05 season to only require 6,000 (not 10,000) seats for membership, Caledonian Stadium was given two new stands in only 47 working days, and was renamed as the 'Tulloch Caledonian Stadium' in honour of the building firm which completed the work.

England v Wales

Despite being in Wales, Newport County have always played in the English football system. This, along with problems obtaining a home ground in their city after re-forming in 1989 led to their nickname of the Exiles. Cardiff City, Wrexham and Swansea City are the three

Deva Stadium, home to Chester City, straddles the border between England and Wales, with the pitch standing on the Welsh side while the main stand is in England!

other Welsh league clubs who ply their trade in England.

Chester City's Deva Stadium straddles the border of England and Wales. Because the club wanted to operate within the English league structure, they made sure their offices were built on the 'English' side.

An 18-point deduction (reduced to three on appeal) was the reward for AFC Wimbledon in 2007 after they signed and played Jermaine Darlington without obtaining international clearance. Darlington, the first man to play for both Wimbledon and AFC Wimbledon, had retired from football after a spell with Cardiff City but was persuaded to return to the non-league game. He had never played outside the English FA-governed system, but AFC officials did not realise that Cardiff's location across the border demanded clearance for the player.

Prior to the Football Association of Wales ejecting their own professional English Football League clubs from the Welsh Cup competition, a number of English clubs took part on a regular basis, e.g. Hereford and Shrewsbury. The latter were beaten in one final by Newport County who qualified for Europe in the process.

England v Scotland

Berwick Rangers are technically in England but play in the Scottish league.

Gretna, the town on the borders of England and Scotland famed for its wedding industry, spent many a season playing in the English football pyramid before being co-opted into the Scottish league. Its rise has been meteoric, funded by Sunderland-born millionaire Brooks Mileson, and they started season 2007–08 with the prospect of top-flight football after three consecutive promotions.

The prospect of Rangers and Celtic one day playing in the English Premiership has long been a topic of debate. It would certainly add spice to the English game having the two Scottish giants in regular competition south of the border, but greatly devalue the Scottish Premier League.

Chapter 3

Lost to the League

Of course, not all those clubs which once graced the rungs of the Football League do so today. For some, simple relegation to the non-league system ended their tenure, for others the end meant the closure of the entire club. Here we commemorate those clubs who, for whatever reason, have been lost to the league…

Lost to the League – England

A cursory glance at the first Football League tables will reveal many of the clubs we are familiar with today, but in amongst them will be found many names that are not so well-known, those that have fallen by the wayside in the intervening years. Some of these clubs simply went out of business, others failed to gain re-election to the league after a disastrous season and yet more went on to achieve greater fame under a different name.

In recent years, automatic promotion and relegation between the Football League and the Nationwide Conference has meant that some more familiar names have disappeared from the Football League after many years, and a few long-established non-league sides have stepped up to make their bid for glory. Here we have a round-up of the clubs whose Football League careers have come to an end, some permanently, some just for the time being…

Aberdare Athletic

Founded in 1892, Aberdare Athletic were Welsh Cup runners-up to Druids in 1904 and Wrexham in 1905, losing both finals 3–0. Otherwise, their early years were relatively uneventful, but they joined the Southern League Welsh Section for the 1920–21 season, and things began to happen. A successful campaign led to their being elected to the new Football League Division Three (South) for the 1921–22 season, the first of

six they would spend as a Football League side.

Despite finishing in respectable mid-table positions, Aberdare struggled to attract the punters, playing as they were in the rugby stronghold of South Wales. After finishing 9th in 1925–26, they suffered a catastrophic dip in form and ended the following campaign at the foot of the table. Some reports say they failed to gain re-election, others that they didn't apply, but either way Aberdare's League career was at an end, with Torquay taking their place.

The following season, Aberdare Athletic merged with Aberaman Athletic and rejoined the Southern League as Aberdare & Aberaman Athletic, but the new club lasted only one season before splitting in two. The Aberdare faction folded, but Aberaman survived, and today's ENTO Aberaman can trace its roots back to the break up of the earlier club in 1928.

Accrington

Founder members of the Football League in 1888, Accrington have no connection to either incarnation of Accrington Stanley, who adopted the town's name only after the collapse of their rivals in 1896.

The earlier club, known as the 'Owd Reds', was formed in 1876, and played at Moorhead Park. In 1884, they joined the revolt against the Football Association over professionalism, having been expelled from the FA for paying one of their players the previous year, but by 1888 they were back in the fold and became one of the 12 clubs in the original Football League. Both Blackburn Rovers and Everton started their league careers with games against Accrington.

By 1893, they found themselves relegated to Division Two, having finished last but one in Division One and lost their Test Match against Sheffield United. Accrington never played another league game, resigning from the Football League rather than face the ignominy of playing in the lower division. They struggled on under increasing financial difficulties for another two years, but threw in the towel after a 12–0 thrashing from Darwen in the Lancashire Senior Cup in January 1896.

Aldershot

One of the more familiar names no longer playing league football, Aldershot Football Club was formed in 1926 and joined Division Three (South) in 1932 following the demise of the short-lived Thames AFC. In a League career lasting almost 60 years, the Shots spent all but five seasons in football's basement, either Division Three (South), or the later Division Four, before falling prey to financial collapse in 1992. Despite last-ditch attempts to rescue the club, Aldershot were declared bankrupt in March 1992, having completed 36 of their Division Four games for the season.

A new Aldershot club was formed very soon afterwards, and from humble beginnings at the foot of the non-league pyramid, the revived Shots are now enjoying considerable success in the Nationwide Conference, and pushing to bring league football back to the town.

Ardwick

Better known these days as Manchester City, Ardwick AFC could trace its roots back to 1880, when St. Mark's Church in West Gorton established its first football team. Renamed Ardwick AFC in 1887, the side went on to win the Manchester Cup twice in two years, and become founder members of Football League Division Two in 1892.

After two seasons, Ardwick AFC changed its name to Manchester City FC, with the aim of creating a club to represent the whole of Manchester, and for many years the Sky Blues remained the city's premier side.

Ashington

Formed in 1883, Ashington AFC is one of the oldest football clubs in the North East, playing in the Northern Alliance, the East Northumberland League and the North Eastern League at various times up until election to the new Third Division (North) in time for the 1921–22 season. The Colliers played just eight years of League football before failing to gain re-election at the end of a disastrous

1928–29 season, during which the side struggled and attendances at their 20,000 capacity ground at Portland Park fell to under four figures. York City took their place.

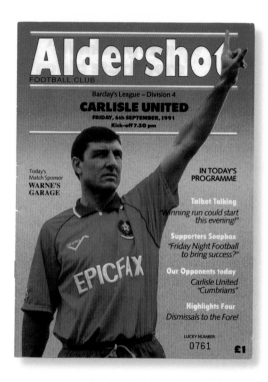

An Aldershot FC programme from the 1991–92 season – the last season the club would experience, going out of business during 1992. Ironically, that day's opponents were Carlisle United, who would finish the season bottom of the league but escaped relegation thanks to Aldershot's unfortunate demise.

After a brief hiatus, a re-launched Ashington rejoined the North Eastern League for the 1930–31 season, since when they've led a largely uneventful non-league existence. In 1958, they were founder-members of the short-lived Midland League, but in recent years they've played their football in the Northern League, and are currently struggling to maintain their place in its upper division.

Most people have heard of Ashington because it is the birthplace of Bobby and Jackie Charlton, although neither ever appeared for their local side. Two famous names have turned out in the Colliers' black and white stripes, though – the Charltons' uncle, Jackie Milburn, who later achieved greatness at Newcastle United, and England cricketer Steve Harmison, who played in central defence at Portland Park until deciding to concentrate on the summer game in 1996.

Barrow

One of the founder members of Division Three (North) in 1921, Barrow remained there until finishing in the lower half of the table in 1957–58 saw them start the following campaign in the newly-created Division Four. Between then and their eventual exit from the League at the end of the 1971–72 season, Barrow managed just two terms in Division Three, their 8th position in 1967–68 marking the high point of their existence.

After periods in both the Football Conference and the Northern Premier League, Barrow now play in the Nationwide Conference North, a new league competition they started in 2004. In recent years, Barrow have gone from the thrill of winning the FA Trophy in 1990 to the despair of going into administration in the opening weeks of 1999, but now (as Barrow AFC) seem to be on a reasonably even footing.

Bootle

Details of their early existence are sketchy, but Bootle were founder members of the Football Alliance in 1889, and, before the arrival of Liverpool, the main rivals to Everton on Merseyside. FA Cup quarter-finalists in 1890, Bootle went on to become founder members of Football League Division Two, created when the Alliance merged with the existing Football League in 1892.

Bootle dropped out after just one season, and seem to have folded almost immediately. Their place in Division Two was, appropriately enough, taken by Liverpool. Today, another club called Bootle FC is playing in the North West Counties League, but this club has no connection with the Victorian side, having been formed in 1953.

Boston United

Boston United were founded in 1933 as successors to Boston FC. They played in various leagues, including the Southern League and the Conference, before gaining admittance to Division Three in 2002. Their centrally located Staffsmart Stadium is loved by many fans but considered not up to standard by others. A local rivalry is conducted with Lincoln City.

In the wake of their promotion, Boston were charged with breaking Football Association rules over the registration of players. Manager Steve Evans and former chairman Pat Malkinson received bans, while the club was fined and docked four points. Had this deduction been backdated their promotion would not have happened.

Few tears were shed then, when, in 2007, Dagenham & Redbridge, the club 'robbed' of league status due to Boston's wrongdoing, were promoted to League Two, whilst Boston were relegated to the Conference in their place. They went into administration ten minutes from time in their last League game to ensure they started the Conference with a clean slate. But financial problems made their survival a matter for debate, and a two-level demotion to Conference North didn't help.

Bradford Park Avenue

Bradford Park Avenue joined Division Two for the 1908–09 season, but just two years earlier they had been members of the Northern Rugby Football Union, and played the oval ball game under the name The Bradford Football Club. What became known as 'the great betrayal' saw the club members elect to abandon the Northern Union game (later known as Rugby League) in favour of Association Football in 1907. Having had their application to join the Football League turned down, Bradford Park Avenue instead spent a year in the Southern League before their second league application met with a positive response.

By 1913, Bradford Park Avenue had achieved promotion to Division One, and completed the final peacetime season in 9th position, their best-ever finish. Soon after the hostilities, the club suffered relegation to Division Two, then Division Three (North) in successive seasons, and never again graced the top flight. By 1963, they had dropped to Division Four, and found it impossible to stop the rot. Having finished bottom of the table for three successive seasons, they failed to gain re-election in 1970 season, and made way for Cambridge United.

In 1973, they were forced to sell Park Avenue and ground-share with Bradford City, but their financial plight was such that even selling the ground could not save them, and the once proud club was liquidated the following year. Since then, a new club, officially Bradford AFC, has risen from the ashes, although fans still refer to the side as 'Avenue'.

Burslem Port Vale

The forerunners of the current Port Vale club, Burslem Port Vale enjoyed two brief spells of league football before World War 1. Founder members of Division Two in 1892, they found themselves back as a non-league side in 1896, after failing to gain re-election. Two years later they were back, but a constant struggle against financial problems finally took its toll and, in 1907, they were forced to resign from the league.

Having moved to a new ground, dropped the 'Burslem' and regrouped, Port Vale were readmitted to Division Two in 1919, taking over Leeds City's place when the latter were expelled from the league in the most famous football scandal of the 20th century.

The Burton Clubs

No fewer than three clubs from Burton enjoyed league status in the first fifteen years of the competition, although one of these was the result of the merging of the other two. Burton Swifts were the town's earliest league representatives, joining the newly-created Division Two in 1892 after previously playing in the Combination and the Football Alliance. They were largely unsuccessful, never achieving better than 6th in Division Two, and after propping up the league at the end of the 1900–01 season, they merged with local rivals Burton Wanderers to form Burton United.

Wanderers had themselves joined the league for the 1894–95 season, but their record was even more unspectacular than Swifts' – three seasons without finishing in the top half of the table, then a failure to gain re-election. They rejoined the Midland League, where they'd started life in 1890, before a disastrous 1900–01 campaign saw them emulate the Swifts by finishing bottom.

The newly-created merger, Burton United, took Swifts' place in Division Two, and started brightly enough – a mid-table finish in their first season seemed to augur well for the future. Things went downhill thereafter, and United finished in the bottom five in each of their remaining five seasons of league football. Voted out of the League in 1907, they spent three further seasons in non-league football before calling it a day at the end of the 1909–10 season.

An unrelated Burton Albion currently play in the Conference.

Cambridge United

A club called Cambridge United existed for a few years prior to World War 1, but the current side has no connection with their earlier namesakes, and can trace its roots back to the formation of another pre-war club, Abbey United. Abbey United started out in 1912 as an amateur side, and remained so until turning pro in 1949. Two years later, they changed their name to Cambridge United, playing in a number of different league competitions until being elected to replace Bradford Park Avenue in the Football League in 1970.

Promoted in 1973, Cambridge were not quite ready for the old Division Three, and suffered immediate relegation back to the basement. Next time it would be different – United achieved two successive promotions in 1977 and 1978, and spent the next six seasons just one step from the top flight, but two successive relegations put them back in the bottom drawer for the 1985–86 season. Remarkably, they would repeat their meteoric rise a few years later, promotion via the play-offs in 1990 being followed by the old Division Three championship the next year. Only defeat at the hands of Leicester City in the 1992 play-offs prevented Cambridge United from becoming the first team ever to go from the bottom division to the top in successive seasons.

Back in the basement by 1995, Cambridge never again rose to such dizzy heights, although a brief spell in Division Two raised hopes for a while. In the wake of the collapse of ITV Digital in 2002, United struggled to survive. Relegation from the Football League in 2005 brought with it a period in administration, but United have pulled through, and continue to play in the Nationwide Conference.

Clapton Orient

As related elsewhere in this book, the club was formed in 1881 as the footballing arm of the Glyn Cricket Club, and underwent several name changes before becoming Clapton Orient in 1898. After joining Division Two for the 1905–06 season, Orient led a largely uneventful life until several years of close calls ended with relegation to Division Three (South) in 1929. The 1930s were difficult years, and when World War 2 called time on league football in 1939, Clapton Orient were fighting for survival.

After the war, and renamed Leyton Orient, the club gradually recovered, and even reached the dizzy heights of top-flight football for a single season in the early 1960s.

Darwen

Darwen Football Club was formed in 1870, although initially they played the oval ball game, and Association rules were not introduced until 1875. Three years later, Darwen opened up the argument about professionalism when they signed Fergus Suter and James Love from Partick Thistle, the English game's first paid players. They were also the first Northern club to achieve significant success in the FA Cup, appearing in the quarter-finals in 1878–79, and the semi-finals two years later.

After playing in the Football Alliance, Darwen joined the newly-expanded Football League in 1891, but failed to impress – they finished with just 11 points from their 26 games, and on the way to becoming the first club to suffer relegation they crashed 12–0 to West Bromwich Albion, still a record top flight defeat. Promoted in 1892–3, and relegated again the following year, Darwen spent the rest of their short league career in Division Two. In 1896–97 they achieved the peculiar feat of going the whole season without drawing a match, still a unique achievement for a league side. In their final Division Two season, they

suffered no less than 18 successive defeats, conceding a staggering 141 goals in 34 games to set two more unbroken League records.

With over 130 years of continuous history, Darwen are still active, these days playing in Division Two of the North West Counties League.

Durham City

Formed in the closing months of World War 1, Durham City joined the League in 1921, one of the founding members of Division Three (North). Their League career was short and none too sweet – after seven seasons without finishing in the top half of the table, they were voted out in favour of Carlisle United.

The club folded in 1938, having spent their final years in the North Eastern League, but the name was revived in 1950, and today the revitalised Durham City can still be found playing in the Northern League at the Archibalds Stadium.

Exeter City

Exeter's recent fall from the Football League coincided with the club's 100th year of existence, so there was little to celebrate down at St James' Park in 2003. It was a bitter blow to a club that had survived a period of administration in the mid-1990s, been forced at one point to sell their ground to avoid going under, and had slowly begun to rebuild for the future.

Formed in 1904 from the merger of two earlier local sides, Exeter City joined the league as founder-members of Division Three in 1920, and spent almost all of their 83 years as a Football League side in its lowest division. They were ever-present in Division Three (South) from its inception in 1921 till the league was reorganised in 1958, then enjoyed only a dozen or so seasons outside the league's basement before relegation to the Conference in 2003.

Exeter survived another period of administration in the wake of relegation, but a takeover by the Supporters' Trust seems to have steadied the ship. They'll be bitterly disappointed not to have regained their League status after losing to Morecambe in the 2007 play-off final, but at least the future now looks brighter.

Gansborough Trinity

Formed as Trinity Recreationalists by the vicar of Holy Trinity Church in 1873, Gainsborough joined the Midland League in 1889, and stepped up to the Football League for the 1896–97 Division Two season. There they stayed for the next sixteen years, at no point finishing higher than 6th, and spending the last few years of their time in the league struggling to compete. In 1912, they failed to secure re-election, and were replaced by local rivals Lincoln City.

Returning to the Midland League, Gainsborough fared slightly better, recording three Championships and several FA Cup wins against league opposition over the years. Founder-members of the Northern Premier League in 1969, this long-established club now play their football in the Nationwide Conference North after gaining promotion in 2004. Neil Warnock used to play for them.

Gateshead

Over the years, the Gateshead name has been associated with several clubs, each rising from the ashes of the one before. The first to bear the name was Gateshead AFC, formed in 1930 after financial problems forced neighbours South Shields to sell up and move to a new ground. South Shields had been playing league football since 1919, so the newly constituted club took their place in Division Three (North), where they stayed until an indifferent performance in the 1957–58 season saw them become founder members of the new Division Four.

Just two years later, Gateshead had to apply for re-election. After 30 reasonably successful years, and with only one previous application for re-election, they were surprisingly voted out. One theory was that the club's geographical location had counted against them, but whatever the thinking, Peterborough United were duly elected to take their place.

Since 1960, the club has suffered several collapses, reforming first as Gateshead Town, then Gateshead United and most recently as Gateshead FC, currently playing in the Unibond League Premier Division.

Glossop (North End)

Formed in 1886, Glossop were originally known as Glossop North End. They joined the North Cheshire League in 1890, moving on to the Combination and then the Midland League before being elected to Division Two of the Football League in 1898. Success was immediate, and they were promoted to Division One at the end of their first season, at which point they changed their name to Glossop FC.

The glory days were brief – relegated after just one season in the top flight, Glossop gradually faded away, inhabiting the lower reaches of Division Two for most of their remaining years in the league. Having finished bottom in the last season before World War 1, Glossop left the Football League, never to return. Ninety years on, and having reverted to their original name, Glossop North End are still plugging away in the North West Counties League.

CLUB FACTS

Glossop claims the distinction of being the smallest town in England ever to have had a Football League team – the 2001 census shows the population of Glossop to be 28,622 – although Nelson, in Lancashire, comes a very close second with a population of 29,010.

Halifax Town

The Shaymen have the unwanted distinction of being the only club to have suffered relegation from the Football League on two occasions, the first in 1993, and the second nine years later.

Formed in 1911, Halifax joined the Football League when the Third Division (North) was created in 1921. Their League career was unspectacular, the vast majority of it spent in the lowest division at the time. In 1969, they gained promotion to the old Division Three, and two years later enjoyed an exciting campaign that saw them miss out on a place in the old Division Two by just four points, but this was to be the high watermark of their time as a league club, and within a few years they were back at the bottom.

Things went from bad to worse, and only once in the next 17 seasons did they finish above 15th in the table. The inevitable loss of league status came at the end of the 1992–93 season, but in 1998, league football returned to the Shay, after Halifax took the (then) Vauxhall Conference championship. It proved to be a short-lived revival – four years later they were relegated again, and have since led an up-and-down existence in the Nationwide Conference.

Kidderminster Harriers

Kidderminster Harriers had been around a long time before League football finally came to the Aggborough Stadium. When the switch to Association Football came in 1886, Harriers had already been in existence for nine years as an athletics and Rugby Union club. They joined the Birmingham & District League in 1889, moved on to the Southern League immediately before World War 2, but resigned in 1960 and went back to the Birmingham League. A further spell in the Southern League lasted until 1983, when Harriers joined the Alliance Premier league, now the Nationwide Conference.

In the years that followed, Kidderminster established themselves as a force in non-league football, reaching the FA Trophy final three times in eight years, enjoying a spectacular FA Cup run in 1993–94, and winning the Conference title at the end of the same season. Denied promotion to the Football League because their stadium was declared below league standard, Kidderminster had to wait until Jan Molby guided them to another Conference title in 2000 for another chance to join the big boys.

When it came, league football proved to be a tough nut to crack. Harriers finished in respectable enough mid-table positions in each of their first three league campaigns, but a string of bad results in the 2003–04 season led to a relatively poor final placing, and the following year they suffered relegation back to the Nationwide Conference.

Leeds City

Formed in 1904, Leeds City joined Division Two of the Football League the following year. In an unspectacular existence, City never progressed past the second round of the FA Cup, and only once managed to finish in the top five of the league, when the legendary Herbert Chapman steered them to 4th position at the end of the 1913–14 season.

As World War 1 drew to a close, evidence of a number of financial irregularities began to come to light, including breaking the ban on paying players during the war, and the subsequent investigation became the biggest scandal to hit British football in the last century. Leeds City were expelled from the Football League just weeks into the first post-war season, and their place, and the results from the eight games already played, given to Port Vale.

The club was dissolved shortly afterwards, the 16 members of the playing staff auctioned off, along with the club's other assets, for the grand total of £9,250. In the wake of the scandal, Leeds United was formed, taking over from Leeds City Reserves in the Midland League. After one season, United were elected to Division Two of the Football League, ironically starting their league career with a game against Port Vale!

CLUB FACTS

The first Conference National Play-off Final introduced to accommodate a second promotion place to the Football League, took place on 10th May 2003 and was contested by Dagenham & Redbridge and Doncaster Rovers. Doncaster won.

Loughborough Town

Loughborough Town FC was formed in 1886, and played in the Midland League from 1891 to 1895. Having finished as champions, the 'Luffs' were elected to Division Two of the Football League, at which point they simplified their name to Loughborough FC.

The club struggled badly in the league, finishing no higher than 12th in any season, and bowing out in 1900 after a catastrophic campaign that saw them win just one of their 34 games. They scored only 18 goals all season, but conceding a staggering 100 on their way to a record low of just eight points.

Their league career over, Loughborough were accepted back into the Midland League, but the club disappeared without ever playing another match.

Maidstone United

Maidstone United's elevation to the Football League in 1989 proved to be the highlight of their career, and the beginning of the end for the Kent side that had started out in the final years of the 19th century. Between 1897 and 1971 they had played in a number of amateur leagues, but then joined the semi-professional Southern League with the stated aim of achieving Football League status within ten years.

Performances and attendances improved, United won promotion to the Southern League's top flight in their second season, and became founder members of the Alliance Premier League (now the Conference) in 1979. In 1984, they were champions, but missed being elected to the Football League. Five years later, they triumphed again, but this time automatic promotion ensured their elevation to Football League Division Four. They'd made it, although it had taken a little longer than originally hoped.

After a shaky start to their first season, Maidstone recovered to reach the play-offs, but lost to Cambridge United. The following season, things took a turn for the worse, and a change of manager brought an unpopular move to a direct and far less attractive playing style than before. Fans drifted away, the club began to find money a problem, and attempts to relocate to a new stadium only made the financial situation worse. By 1992, the club had been forced into liquidation, and resigned from the league at the start of the 1992–93 season.

In the wake of the meltdown, Maidstone United's youth side formed the nucleus of a new club, who are now enjoying life in the Ryman Premier Division after winning the Ryman League Division One title in 2007.

Merthyr Town

Formed in the early years of the 20th century, Merthyr Town, like several other Welsh professional clubs, joined the Southern League in 1909. In 1920, when the Football League was extended to three divisions by the simple expedient of absorbing the Southern League's top division, Merthyr began a nine year league run that started reasonably enough, but simply petered out.

After a succession of poor placings, Merthyr finished the 1929–30 season nine points adrift at the foot of Division Three (South), and were voted out of the league, making way for the short-lived Thames AFC. By 1934, the club had folded, and today's Merthyr Tydfil FC has no connection with this earlier incarnation.

Middlesbrough Ironopolis

The splendidly named Middlesbrough Ironopolis came into being in 1889 after some members of Middlesbrough FC, then an amateur side, decided they would like to form a professional club. Ironopolis joined the Northern League in 1890, and topped the table in each of their first three seasons. The resignation of Accrington in 1894 provided a place in Division Two of the Football League for Ironopolis, who seemed to have a bright future.

Unfortunately, things didn't work out that way – crowds were sparse, gate receipts didn't even cover the players' wages, and travelling expenses from the North East were unsustainable. Unable even to afford the rent for their ground, the 'Nops' were wound up on June 5th, 1894 after just the one league campaign.

Nelson

Founded in 1881, Nelson played their football in the Lancashire League (later the Lancashire Combination) from 1891 until 1916, when the club was closed down until hostilities were over. After the war, Nelson briefly joined the Central League, then became a founder member of the Football League Division Three (North) in 1921.

The next few years could best be described as unpredictable – Nelson were promoted in 1923, relegated the following year, and narrowly missed being promoted again the year after that. As the 1920s drew to a close, Nelson began to struggle, finishing in the lower reaches of the league in each of their last four seasons. A failure to gain re-election in 1931 saw them drop to the Lancashire Combination, and in 1936 the club went out of business. In 1946, a re-formed Nelson FC picked up where the earlier club had left off, and continues to this day.

New Brighton

New Brighton could trace their origins back to 1910, and the formation of South Liverpool FC. South Liverpool ran into financial problems and were declared bankrupt in 1921, but as so often happened another club was immediately formed to take its place. New Brighton initially stepped into the old club's shoes in the Lancashire Combination, but in 1923 made a successful application to join the newly-expanded Football League Division Three (North).

Their entire league career was spent fairly uneventfully in the same division, until a poor showing in the 1950–51 season led to their being voted out of the Football League and Workington being elected in their place. However, there were some highlights in New Brighton's story, with three FA Cup fourth round appearances to cheer fans. The 1956–57 run was particularly impressive, the club overcoming league opposition three times before crashing out 9–0 at Burnley.

Thirty years of non-league football ended in 1981, when the club finished bottom of the Cheshire County league, and folded. The name was revived in 1993, and these days New Brighton play in the West Cheshire League, but the current club has no connection with the former League side.

New Brighton Tower

Like Chelsea and Thames AFC, New Brighton Tower FC were unusual in being a club formed to play at an already-built stadium. The New Brighton Tower was a seaside attraction built on Merseyside to rival the famous Blackpool Tower, and when its owners decided there was a need for some out-of-season entertainment a stadium was added to the complex.

New Brighton Tower FC was formed to provide the entertainment, and began life in the Lancashire League at the start of the 1896–97 season. Success was immediate, and the new club finished top of the league in their first season. Duly elected to Football League Division Two, the club embarked on a signing spree, bringing in several ex-international players to bolster the side.

Despite some good results, and three top half of the table finishes, crowds at the 80,000 capacity stadium averaged around 1,000, and the ongoing cost of maintaining the side proved to be too much for the Tower's owners. The club was disbanded in 1901, and replaced in the League by Doncaster Rovers.

The tower was dismantled just after World War 1, rendered unsafe by years of neglect, but the stadium continued in use for many years, staging the World Cycle Championships in 1922, and hosting some of the matches played by the later New Brighton football club. Today nothing is left of the complex, the remainder having been destroyed by fire in 1969.

Newport County

Formed in 1912, and immediately accepted into the Southern League, Newport County were among the Football League Third Division's founder members in 1920, moving to the Third Division (South) when the League expanded further the following year. There they stayed until the outbreak of World War 2, finishing as champions in the last peacetime campaign.

After the war, despite looking forward to life in Division Two, County often found themselves outclassed, including a league record 13–0 defeat at Newcastle in October. The club spent the remainder of their time as a Football League club in the lower divisions, although they enjoyed a brief spell of relative success under Len Ashurst in the early 1980s. By the end of the decade, County were in decline, successive relegations in 1987 and 1988 leading to the loss of league status after almost 70 years.

Newport failed to complete their first season of non-league football, and were officially wound up in February 1989. A new club was formed within months, starting anew in the Hellenic League. Now in the Conference South, the revived County are continuing the quest to bring league football back to Newport.

Newton Heath

Manchester United's rise to pre-eminence in the English game began 130 years ago in 1878, when men at the Lancashire & Yorkshire Railway depot in Newton Heath decided to form a works football team.

Known at the outset as Newton Heath LYR FC, the team severed its links with the railway twelve years later, and became Newton Heath FC. In 1892, they joined the Football League when Division One was expanded to 16 clubs, but finished last in each of their first two seasons, and were relegated in 1894.

Newton Heath remained a reasonably successful Division Two side for the next few years, but at the turn of the century, they began to suffer the financial problems that affected so many clubs in the early days. John Henry Davies, a wealthy brewery owner, took the club over in 1902. He changed the club's name to Manchester United (although Manchester Central and Manchester Celtic were also considered), and replaced their green and yellow halved shirts with the red strip now famous the world over.

Northwich Victoria

One of the older clubs still in existence, Northwich Victoria can trace their history back to 1874, when the club was founded and patriotically named in honour of the reigning monarch. For some years, they played only friendly matches, but joined the Combination at its inception in 1890. Two years later, the 'Vics' began their short stay in the Football League when they became one of the founding members of the new Division Two, but professionalism proved too great a financial burden, and Northwich returned to non-league football after just two terms.

For over 125 years, Northwich played their football at Drill Field, but were forced to sell up in 2002 and ground share with local rivals Witton Albion. Having survived a period in administration, they moved to a new home, Victoria Stadium, in 2005, and in their first season at the new ground gained promotion to Nationwide Conference, leaving them one promotion away from a long-awaited return to league football.

Oxford United

Loss of their League status in 2006 after 44 years came as a bitter blow to fans of a club that had been in the top flight of English football just 20 years earlier. Their rise to the old Division One was all the more remarkable given their relatively late entry into the Football League, which came after the collapse of Accrington Stanley in 1962.

For almost 60 years after their formation in 1893, Headington United remained a small amateur club, but they turned professional in 1949 after their application to join the Southern League was successful. Headington were ambitious, and followed their first Southern League title in 1953, and an impressive FA Cup run in 1954, with a ground improvement scheme that made the Manor one of the best non-league venues in the country. In 1960, Headington raised their profile by changing their name to Oxford United, and two years later brought league football to the city for the first time.

Promotions in 1965 and 1968 saw Oxford into the old Division Two, although they suffered their first ever relegation eight years later. Money became tight, but with the help of controversial tycoon Robert Maxwell, the club survived. In 1984, they were back up again as old Division Three champions, and in 1985 they achieved what had seemed unthinkable only 20 years earlier – promotion to the top flight. What's more, they achieved it with a second successive championship, the first club ever to do so, and added the Milk Cup to the trophy cabinet for good measure.

Three seasons later, they were relegated again, and the glory days were over. A gradual decline in the club's fortunes saw them slip ever further down the league, and by 2001 they were back in the bottom division. Managers came and went, cash remained an issue, and five years later the battle for league survival was lost. At the end of the 2006–07 season, Oxford narrowly missed out on an immediate return to the league, finishing second in the Nationwide Conference, but losing 2–1 to Exeter in the play-off semi-final.

The Rotherham Clubs

Like Burton, the town of Rotherham has been represented in the league by three clubs, but, like Burton, one was a result of the amalgamation of two earlier sides.

First came Rotherham Town, formed in 1870, and one of the founder members of the Midland League in 1889. Their brief period in the league lasted just three seasons between 1893 and 1896. Spent entirely in Division

Two, it was an unspectacular stay by any measure, the high point being 12th place in their second term. After finishing last but one in 1896, Rotherham Town were voted out of the league. In 1904, they were back in the Midland League, where they remained until merging with Rotherham County in 1925.

Rotherham County had also done time in the Midland League, joining in 1903 and staying until elected to Division Two of the Football League in 1919. Relegated to Division Three (North) in 1923, County soon found life difficult, and a merger with their near neighbours seemed to be the best option for both clubs. The newly merged Rotherham United competed in the League from the 1925–26 season, and are still active in League One today.

CLUB FACTS

Oxford is the largest city in England without a Football League side, closely followed by York and Gloucester. Wigan is the smallest town to boast a Premiership side, while Barnsley is the smallest with a team in the Championship.

Rushden & Diamonds

Rushden FC had been in existence since 1889, competing in the Midland League, the Northants League and the United Counties League before being elected to the Southern League Midland Division in 1983. At the end of the 1990–91 season, Rushden were promoted to the Southern League Premier Division, but their Hayden Road ground was declared not to be of the required standard, and they were relegated again by order of the football authorities despite a mid-table finish.

Irthlingborough Diamonds, meanwhile, had been an under-18 side from their formation in 1946 until moving up to the United Counties League in 1964. After enjoying some success in both the league and FA Vase competitions during the 1970s and 1980s, Diamonds' fortunes went into decline, and in 1991 local businessman Max Griggs was approached for a possible sponsorship deal.

Griggs suggested a merger with Rushden, and despite some initial scepticism both parties agreed. Griggs put up the cash to bring Diamonds' Nene Park stadium up to scratch, and, the new club took over from Rushden FC in the Southern League Midland Division at the start of the 1992–93 season. By 1996, they were in the Southern League Premier Division, and in 2002, Rushden & Diamonds' Football League career began with promotion to Division Three.

There, they made an immediate impact by topping the table at the end of their first season. This meteoric rise was followed by an equally spectacular fall – the new club suffered immediate relegation, endured a nail-biting fight against a second successive relegation in 2004–05, and finally relinquished their League Two place in favour of the returning Hereford United in 2006.

Scarborough

When Lincoln City became the first victims of automatic relegation from the Football League in 1987, the team that stepped up to take their place was Scarborough.

Scarborough are one of the oldest clubs in the country, having been formed in 1879 by members of a local cricket team. Unsurprisingly, their early matches were played at the cricket club's ground, but in 1898, Scarborough FC moved to the Athletic Ground in Seamer Road, latterly known as the McCain Stadium.

Between 1898 and 1927, Scarborough played as amateurs in the Northern League, after which they turned pro and joined the Midland League. Moving up to the Northern Premier League in 1968, Scarborough began the most successful period of their history, winning the FA Trophy three times in five years, and two impressive runs in the FA Cup in 1975–76 and 1977–78. Another step up, to the Alliance Premier League, followed in 1979, and in 1987 Scarborough topped the now renamed Vauxhall Conference to secure a place in the Football League.

Scarborough's stay in the League lasted twelve seasons, during which time they reached the play-offs twice, but spent several seasons struggling to avoid the drop. There were some notable League Cup runs to cheer the fans, but a desperately close relegation dogfight in 1999 saw Scarborough finish in last position and making a return to non-league football. Since then the club has struggled to survive, and the 2006–07 season saw them relegated from the Conference North. Now defunct, they have been succeeded by Scarborough Athletic.

Small Heath

Formed in 1875 by the cricketers of the Holy Church team in Bordesley Green, Birmingham, Small Heath Alliance had turned professional and shortened their name to Small Heath by the time they became founder members of the Football League Division Two in 1892.

The Heathens were champions in their first season, but missed out on promotion after losing their Test Matches against Newton Heath. They had better luck against Darwen the following year, but found it difficult to compete and suffered relegation two years later. It was a pattern that would be repeated several times in the club's history.

In 1905 they changed their name again to become Birmingham FC, and the following year completed the move to their current home at St Andrews. A final change of name saw them become Birmingham City in 1946.

South Shields

Three distinct clubs have used the South Shields name, the first, and only one to taste league football, having been formed in 1907 as South Shields Adelaide. Under this name, the team played one season in the Northern Alliance, then transferred to the North Eastern League, dropping the 'Adelaide' from their name in 1910.

After World War 1, South Shields joined Football League Division Two, where they played for nine seasons before suffering relegation to Division Three (North). Two years later, in a bid to stave off financial collapse, South Shields sold their ground and relocated nine miles west to become Gateshead FC (see page 62).

A second South Shields club was formed in 1936, but incredibly history repeated itself in 1974, when this incarnation of the club also moved to Gateshead and became Gateshead United FC. A new club, initially called South Shields Mariners, was formed almost immediately, and continues to the present day. They are currently playing in the second division of the Northern League.

Small Heath, who would in 1905 change their name to Birmingham City. Seen here is the team for the 1892–93 season.

Southport

Another of the more recent names to disappear from the league, Southport have a continuous history going back to 1881, although their league career didn't begin until some forty years later.

Founder members of the Central League in 1911, Southport hold the distinction of being the first club to bear the name of a sponsor, when they played the 1918–19 season under the patronage of the Vulcan Motor Company, and duly changed their name to Southport Vulcan. By 1921 they were known simply as Southport once more, and began their Football League career in the new Division Three (North).

Ten years later, they became the first Divison Three club to reach the sixth round of the FA Cup, losing 9–1 in a replay against that season's Division Two champions, Everton. There were other FA Cup runs of note, but success in the league was elusive – their best finish was 8th in the old Division Three in 1969. By the mid-1970s, Southport were struggling, and finished last but one in each of their last three seasons in the league. Finally, in 1978, they failed re-election, and Wigan Athletic stepped into the breach.

Since then, Southport have played in a number of competitions, and briefly harboured hopes of a return to league football after achieving promotion to the Nationwide Conference in 2006. Sadly, the side struggled badly, and suffered immediate relegation back to the Nationwide Conference North.

Stalybridge Celtic

Another club with a long history, but only a fleeting period of league fooball, Stalybridge Celtic FC was formed by Herbert Rhodes, a local businessman and philanthropist, in 1909. Rhodes put a lot of money into developing the club and its ground, Bower Fold, as well as turning out for them in their early years.

Until 1911, Celtic played as an amateur side in the Lancashire and Cheshire Amateur League, then turned pro and moved on to the Lancashire Combination. Before World War 1 put the brakes on English football in 1915, Celtic also spent time in the Southern and Central Leagues, and it was in the Central League that they resumed playing at the beginning of the 1921–22 season. After finishing as champions, they were elected to the Football League as members of the new Division Three (North).

It was a short stay – performances were patchy, local support proved difficult to sustain, and the club soon found itself financially challenged. Lacking the funds to compete for a third season, Stalybridge Celtic resigned from the Football League after the 1923–24 season, and were accepted into the Cheshire County League. Still in business, and fast approaching their centenary, Celtic now play in the Nationwide Conference North.

Thames AFC

Thames AFC was formed in 1928 in much the same way as Chelsea and New Brighton Tower, to play at a stadium that had already been built. The West Ham Stadium, with a capacity of over 100,000, had been built with a view to staging greyhound and speedway events, but these were not held on Saturdays, so a football team seemed the obvious way of making more use of the stadium.

Thames AFC joined the Southern League soon after being formed, and achieved a mid-table finish in their first season. Their second was far more successful, and their third place was enough to gain them admission to the Football League's Division Three (South), where they took the place of Merthyr Town prior to the 1930–31 season. To mark the occasion, Thames AFC shortened their name to Thames.

It was downhill all the way from here. Thames found it impossible to compete with established local sides like Clapton Orient, Charlton, West Ham and Millwall, and the huge stadium, the largest in England to host regular football matches, remained virtually empty on match days – just 469 fans turned out to watch the match against Luton Town in December 1930. Results were equally poor – Thames finished 20th and 22nd (of 22) in their two League campaigns, and the club's directors soon decided to abandon the idea and wind the club up. When Thames failed to apply for re-election, their place was awarded to Aldershot.

Torquay United

Old boys from local colleges decided, whilst they were listening to the band in Princess Gardens, to form a football club. Officers were later elected at a meeting held at the Tor Abbey Hotel, and in 1899 a football team was produced. Torquay at first played in local leagues, and at a number of grounds. For some time they were known as Torquay Town, and they moved to Plainmoor to ground-share with Babbacombe FC in 1910.

The name Torquay United was adopted in 1921, when the club finally merged with Babbacombe and turned professional. An application to join the League Division Three South was accepted in 1927 when Aberdare United were cast out after a tied vote. Perennial under-achievers, Torquay failed to rise beyond the third level of the league structure, and finished perilously close to the bottom of the pile on several occasions. The inevitable happened in 2007, whereupon they re-employed Leroy Rosenior, the manager under whom they'd enjoyed their most recent success (promotion to League One in 2004). Within days the club had been taken over by a consortium led by another former Plainmoor boss, Colin Lee, and it was all change again!

The club beloved of Helen Chamberlain of Sky TV's *Soccer AM* fame will hope to reclaim their 80-year league status with the briefest of gaps.

Wigan Borough

Wigan Athletic can trace their origins back to the town's earlier league representatives Wigan Borough, who spent ten seasons in Division Three (North) from its inception in 1921. Until the move to the JJB Stadium in 1999, Athletic played their home games at Springfield Park, which had been their predecessors' ground.

Borough were far from the first football club to represent Wigan, though – prior to their formation in 1920, Wigan County, Wigan United and Wigan Town had all come and gone – but Borough were the first to achieve League status. Initially playing as Wigan Association, then changing their name to avoid confusion with the town's Rugby League side.

They finished 17th of the 18 teams in the Lancashire Combination in 1921, but still decided to push their luck and apply for membership of the new Football League Third Division (North). Incredibly, they were voted in, apparently because the FA were anxious to promote soccer in rugby strongholds, and the town of Wigan fitted the bill perfectly.

Borough's league career was fitful, and for the most part unspectacular. Attendances were low, and the club always struggled financially. By 1931, Wigan Borough were in serious trouble, and it was only a matter of time before the axe fell. Unable to meet their debts, Borough resigned from the league on October 26th and went into liquidation. Six months later a new club, Wigan Athletic FC, rose from the ashes, although it would be almost 50 years before they brought league football back to the town.

CLUB FACTS

Torquay United right back Jim McNichol was the victim of one of football's most unusual injuries during his side's game against Crewe Alexandra on the final day of the 1986-87 season. As he cleared the ball upfield from the touchline, a nearby police dog, presumably under the impression that McNichol was about to attack his handler, bit the hapless defender on the thigh. McNichol was able to continue after treatment, and Torquay went on to draw the game, ensuring their survival as a league club, and condemning fellow strugglers Lincoln to the first-ever automatic relegation to non-league football. Twenty years on, and after 80 years in the league, Torquay have now met the same fate.

Workington

Founded sometime in the early 1880s, Workington played only friendly games and entered local cup competitions until joining the new Cumberland Association League in 1890. Over the next 20 years, the Reds featured in a succession of northern league competitions, but economic factors led to the club being disbanded in 1910.

Reformed in 1921, the club led a largely uneventful non-league existence until being elected to the Football League Division Three (North) in 1951. Initially, life in the league proved to be a struggle, but with the arrival of Bill Shankly as manager in January 1954, things gradually improved. Shankly moved on to Huddersfield two years later, and after a poor showing in 1957–58, the Reds found themselves effectively relegated to the new Division Four.

Hampered by a lack of funds throughout their time in the league, Workington never made much impression, although a brief period in Division Three lifted supporters' spirits in the mid-1960s. By the mid-1970s they were struggling badly, and had to apply for re-election in each of their last four seasons in the league. In 1977, the axe fell and Workington were voted out.

After surviving several extremely lean spells, Workington have recently seen something of a renaissance, and are now riding high in the Nationwide Conference North.

CLUB FACTS

There were more chiefs than Indians at Workington in 1966, when the addition of a thirteenth board member meant the club had more directors than full-time players.

York City

Formed in 1922, York City played in the Midlands League until elected to the Football League Division Three (North) in place of Ashington in 1929. City started brightly, finishing in 6th place in their first season, but this was to be their best performance until 1952–53, when they ended the campaign in 4th place. In 1954–55 they repeated the feat, with the added bonus of an FA Cup semi-final appearance against eventual winners Newcastle United. York held the Magpies to a 1–1 draw at Hillsborough before losing 2–0 in the replay at Roker Park.

York remained in the Third Division (North) until the Football League reorganization of 1958 left them in the newly-created Division Four. From then on, City led an unpredictable league existence, enjoying six promotions, suffering six relegations, and having to apply for re-election on six occasions (including three consecutive seasons at the end of the 1960s) before finally losing their league status after 75 years at the end of the 2003–04 campaign.

Like Oxford United and Exeter City, York City ended the 2006–07 season in one of the Nationwide Conference play-off positions, but all three former league clubs will have to endure another season of non-league football after Morecambe secured the coveted promotion to League Two.

Meltdown Mania

Sadly, clubs continue to struggle to this day and there are those whose perilous position suggests they may soon be joining the list of those whose names have already passed out of football history. For some, new management, a relocation, a change of name or a drop down the league may be enough to ensure survival – we can only hope that is true of the following clubs currently facing difficulties of the worst kind.

Canvey Island

In 2006, owner-manager Jeff King, who had been in charge since 1992, withdrew his financial support, which had seen the Essex club climb to the unlikely heights of Conference National. They accepted voluntary relegation to the Isthmian League First Division North in the 2006–07 season, starting afresh with new management and a whole new playing squad. King moved to nearby Chelmsford.

Crawley Town

Crawley Town of the Conference had hit tough times before, having endured a couple of months of administration in 1999, but had been dragged out of the mire by John Duly who took them through a very successful period in their history. In mid-2005, new owners the SA Group decided that they would now preside over a full-time club and money started to be spent, which heralded the onset of problems both on and off the pitch. In the 2006 close season the club were fined £10,000 and deducted three points for financial irregularities, which heralded another spell in administration.

A Supporters Trust came in with an offer to take over the club should creditors not accept what was on offer from SAG. So the 2006–07 season commenced with the club in total chaos, the team having to make up for a ten-point deduction due to the administration issue. They survived, but were docked six points in 2007–8.

Farnborough Town

Owner-manager Graham Westley used the proceeds of a 2003 FA Cup fourth round match with Arsenal (switched to Highbury for safety reasons) to withdraw his loans to the club and move on a week later to Stevenage with half of the first team in tow. The FA subsequently banned FA Cup ties being switched for financial gain. The club was liquidated in 2007, reforming as Farnborough FC two 'rungs' down the pyramid.

Hornchurch

Carthium Ltd, the company behind Hornchurch FC, had debts of over £7 million when they folded during the 2004–05 season, leaving the club no alternative but to go into administration, a sad day for a club with a history going back to 1923. Liquidation followed, but out of the ashes emerged AFC Hornchurch, whose inaugural season in 2006–07 found them triumphant in Ryman Division 1 North.

Weymouth

Sports journalist Ian Ridley had planned to take his hometown club to the league but lacked the resources to see the dream through. He yielded to board member Martin Harrison, a local hotel owner, but in 2007, the club shed manager Garry Hill and most of its higher-paid players, reverting to part-time status and seeing out the season with enough points to avoid a swift return to the Conference South.

Lost to the League – Scotland

Life for many of the Scottish League clubs has often been a struggle. Based in smaller communities than their southern counterparts, and often many miles from their nearest neighbours, money has always been an issue for all but the biggest names.

In the early days of the Scottish League, clubs came and went with even greater frequency than they did south of the border, and the economic problems that affected all aspects of life in Britain in the 1920s took a particularly heavy toll on football clubs in the far north. An attempt to introduce a third division to the Scottish League in the middle of the decade turned into a disaster, lasting just three seasons before ending in chaos. For many of the clubs involved, the financial repercussions proved terminal. Many sides ceased to exist altogether, while other followed a route more common in Scotland than in England, and turned to Junior League football. Either way, many unfamiliar names made a fleeting appearance in the League around this time before disappearing again.

In this section, you'll find a round-up of the clubs who once played Scottish League football, some familiar, some no more than a footnote in the annals of the game.

Abercorn

Abercorn were the second football club to spring up in Paisley in 1877, starting life just a few months after their more famous neighbours St Mirren. In 1887, Abercorn reached their first Scottish Cup semi-final, but lost 10–1 to Cambuslang, still a record margin for that stage of the competition. Three years later, they became one of the eleven founder members of the Scottish Football League, finishing one place above local rivals St Mirren in the first season.

Abercorn remained in the Scottish Football League until 1915, the only real highlights of their stay being the Division Two championships secured in 1896 and 1909. Because automatic promotion and relegation between the two divisions wasn't introduced in Scotland until after World War 1, the Division Two champions still had to rely on being voted into the top flight by the clubs already there – Abercorn were lucky in 1896, but not so lucky the second time around, and remained in Division Two for the rest of their time in the League.

Abercorn's undistinguished League record allowed St Mirren to become the predominant side in Paisley, and the smaller club effectively died as a result. Between 1915 and 1920, they played in the Western League, but chose not to renew the lease on their ground at the end of their final season. Their last-ever game was an 8–2 defeat by Vale of Leven in the 1920–21 Scottish Cup competition, and in 1922 the club, effectively already defunct, was barred from the Scottish FA for having no home ground.

Airdrieonians

Airdrieonians FC, more commonly known simply as Airdrie, went out of business at the end of the 2001–02 season, after 124 years in existence. In their final season, Airdrie finished a creditable second in the Scottish League Division One, but crippling debts sealed the fate of the Lanarkshire club and set the stage for one of the most bizarre and controversial takeover bids in football history.

Founded in 1878, Airdrieonians were initially known as the Excelsior Football Club, adopting their more familiar name in 1881. Thirteen years later the club joined the Scottish League Division Two and in 1903 they won promotion to the top flight for the first time. After a shaky start, Airdrie soon established themselves as serious contenders for the game's major honours, and finished in the upper reaches of the table on several occasions before World War 1. In the 1920s they did even better, finishing as runners-up for four consecutive seasons in the middle of the decade, and recording their only Scottish Cup victory in 1924.

Airdrie spent most of the remainder of the twentieth century in the top division, although it was only much later that they again enjoyed the kind of success they had before World War 2. In 1975, Airdrie missed out on being founder members of the new Scottish Premier Division by a whisker, finishing 11th in the old Division One on goal average behind Motherwell. But under Alex MacDonald in the 1990s, Airdrie made two Scottish Cup final appearances and regularly challenged for a return to top flight football. Ironically, it was the possibility of promotion that effectively killed the club.

By the 1990s, Airdrie's Broomfield Park ground was no longer of the required standard for Premier League football, so the board decided to sell up and build a new stadium in readiness for promotion. It proved a costly misjudgement. Airdrie suffered four years of ground-sharing with Clyde in Cumbernauld before they could move to the new Excelsior Stadium, and with attendances inevitably down, it wasn't long before the club was in dire financial straits. Crippled by debt, Airdrie went out of business in May 2002.

In the wake of the collapse, Airdrie fan Jim Ballantyne attempted to have a newly-formed club under the name Airdrie United elected to the Scottish League, but failed, as Gretna had already been voted in. A controversial deal was then engineered in which Ballantyne took over the failing Clydebank FC, moved it lock, stock and barrel to Airdrie, and renamed the club Airdrie United, who simply carried on where Clydebank left off in Division Two.

Armadale

Formed in the 1890s, this West Lothian side initially played in the Eastern Football Alliance, but later switched to the Central League. In the years immediately before World War 1, Armadale dominated the league, finishing as champions in 1914 and 1915.

In 1921, when the Scottish League reintroduced a second division by absorbing the Central League, Armadale were founder members of the new tier. After an encouraging first season, finishing third, the fortunes of the club declined, and by the end of the decade they were struggling to make any headway.

Armadale's final full season in Division Two was 1931–32, and although they played the first 17 games of the following campaign, their finances were in disarray, and they were unable to provide the match guarantees – the minimum amount to be paid to visiting teams – required by the Scottish FA. Expelled from the League, Armadale ceased to exist shortly afterwards.

Arthurlie

Formed in Barrhead, Renfrewshire, in 1882, Arthurlie turned professional in 1890 with a view to joining the new Scottish Football League. Having failed to secure membership, Arthurlie joined the Scottish Federation, one of a number of leagues that sprang up in imitation of the 'official' version around this time. They were almost immediately successful, winning the title in 1892, and four years later reached the pinnacle of their achievements by knocking the mighty Celtic out of the Scottish Cup.

Expansion of the Scottish League Division Two in 1901 meant that Arthurlie finally got their chance to join, but they never made much of an impression apart from finishing second in the 1906–07 season. Unfortunately, automatic promotion and relegation was still a long way off, and Arthurlie were not elected to the top flight.

Division Two was suspended for the duration of World War 1, and so Arthurlie joined the Western League pending the resumption of League football. The refusal of the Scottish FA to reinstate Division Two after hostilities ended led to the resignation of all the former member clubs in 1920. Arthurlie continued in the Western League, only to see a new Division Two created the following year from the old Central League. Two years later, the creation of a third tier of Scottish League football saw Arthurlie back in the league, and they made an immediate impact. Finishing as champions in the first season, Arthurlie regained their Division Two status, but money was tight, and by 1929 the club found it impossible to continue.

Having resigned from the league near the end of the 1928–29 season, Arthurlie spent two years as an amateur side, then moved to junior football, where they continue to this day.

The Ayr Clubs

Like Burton and Rotherham south of the border, Ayr is another town that has been represented by three different League clubs, and once again the third was the result of a merger of two earlier sides, Ayr FC and Ayr Parkhouse.

Ayr FC was formed in 1879, and was itself the result of the joining of two earlier sides, Ayr Academicals and Ayr Thistle. Ayr Parkhouse was formed in 1886, taking its name from the farm where its players trained. For a while, the two sides coexisted peacefully, but by the early 1890s they had become bitter rivals. The origins of this rivalry lay in an attempt by Ayr FC to entice Parkhouse's best players to join

them, and the strength of feeling between the two sides would bring them into conflict many times in the years to come.

In 1897, Ayr were admitted to the Scottish League Division Two, but initially found life difficult and had to seek re-election twice in their first three seasons. Ayr Parkhouse joined them in 1903, but fared badly, and finished bottom in their first season. They failed to gain re-election, due in no small part to a vigorous campaign by the board of Ayr FC to have them thrown out.

As Ayr's fortunes improved, Parkhouse were re-elected to Division Two, and for a few seasons the two sides were both moderately successful without ever seriously threatening to achieve promotion. By 1909, both had begun to go into decline and it was widely agreed that Ayr couldn't realistically support two senior clubs. The logical solution was a merger, an initially unpopular idea that gained much-needed momentum after Parkhouse slumped to the bottom of Division Two as the 1909–10 season drew to a close.

The merger proved to be just the boost the town's football needed. The new club, Ayr United, finished as runners-up in their first season, and then topped the table twice before being elected to Division One. Almost a hundred years later, Ayr United are still playing Scottish League football, although these days they are languishing in its third tier.

Bathgate

Formed in 1893, Bathgate played in a number of minor league competitions in the years leading up to World War 1, but were founder members of the reformed Scottish Division Two in 1921.

For a while, the side performed well, finishing in the top five in each of their first three seasons, but thereafter the club suffered a downturn in their fortunes, and in each of their remaining league seasons they finished in the bottom five. The 1927–28 season proved to be the last they would complete, and Bathgate resigned from the league in 1929 with ten of the season's games still to play.

The club survived for almost another ten years outside the league, but were eventually wound up in the autumn of 1938.

Beith

Beith's early history is curious in that the club was formed in 1875, disbanded in 1883, and then re-formed the following year. However, the club seem to have played no more games until 1888, when another revamp occurred. Between 1891 and 1923, Beith played their football in the Ayrshire League, the Scottish Combination, and finally the Western League, where they were when the Scottish Football League decided to create a new Division Three. Along with most of the clubs in the Western League, Beith became founder members of the new division.

Having finished in a mid-table position in the inaugural season, Beith were lacklustre the following year, and no better the year after that. As the 1925–26 season wore on, it became obvious that some of the poorer Division Three clubs would be unable to complete the season, and the competition collapsed in disarray with games outstanding.

The loss of league status saw Beith move to the Scottish Alliance, where they played as a senior side for another twelve years. However, in 1938 the side was disbanded, and reconstituted as Beith Juniors FC, who are still active today.

Bo'ness

Formed in 1882, Bo'ness were founder members of the Eastern Alliance in 1891, but the new league collapsed before all the first season's games were played and Bo'ness went back to another ten years of friendlies and cup competitions. In 1901, however, they took the plunge again, joining the Central Combination. There they stayed until 1921, when the Combination was absorbed into the Scottish League as the new Division Two.

Bo'ness featured strongly in the League, and finished in the upper reaches of the table most years. In 1927, they won promotion to Division One, but it was to be a short stay, as they made an immediate return to the lower division for the 1928–29 season. Never again did Bo'ness look likely to challenge for promotion, although performances were far from disastrous, and the side generally held its own.

Off the field, it was a different matter. Financially, the club was in a mess, and it was soon unable to meet the minimum payment required by visiting teams – the so-called match guarantee – under Scottish FA rules. After several weeks of the 1932–33 season, the Scottish FA took the decision to expel Bo'ness, and their time as a League club was over. Between then and the end of World War 2, Bo'ness plied their trade in a number of minor league competitions, before being merged with Bo'ness Cadora JFC to become Bo'ness United, these days one of the strongest junior sides in Scotland.

Broxburn United

Formed in 1912 after a merger between Broxburn FC and Broxburn Athletic, both long-standing senior sides, Broxburn United played mostly in the Central League until it was incorporated into the Scottish League in 1921 as the new Division Two.

Their brief league career was generally unspectacular, but a severe dip in form left them bottom of the table in 1925–26, and they were forced to seek re-election in the wake of the collapse of Division Three. Surprisingly, given that their earlier performances had been far from dreadful, Broxburn were given no second chance, and they were voted out.

After one season in the Scottish Alliance, Broxburn relinquished senior status and moved to the Midlothian Junior League, but the club was not a success, and closed down in 1932.

Cambuslang

In a little over 20 years of existence, Cambuslang enjoyed more than a little success in a number of competitions, winning the Lanarkshire Association Cup two years running in the mid-1880s, coupling a Glasgow Cup win with a Scottish FA Cup final appearance in 1888, and then opening their Scottish League account with an 8–2 win over the highly-respected Renton in the opening game of the inaugural season.

But their stay in the league lasted just two seasons, and after finishing last but one in 1892, Cambuslang joined the Football Alliance. They played just two seasons there as well, but the glory days were long-gone, and in 1897 the club was formally disbanded.

Clackmannan

Another of those clubs to lead a nomadic early life, Clackmannan had been in existence for 30 years and competed in the Midland League, the Central Combination and the Eastern League, before achieving Scottish League status when the Central League became the new Division Two in 1921.

Their initial experience of life in the league was not a good one – after finishing at the foot of the table, they decided not to apply for re-election. Instead, they waited a year, and applied to rejoin for the 1923–24 term, but were rejected. Shortly afterwards, they were, however, accepted into the newly-created Division Three.

Their second taste of life in the Scottish league was no sweeter than the first – after three indifferent seasons, Clackmannan found Division Three collapsing around them with the club stranded near the bottom of the table. Their league career over, Clackmannan struggled on for a few more years before folding in 1931.

Clydebank

The history of football in Clydebank is convoluted, to say the least. In the late nineteenth century, a club known as Clydebank FC existed for around 15 years, but by 1902, it had ceased playing. Between 1914 and 1931, a second Clydebank FC spent a dozen or so years in the Scottish League, but neither of these has any connection with the Clydebank club that played league football between 1965 and 2002. The third Clydebank FC had its origins in a merger between East Stirlingshire and Clydebank Juniors, a long-established club that had been active throughout the twentieth century.

East Stirlingshire's owners, the Steedman brothers, controversially merged the two sides in 1964 to form a new club, generally known as ES Clydebank, to take over from East Stirlingshire in the Scottish League Division Two. They moved the new club from Falkirk to Clydebank, but East Stirlingshire supporters mounted a legal challenge to the merger and the move, and after one season East Stirlingshire were back in Falkirk, leaving Clydebank without a senior club once again.

The Steedmans decided to stay in Clydebank and form a new Clydebank FC from the remnants of Clydebank Juniors. The new club was elected to the Scottish League Division Two in 1966, and spent 35 comparatively successful years in the league, including several seasons of top-flight football, before another controversial business deal led to the final disappearance of the Clydebank name in 2002.

The seeds of Clydebank's demise were sown when their home ground was sold in 1996. For the last six years of their existence, the team played at a variety of venues, support dwindled and the club finally went into administration. Meanwhile, the collapse of Airdrieonians, and the subsequent failure of a newly constituted club, Airdrie United, to get into the Scottish League, led to United's backers taking over Clydebank FC and relocating the club to Airdrie under the United name. In real terms, the current Airdrie United FC is a logical continuation of Clydebank FC, but the name itself has gone.

Cowlairs

Formed 1876, Cowlairs must have made some sort of impression during the early years of the Scottish game, because they were amongst the clubs invited to join the new Scottish League when it started up in 1890. Whatever hopes people may have had for the club at the beginning of the season, they must have all but evaporated by the end, because Cowlairs finished bottom of the league with only three wins from their 18 games. They were duly voted out and Leith Athletic took their place.

Two years later, the Glasgow side returned to the league as founder members of the new Division Two, and this time it seemed they might fulfil their promise. After finishing second in their first season, though, things went badly wrong, and in 1894–95 they once more finished bottom of the table, and once more they were voted out. This time there was no way back, and the club folded shortly afterwards.

Dumbarton Harp

One of the many clubs formed amongst Scotland's Irish communities in the late nineteenth century, Dumbarton Harp started life in 1894 as a junior side, and remained so until 1908. Thereafter, they played senior football, first in the Scottish Union, and then in the wartime Western League, from which many of the clubs that made up the new Scottish League Division Three were taken in 1923.

Harp duly became league members, but soon found that the increased overheads of running as a league club, particularly the travelling costs, consistently outstripped their income. Harp completed only one season as a league side, finishing just below the middle of the table, before the inevitable happened and the club were forced to resign from the league after completing around half of their fixtures for the 1924–25 season. The club was wound up shortly afterwards.

Dundee Wanderers

The names of Dundee and Dundee United will be familiar to all followers of the Scottish game, but at the end of the Victorian era, another club briefly represented the town in the Scottish Football League. They were known as Dundee Wanderers, and were formed in 1885. Having changed their name to Johnstone Wanderers in 1891

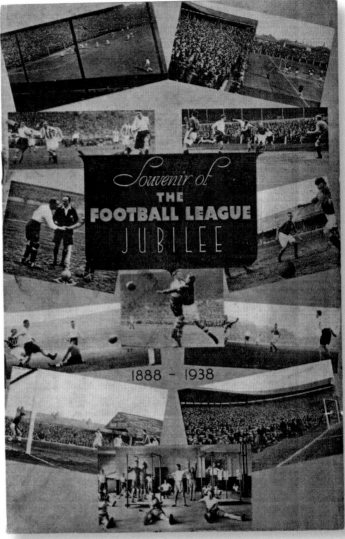

in the wake of a merger with Strathmore FC, the new club spent three years in the Northern League, before being elected to Division Two of the Scottish League, at which point the name was changed back to Dundee Wanderers.

A single season in the Scottish League proved too much for Wanderers, who must have harboured high hopes for the future when voted in for the 1894–95 season. In the event, they were never able to compete, and finished the campaign ninth out of ten before failing re-election.

Back in the Northern League, Wanderers finally tasted success in 1900, when they finished as champions, but by 1910 the club was struggling, and they resigned. The following season they were back, but the revival was short-lived, and the club folded during the 1912–13 season.

Dykehead

Formed in 1880, Dykehead waited a long time to bring Scottish League football to the mining town of Shotts, only to see the collapse of the ill-fated Division Three snatch it away once more.

The club's early days are poorly documented, but by 1894 they had joined the Scottish Alliance. After the abandonment of the Alliance two years later, Dykehead appear to have been without regular games until 1903, when they joined the Eastern League. Periods in the Scottish Football Combination and the Scottish Union followed, and during World War 1, Dykehead played in the Western League, and were still there when the Scottish League Division Three was formed from the Western League in 1923.

In common with almost all the clubs who made up the new third tier of Scottish League football, Dykehead's league career was restricted to the three seasons for which it operated. They performed reasonably well, twice finishing in the top five, but lasted only a few years after Division Three was discontinued. Having returned to non-league football, Dykehead survived until 1928, when the club folded.

Edinburgh City

There's a modern senior club calling itself Edinburgh City, but the current version bears no relation to the former Scottish League side which was formed in 1928 and elected to the Scottish League Division Two in 1931 in place of Clydebank FC.

Before this, they had spent two seasons in the East of Scotland League and one in the Edinburgh District League, and judging by their performances in Division Two during the years that followed, it's possible that they might have been better remaining at the lower level. In the years leading up to World War 2, Edinburgh City had to apply for re-election almost every season, and it was no surprise that they were placed in the new third tier of the Scottish League, known as Division C, when football resumed in 1946.

Things got no better, and City finished in the bottom two of the new division for the next three seasons before resigning from the league at the end of the 1948–49 season. Several years as a junior side followed, but in 1955 City closed down for good. The name was brought back into use in 1985, when Postal Union FC successfully applied to adopt it, and it is this version that continues to this day.

Galston

Formed in 1891, Galston played in local Ayrshire leagues between then and 1897, when the Ayrshire Combination was abandoned. They later joined the North Ayrshire League, before appearing in the Scottish Football Combination and then the Scottish Football Union in the years leading up to World War 1.

After the war, Galston joined the Western Union, and became one of the clubs included in the Scottish League Division Three at its inception in 1923. Like many of the smaller clubs, Galston found the increased costs associated with being in the new competition difficult to meet, and by 1925 they found it impossible to continue. Halfway through the 1925–26 season, Galston resigned and turned to junior football as a way to carry on. They continued in this form until the outbreak of World War 2, but disbanded for good in 1940.

Helensburgh

Several clubs called Helensburgh FC existed in the early years of Scottish football, the earliest being recorded in 1874. This incarnation actually made it to the semi-final of the Scottish FA Cup in 1879, but the team that carried the town's name into the Scottish Football League was formed over 20 years later, in 1896.

Overshadowed by their established near-neighbours Renton, Dumbarton and Vale of Leven, Helensburgh remained a small amateur club for many years, but after World War 1 they joined the Western League, from where they were inducted into the Scottish Football League with the formation of Division Three in 1922.

Inevitably, money soon became a problem, with running costs and travelling expenses regularly exceeding gate receipts. League status had done nothing to improve attendances, even though Helensburgh were sitting proudly at the top of the table when the division was wound up in 1926. They were, in fact, the only club to complete all their fixtures for the season.

For 1926–27, Helensburgh joined the Scottish Alliance, but the following year took the decision to convert to a junior club. The change of status did nothing to improve the club's fortunes, and the following year Helensburgh FC ceased operations.

Johnstone

Formed in the late 1870s – some records say 1877, some 1878 – Johnstone were a new club for a new community, the town itself having only recently developed. After some years playing only local sides, Johnstone joined the Scottish Alliance in 1894, then moved to the North Ayrshire League and, in 1898, the Scottish Football Combination. By 1905, they were members of the highly-regarded Scottish Football Union, so when the Scottish League Division Two was extended in 1912, Johnstone were successful in applying for one of the two places on offer.

In the seasons prior to World War 1, Johnstone struggled to make any impact, and things hardly improved when Division Two football resumed in 1921. Only once did they finish in the top 10, and in 1924–25 they suffered a disastrous campaign that saw them relegated to the recently-formed Division Three. The division's demise marked the end of Johnstone as a League club, and after one further season of Scottish Alliance football, the club was disbanded.

Leith Athletic

Formed in 1887, Leith Athletic had a lengthy and complex history that included many years of Scottish League football in a number of separate spells, but never really achieved a great deal. Their first period in the Scottish League started in 1891, when they were elected to replace the ailing Cowlairs. When Division Two was created in 1893, Leith remained in what was now Division One, but their time amongst the top clubs came to an end in 1895 when they were relegated.

For the next 20 years, they remained in Division Two (renamed Division B for the final 'pre-war' season, 1914–15), although the club underwent a revamp in 1905, when Leith Athletic FC was liquidated, and a new club, Leith FC took over its assets and its place in the League. Leith FC twice finished as Division Two champions, but with automatic promotion and relegation yet to be put in place, a failure to amass the votes required to go up meant they remained in Division Two.

Leith FC closed down during the war, reforming in 1919 under the old Leith Athletic name. Their second spell of League football began in 1924, when they were elected to the new Division Three, and it ended when the division was dissolved three years later. Leith Athletic then made an unsuccessful application to join Division Two, but the failure of Nithsdale Wanderers the following season created a vacancy that Leith were invited to fill. Promotion in 1930 gave them a second taste of life at the top, but it lasted only a couple of seasons, and they spent the rest of the decade as a middle–order Division Two side.

In 1946, when football resumed after World War 2, Leith were placed in the new third tier, Division C, although expansion of Division Two in 1947 saw them take one of the new places there. They suffered immediate relegation, and found themselves back amongst the reserve sides that made up most of Division C. Athletic's directors tried to persuade the Scottish FA that the few full sides in Division C should be allowed to join Division 2, but to no avail. Things came to a head in 1953, when Leith effectively went on strike – their refusal to play any more games led to their expulsion from the League, and, unable to secure regular games elsewhere, the club collapsed two years later. The current youth team bearing the Leith Athletic name has no connection with the former club.

Linthouse

Formed in 1881, Linthouse hailed from the Govan district of Glasgow. They joined the Scottish Football Alliance in 1891, and were elected to Division Two of the Scottish Football League in 1895. Surprisingly, given their form in the previous few seasons, they fared badly in their first campaign, finishing last and having to apply for re-election. The club narrowly survived the ballot and went on to four more seasons of league football, but finishing last but one in 1899, and last in 1900 persuaded the club's directors that continuing was pointless, and Linthouse resigned from the league. Within a few months, the club had gone out of business.

Lochgelly United

Formed in 1890 from the amalgamation of two earlier sides, Lochgelly Athletic and Fife Hibernian, Lochgelly United were initially the premier side in the area until their great local rivals East Fife came into being in 1903. Apart from a couple of years in the Central League in the late 1890s, Lochgelly played only in friendly games and the odd cup competition until 1902, after which they re-entered non-league football until gaining election to the wartime Division B in 1914.

After a period in the Eastern League during World War 1, and the Central League thereafter, United rejoined the Scottish FA, and took up a place in the reconstituted Division Two in 1921. They were subsequently relegated to Division Three in 1924, and lost their league status when the third tier was discontinued in 1926. By 1928, the club had ceased operations, and the name died with them.

CLUB FACTS

All football clubs go through lean patches from time to time, but Crewe Alexandra's record in the mid-1950s takes some beating. At one point, they went 56 away games without a win, and in the 1956–57 season, they went without a win of any description for 30 games, their 2–1 victory over Scunthorpe on September 19th 1956 being their last until they beat Bradford City by a solitary goal to nil on April 13th the following year. They propped up Division Three (North) for three consecutive seasons, winning only 23 of their 138 League games in that time. Next time you think it can't get any worse, spare a thought for those long-suffering Crewe fans all those years ago...

Meadowbank Thistle

When workers at the electronics company Ferranti, in Edinburgh, formed a football team in 1943, they chose the name Ferranti Thistle and entered the Eastern League. There they stayed until the Scottish Football League was restructured in 1974 in readiness for the start of the new Premier Division the following year. Ferranti were controversially elected to join Division Two of the League – they were not only preferred to Hawick Royal Albert and Gateshead United, but also several long-established Highland League clubs who

believed they had a better claim to the spot, and which objected strongly to the result of the election.

The suspicion arose that the Ferranti team had been preferred simply for geographical reasons, but worse still was the realization that Ferranti had succeeded even though their City Park ground (formerly Edinburgh City's) was not of the required standard for league games. There was also the issue of a league side bearing the name of a commercial entity, not allowed under contemporary SFL sponsorship rules. In the end, these side-issues were laid to rest by hiring the Commonwealth Stadium for home fixtures, and changing the club's name to Meadowbank Thistle, chosen after the *Edinburgh Evening News* invited readers' suggestions.

Thistle struggled for a while, but by the mid 1980s things were looking up, and the club enjoyed five seasons in Division One (tier two). Further league restructuring meant they were relegated to Division Two in 1994, and dropped to the basement division the following year. It was by now obvious that Meadowbank were never going to be able to compete with Hibs and Hearts, and with financial disaster looming, a radical rethink was required.

The solution was as controversial as Meadowbank's entry into the league 30 years earlier – after a takeover by local businessman Bill Hunter, the club was relocated to Livingston in West Lothian, renamed Livingston FC, and given a new badge and playing strip. Meadowbank Thistle was no more.

Mid-Annandale

Until the arrival of Gretna in 2002, Mid-Annandale were the most southerly team ever to play in the Scottish Football League, hailing as they did from Lockerbie, Dumfries & Galloway. The club's origins lay in an earlier side, Vale of Dryfe FC, who flourished briefly in the late 1890s, but had been largely inactive thereafter. In 1910, a revitalised club, renamed Mid-Annandale, emerged and joined the Southern Counties League.

Like a number of other small clubs, Mid-Annandale's league career was spent entirely in the abortive Division Three, after which they returned to non-league life in the Scottish Alliance, then the Provincial League and finally the Southern Counties League. By 1936, the club had been wound up, but the name was revived as recently as 2003, when a new Mid-Annandale joined the South of Scotland Football League, playing in the same strip as their earlier namesakes.

Nithsdale Wanderers

Formed around 1896, Nithsdale Wanderers came from the town of Sanquhar, Dumfries & Galloway, one of the smallest towns in Scotland ever to produce a Scottish Football League side. For the first dozen or so years of their existence, Wanderers restricted themselves to friendly games and cup competitions, but briefly joined the Scottish Football Combination before moving to the Southern Counties League in 1910 for the remaining seasons before World War 1. Like many of the smaller clubs, Nithsdale Wanderers suspended operations for the duration, but resumed in the Western League in 1921, thereby becoming part of the new Scottish League Division Three the following year.

They were an immediate success, finishing sixth in the first season, and topping the league the year after. Sadly, Division Two proved to be a step too far for the Wanderers, who found life difficult in their first season there, and impossible in their second. Having finished a poor last in 1926–27, and with the lower division by now abandoned, Nithsdale were voted out of the League.

Unlike many of the other former Division Three clubs, Nithsdale were still financially solvent, and made several applications to return to the league in the years that followed, but it was not to be, and although Nithsdale continued as a senior side until 1950, they remained a non-league outfit. Having regrouped as a junior side, the Wanderers continued until 1964 before disbanding altogether. The name, however, was revived by a new senior side in 2001, playing in the South of Scotland League.

Northern

Very little information about this early Glaswegian side seems to have survived, but we do know that they were formed in 1874 in the Springburn district, and played home matches at Hyde Park. They were founder members of the Scottish Alliance in 1891, and two years later became founder members

of the new Scottish League Division Two.

Their only season as a league side was uninspired, to say the least, and they finished in joint eighth position (out of 10) with just nine points from 18 games. Only Thistle had fared worse, and it came as no surprise that both clubs were voted out of the League. Northern were accepted back into the Scottish Alliance, but completed only two more full terms before resigning halfway though the 1896–97 campaign and closing down.

Peebles Rovers

Peebles Rovers were another of the clubs whose only league appearances were in the short-lived Division Three, and like many of them, its collapse triggered the collapse of the club.

Formed in 1893, Peebles Rovers joined the Border League in 1902, and switched to the well-respected Scottish Football Union seven years later. In the years that followed, standards in the SFU declined, and when war broke out, the league was discontinued, and Rovers went into hibernation until rejoining the Border League after peace was restored in 1919.

Short spells in the Eastern League and the Western League followed, before the latter was incorporated into the Scottish Football league as Division Three. When the new division collapsed in the spring of 1926, Rovers collapsed with it, going out of business without completing their fixtures. A new club rose from the ashes almost immediately, and continues to this day, although it has switched on several occasions from the junior to the senior game along the way.

Port Glasgow (Athletic)

Some sources give their date of formation as 1877, others as 1880, but we do know that Port Glasgow Athletic were originally known as Broadfield FC, and changed their name in 1881. Ten years later, they joined the Scottish Alliance, playing two seasons there before it was absorbed into the Scottish Football League as the new Division Two.

Port Glasgow found the new league to their liking, and finished in the upper reaches of the table each year until 1902, when they finished as champions and were elected to Division

One. Here, however, they found life more difficult, and had to apply for re-election at the end of their first season, something that the club would have to do on three more occasions in the next eight years.

Away from the league, Port Glasgow experienced the odd highlight, most notably Scottish Cup semi-finals in 1899 and 1906, the year in which they recorded an historic victory over the mighty Glasgow Rangers in the previous round.

By 1910, the club was in decline, both on and off the field. Having finished last in Division One, and with mounting debts, they decided not to seek re-election, and accepted relegation to Division Two. Unable to stop the slide, Port Glasgow played just one more indifferent season before going out of business in 1912.

Renton

One of Scotland's earliest clubs, Renton FC was formed in 1872, and quickly established itself as one of the biggest names amongst the first wave of Scottish footballing sides. They reached the semi-finals of the very first Scottish FA Cup competition in 1874, then went one better the following year, but lost both times to Queen's Park. Several quiet years followed, but in 1885 Renton were finally successful, beating fierce local rivals Vale of Leven 3–1 after a replay. Three years later, Renton won the trophy again, demolishing Cambuslang 6–1 in the final – still a record winning margin.

Renton also became 'World Champions' in 1888, when a match between the cup winners in England and Scotland was billed as being to determine 'the Championship of the UK and The World'. Renton ran out 4–1 winners against West Bromwich Albion, fielding a team that featured no less than eight players who represented Scotland during the year. Although the 'World Champions' title was rather fanciful, Renton's footballing prowess was evident in the fact that they also beat Preston North End and Sunderland during 1888, both teams recognised as being amongst England's finest at the time.

In 1890, Renton were naturally chosen as one of the clubs that would form the new Scottish Football League, but you won't find their name amongst those in the first league table – Renton were suspended from all football after a handful of games when it was discovered that they had played a friendly match against 'Edinburgh Saints', who turned out to be St Bernard's, a club already suspended by the Scottish footballing authorities for making payments to their players. Following a legal challenge, Renton were allowed to rejoin the league for the 1891–92 season.

When the Scottish FA finally embraced professionalism in 1893, it effectively killed off village sides like Renton. Unable to retain its best players in the face of the money on offer from wealthier, metropolitan sides, Renton quickly went into decline, and were relegated from Division One in 1894 having won only one game all season. They fared slightly better for a while in Division Two, and reached the 1895 Scottish Cup final, but this was their swansong. Amid mounting debts, they resigned from the league after a few weeks of the 1897–98 season, and their place was given to Hamilton Academical.

Renton continued in non-league football until 1920, when the club resigned its place in the Western League and was disbanded.

Royal Albert

Another of the clubs whose league career took place entirely within the ill-fated Division Three, Royal Albert were formed in 1878 in Larkhall, South Lanarkshire. Until World War 1, they played in a number of different league competitions, then joined a number of former Scottish League Division Two clubs to form the wartime Western League in 1915.

Like many others, Royal Albert remained in the Western League until 1923, when it became integrated into the Scottish Football League as their new Division Three. Those that survived the three disastrous years of life in Division Three mainly joined the Scottish Alliance, but like so many of these, Royal Albert had been fatally damaged by the experience, and called it a day in 1927.

A new, junior side was formed almost immediately, and assumed the name Royal Albert Athletic JFC. Eighty years on, the club is still in existence, and still playing at junior level.

Solway Star

Another club from the Annan area of Dumfriesshire, Solway Star were relative latecomers to Scottish football, having been formed in 1911. Like many provincial clubs, Solway Star relied on friendly games and cup competitions during the early days of their existence, but took the plunge and joined a league competition in 1914 when they became members of the Southern District League.

During the First World War, Solway Star appear to have been inactive, or at least not to have played in any of the wartime leagues, but in 1921 they re-emerged in the Southern Counties League for one season, before joining the Western League in 1922. As a result, they found themselves in the new Scottish League Division Three at the start of the 1923–24 season.

Solway Star started modestly, finishing just below mid-table in their first season, then enjoyed a much better second term, finishing third. That was as good as it got, and in Division Three's final, chaotic term, the club ended up towards the lower reaches of the table once more. After 1926, Solway Star featured in a number of non-league competitions, finally resigning from the South of Scotland League in 1933 and concentrating on friendlies and cup competitions. Eventually, not long after World War 2, Solway Star ceased operations for good.

St Bernard's

St Bernard's were one of a number of Scottish football clubs whose origins lay in the military. Started in 1878 by members of an earlier side formed by members of the Third Edinburgh Rifle Volunteer Corps, they took their name from St Bernard's Well, a famous local landmark. In 1880, they joined the Scottish FA, becoming one of the country's more successful sides in the years that followed. However, success proved problematic – unable to pay their players under Scottish FA rules, clubs like St Bernard's saw the best of them taking their skills to professional clubs south of the border. Illegal payments became widespread, and in 1890, St Bernard's were found guilty of the practice and banned from all competition for 12 months. To get around

the ruling, they played games under the name 'Edinburgh Saints', one such encounter with Renton in the opening weeks of the inaugural Scottish League season leading to Renton's suspension.

In 1893, after two successful seasons in the Scottish Alliance, St Bernard's joined the Scottish League, taking over a Division One slot vacated by one of the two clubs voted out that season. Finishing third in their first season, and winning the Scottish FA Cup in 1895, these were St Bernard's glory years. After losing their top flight status in 1900, they spent the remaining years up to World War 1 in Division Two. Two top-of-the-table finishes in 1901 and 1907 went unrewarded, and St Bernard's never again tasted the high life.

For the rest of their time in the league, St Bernard's remained in the second tier. The 1920s proved to be a particularly lean period, but there was some improvement in the club's fortunes in the decade that followed. However, fate dealt the club a fatal blow in 1943. The death of a club director led to his executors demanding the return of his investment in the club – St Bernard's were forced to sell up to settle the claim, and the name disappeared from Scottish football.

Third Lanark

Formed in December 1872 by members of the Third Lanarkshire Rifle Volunteers, this famous old club soon became one of the predominant sides in the early years of Scottish football, reaching the Scottish Cup final in 1876 and 1878, and finally winning the trophy for the first time in 1889 by beating the mighty Glasgow Celtic. Their sad demise almost a hundred years later has been the subject of fierce debate ever since, with accusations of boardroom skulduggery and financial mismanagement persisting to this day.

Their early success naturally led to their inclusion in the new Scottish Football League in 1890, and in the decade that followed they turned professional, won the Glasgow Cup on three occasions, and performed consistently, if unspectacularly, in the league. In 1903, they severed their links with the regiment and renamed themselves the Third Lanark Athletic Club, winning the Scottish League Championship for the only time at the end of the 1903–04 season. The following year they took the Scottish FA Cup again, this time defeating the other half of the Old Firm in the final, and in 1906 won the Glasgow Cup, but these were to be the club's last honours. For the next 20 years, Third Lanark remained an average First Division side, but they finished last at the end of the 1924–25 season, and were relegated.

Promoted and relegated again several times before World War 2 interrupted play, the only real highlight of the 1930s was a return to the Scottish FA Cup final in 1936, but Rangers finally got their revenge for 1905 by running out 1–0 winners. After the war, the 'Thirds' played in the top flight until 1954, when they were again relegated, but promotion in 1958, the League Cup final in 1960, and a third-place finish in Division One in the 1960–61 season all pointed to a bright future.

It wasn't to be. Third Lanark's fall from grace was as quick as it was spectacular. In 1964–65 they lost 30 of their 34 Division One games, and were relegated with only seven points. Two mediocre seasons in Division Two followed, but all was far from well off the field. Infighting, power struggles and potential development deals centred on the club's ground at Cathkin Park all took their toll, and after a Board of Trade enquiry, the club was declared bankrupt and liquidated in 1967. Rumours persist that the club's chairman engineered its demise in order to profit from the sale of the ground, but Cathkin Park remained derelict for years afterwards. Even today, the last remains of the terracing stand as a monument to a once-mighty club.

Thistle

Formed in Glasgow in 1875, Thistle have one of the shortest Scottish League careers, playing in Division Two for a single season in 1893–94. Prior to this, they had spent two years in the Scottish Alliance, and when the Alliance was incorporated into the Scottish Football League to form a new Division Two, Thistle became one of its founder members.

Their only season was a complete failure – they won only two of their 18 games, finished bottom of the table, and failed to get re-elected. So traumatic was the whole experience that Thistle decided not to continue in any form, and were disbanded shortly afterwards.

Vale of Leven

Vale of Leven FC was formed in the town of Alexandria in 1872, and soon became a major force in Scottish football. They won the Scottish Cup three years running – in 1877, 1878 and 1879 – the first of these victories marking the first time the Scottish Cup had been taken out of Glasgow. During the following decade, they made three more consecutive Scottish Cup final appearances, but were defeated each time.

In 1890, Vale of Leven made their last Scottish Cup final appearance, losing to Queen's Park, but later in the year they became founder members of the Scottish Football League, and a new chapter in their history began. Unfortunately, the rise of professionalism in the game coincided with the start of the new league, and teams from the smaller Scottish towns found it difficult to compete with the big city clubs. Vale of Leven lasted only two largely depressing seasons in the Scottish Football League, and their second term must rank amongst the worst any club had to endure – they went without a win all season, conceded 100 goals in their 22 matches, and finished five points adrift at the bottom of the table.

After a single season in the Scottish Alliance, Vale of Leven withdrew from league football for almost a decade, but returned to the Scottish Football Combination in 1903, and were accepted to fill one of two Scottish League Division Two places created when the division was extended in 1905. Apart from a spell in the Western League while Division Two was inactive during the war, Vale of Leven stayed there until relegated to Division Three in 1924. When Division Three collapsed two years later, their league career was over, and aft a brief spell in non-league competition, this famous old club was finally disbanded.

The name was revived a decade later, a new junior side being formed to play at the earlier club's former home at Milburn Park. Almost 70 years later, Vale of Leven JFC are still active.

PART II: Identity

Chapter 1

Showing Your Colours

The colours a club plays in are an intrinsic part of its make-up. Up until the 1970s, shirts tended to be plain with the club badge on the left breast. Several factors have since combined to make the shirt less of a necessity and more of a must-have fashion item that needs to be updated each season.

The replica shirt industry has increased several-fold the number of changes clubs have made to their kit, in order to keep it 'current' and encourage repeat purchases. Home shirts tend to remain the same colour, but details will vary in terms of collar style and trim. Contrasting panels and other details have been regularly used to 'spice up' plain designs.

Commerciality has demanded that the name of the sponsor now appears on shirts in larger type than anything identifying the team. Even the kit manufacturer's logo is guaranteed prominence as the biggest names in sportswear vie for the top clubs' patronage. The once humble shirt is now an item of 'branded sportswear'.

If home kit tends to be traditional, in base colours at least, the same cannot be said for away kit. These shirts are often bought as fashion items, so many clubs have run the gamut of colours over the years – though those with close city rivals will tend to steer clear of any kit resembling their neighbour. Stripes, checks and other 'trendy' designs come into play here. A good example was the

Adidas-produced 1991 away kit for Arsenal which featured a navy-blue zig-zag pattern topped with a subtle shadow design. Nicknamed 'the bruised banana' due to its appearance when seen from the terraces, the shirt became the fashion must-have in early-1990s North London.

Some clubs have even created a special 'third kit' to wear when their away kit clashes, or one that may be pressed into service for an historic cup tie as a 'limited edition'. Manchester United followed this course in 1998 by launching a home kit designed solely for Champions League action. With a simple white collar, no superfluous trim and traditional white socks It was to feature in one of the greatest evenings in the club's history, the 2–1 victory over Bayern Munich in the final, echoing the Matt Busby team's triumph three decades or so earlier.

Most clubs derived their original colours from a local connection like the founder's old school or a colour associated with the heraldry of the area. (Arsenal adopted red due to a kind donation of kit from Nottingham Forest, but would customise it with white sleeves.) It's rare for a team to change colours completely as Leeds United did in the 1960s in homage to the great European Cup-winning Real Madrid side.

The world football scene impacted on English team colours in the 1970s, many sides adopting yellow as an away strip as a tribute to the recent Brazilian World Cup winners. Other away colours have proved

Two ardent Aldershot Town supporters display the full range of club colours.

somewhat less vibrant, Alex Ferguson famously blaming his Manchester United team's all-grey shirts for a poor performance against Southampton in the 1995–96 season. This kit was dropped after Manchester United failed to win a single game while wearing it. According to the players, the kit wasn't visible enough which led to poor passing accuracy and hence bad results.

The current millennium has seen Bolton and Charlton both celebrate their centenary years with launches of one-off 'retro' home kits. The clubs were given special dispensation by the Premiership for the kit to be worn just once in a league fixture, while 1999–2000 saw Blackburn Rovers commemorate 125 years of existence with a purple design with red diagonal band that

was unlike anything previously worn by their players!

Wearing your team's shirt has become part of belonging to a tribe. Here's the history behind the colours you and your fellow supporters wear each week with pride.

Accrington Stanley

In their second stint as a Football League club the resurrected Accrington Stanley have retained their familiar red shirts, albeit with a white slash down the right hand side and white shorts. Apart from the red socks, which substitute for white, there are few changes from the strip the club unveiled when re-emerging in 1970. It should be noted that the original Accrington FC, a founder member of the Football League, also played in red shirts.

Howard Vaughton, who played for Aston Villa throughout the 1880s. Note the striped kit, which predates today's more familiar claret and light blue. After retiring from football, Vaughton ran a silversmith's and was at one stage charged with producing a replacement FA Cup.

Arsenal

Those watching Arsenal from the 1930s onwards became reconciled to the bright red shirts with the almost unique white sleeves that constituted a staple of the club kit, so many would have been taken aback at the deeper tones adopted for both shirts and socks in the 2005–06 season. However, anyone digging back into history will show the darkening actually looks like a throwback to the strip employed by Arsenal in its previous manifestations. For 2006–07, the lighter red and white sleeves had returned, adorned with two thin yellow strips running from armpit to the waistband of the white shorts, which have minimal red decoration at the two front corners.

CLUB FACTS

Arsenal owed their selection of colours to Nottingham Forest, two of whose players Morris Bates and Fred Beardsley played for their forerunners Dial Square. As the newly formed club was tight for funds, Beardsley wrote to Forest for assistance and they provided them with a set of red jerseys and a ball. Dial Square, the name of one of the workshops at the Royal Arsenal, briefly became Woolwich Reds before officially being re-christened Woolwich Arsenal. They cut their ties with the area and moved to north London in 1913.

Aston Villa

Aston Villa's famous claret and light blue club colours emerged in the early 1890s after a decade and a half which encompassed at least five different strips. The principal appearance of the shirt has not changed dramatically for over a century, the shirt body invariably claret, the arms light blue. The white shorts have been more or less a permanent fixture, allowing for the odd experimentation with both claret and light blue.

Barnet

Early manifestations of the Barnet club played in black and white, violet and white and green and white before the amber and black combination we know today was settled upon two decades into the twentieth century. Over the years the amber darkened somewhat and over the last couple of years black has become the more dominant colour. The current kit has the shirt body in amber with black shoulders and arms plus black shorts carrying a thin amber line close to the short sides which have a broken white decoration.

Barnsley

Apart from the very early days of the club, when blue and white stripes were order of the day, Barnsley have played in red shirts and white shorts for virtually the whole of their Football League life. In fact the club's kit remains one of the least tinkered with in existence, for apart from the odd dash of white on the shirt, the change of sponsor and the varied colour predominance in the socks, the basic strip has been stable for close to seventy years.

Andy Liddell shows off the Barnsley kit of 1994. The South Yorkshire side's kit has tended to be one of the least changed of any club throughout the years.

Birmingham City

The current Birmingham strip of blue shirts and white shorts had its antecedents in the very first kit used by Small Heath Alliance,

a former name of the club, which had a white diagonal crossing the blue shirt. Apart from brief dalliances with light blue and black with amber, the dark blue and white have been associated with the club for close to a hundred years. The intrusion of yellow for a brief period in the early 1990s should be regarded as an aberration.

Blackburn Rovers

The original famous halved shirts of Blackburn Rovers were actually half light blue which reflected the Cambridge University backgrounds many of its founders could boast. By 1920, a darker blue had been introduced to contrast most effectively with its white counterpart. Apart from the 2004–05 season when blue was introduced, white has always been the colour of the shorts, even when, for a couple of years at the turn of the century, light blue made a brief return to the shirts.

Blackpool

Up until 1923, when Blackpool's famous tangerine shirts were introduced, there had been many changes in club colours with red, white and blue all dominating the kit. A particularly fetching combination of red, yellow and black stripes as a shirt design was also in brief evidence. Although initially the tangerine was matched with black shorts, by the 1930s white shorts had taken over, only occasionally to be displaced by tangerine ones in the 1980s and 1990s.

Bolton Wanderers

Under the name of Christ Church the club had favoured red in its colours and for the first few years of the Bolton Wanderers club it reappeared in very strange fashion. The red spots on a white background of 1884 looked more appropriate for the horseracing track and the red white and blue stripes of a year later could have doubled as a pyjama pattern. The eventual establishment of blue and white as club colours may have looked staid by comparison but was more appropriate. The current kit of all-white with a blue panel running down the right arm and a nick of blue and red at the bottom of the left leg looks decidedly sober.

AFC Bournemouth

The cherry-red and white shirts of the Boscombe club were retained by the newly named Bournemouth & Boscombe Athletic when they joined the Football League in 1923, the shorts colour changing from blue to black. Slowly but surely the white has disappeared from the strip and the 2006–07 season had black and red striped shirts matched with solid black shorts. Their red and black kit introduced in 1971 was based on the old AC Milan strip. The team reverted to predominantly red for the 2004–05 and 2005–06 seasons before announcing a return to the stripes for the 2006–07 season due to fan demand.

Bradford City

Claret and amber have always been Bradford City's colours. Even during the 1980s and 1990s when all white kits were adopted, the trimmings were always in those colours. At the club's formation hooped shirts were favoured, soon to be replaced by stripes which have certainly been a recurring feature throughout the club's history. At the commencement of the 2006–07 season, broad stripes on the body of the shirt were flanked by solid claret sleeves, while the shorts of solid claret had amber trim.

Brentford

The associated red and white striped shirts and black shorts were not adopted at Brentford until the mid-1920s. For the previous thirty-five years they had played in an array of colours, from the Oxbridge-inspired hooped shirts of claret, light blue and salmon

to white solid shirts and blue shorts. Currently the stripes are fairly broad broken by a white panel to display the sponsor's name and the shorts have narrowing red trim at the top on both sides.

Brighton and Hove Albion

The blue and white stripes associated with Brighton & Hove Albion were introduced in 1904, long before they became members of the Football League. There have been periodic deviations from this style of shirt, for instance in the 1930s when a red stripe was added to the mix or the odd flirtation with solid blue which has subsequently been rejected. The contemporary shirt has a broader blue stripe running down the arm and white shorts sporting blue edging.

Bristol City

Since 1897, the predominant colour in the City kit has always been red, the shirts often solid and the shorts invariably white with the occasional red trim. In 1999, red shorts took hold, which looked like becoming the norm until 2006–07, when the kit comprised solid red shirts, interrupted by a white panel running from the neck to the bottom of the arm and white shorts, again with red edging.

Bristol Rovers

It was not until the early 1930s that Rovers turned to dark blue and white quarters for their shirt design, the manager believing this made his players look bigger (a theory which presaged Bill Shankly's all-red reasoning by some thirty years). Up to that time, playing under three other names, they had utilised black and white stripes, buff and green halves and even all black with a yellow diagonal across the shirt. The current shirt displays a departure in so far as light blue is now teamed with white over white shorts.

Burnley

Claret and light blue was far from being Burnley's first colours, for they dabbled with stripes in four different combinations, solid red shirts and apparently much disliked green shirts before settling on Aston Villa's famous strip in 1910. They have now of course stuck with their choice for close to a century, the only break being in the mid 1930s when black and white made a brief appearance. The 2006–07 season witnessed claret as the overwhelming colour, the blue only in a panel on the right hand side of the shirt and down the arm.

Bury

Blue and white became Bury's colours before the turn of the twentieth century, replacing the light blue and chocolate favoured in their early days. White shirts and blue shorts with design modifications have been the club colours ever since. The current strip sees a white-bodied shirt with blue arms split by thin blue then white panels. The shorts are blue, edged from top to bottom by white.

Cardiff City

As Riverside FC, the soon to be Cardiff City played in quartered chocolate and amber shirts but upon renaming themselves, the club reverted to blue shirts and white shorts which suits their nickname, the Bluebirds. This combination remained virtually intact until the twenty-first century when blue shorts were introduced, and the current kit is solid blue with white trimming to both shorts and shirts. The shirts also have white panels which run from neck to armpit.

Carlisle United

The latest Carlisle kit has blue shirts with white epaulettes which extend the length of the sleeve where they are joined by red and blue stripes finished with blue edging. The shorts are white with two blue diagonal stripes running across them. Despite its contemporary appearance the ensemble is not that far removed from the club's very first strip in 1928, which had solid blue shirts and white shorts.

Charlton Athletic

Charlton's red and white has been virtually a permanent feature since their earliest playing days in 1905. The only times that tradition has been broken was for a season in the 1920s when light and dark blue stripes made a brief appearance, plus during the 1969–70 campaign when an all red strip took centre stage. The latest offering sees

the red shirt broken by white epaulettes and white trim at wrist level; the white shorts have thin decorative strips down the middle of each leg.

Chelsea

For the first three decades of their existence Chelsea played in light blue shirts and white shorts, except for a very brief interlude where dark blue was introduced. It was not until the mid-1930s that the deeper colour became the norm for the club and has remained so to this day. In 1963, matching blue shirts and shorts became the club colours, which allowing for the odd piping incursion, as in the 2006–07 season and a misguided hoop concoction in the 1980s, have remained in place.

Cheltenham Town

When entering the Football League in 1999, Cheltenham were already sporting their colours of red and white striped shirts with white shorts, which with minor design alterations were still intact in the 2006–07 season, after a couple of years of wearing black shorts. Decades before their elevation, red had always been an integral colour in the club's kit, most strikingly used in the hooped shirts introduced in the late 1930s.

Chester City

Blue and white stripes have been in vogue at Chester for more than 70 years, a far cry from the black and white hoops used under the early guise of Chester Rovers. Solid colour shirts of blue, green and red have also been used over the decades. The present strip has blue and white stripes running down the body of the shirt with thicker bands running down the arms; the shorts are blue, edged on both legs by white.

Chesterfield

In the 1892–93 season, Chesterfield surely claimed a little bit of history, being the only club ever to have used the union jack as part of their basic colours. The flag was there for all to see, emblazoned on the body of the shirt. Although they have never had another kit making such impact, the current strip does utilise red, white and blue, albeit with a blue shirt with white strips at the sides plus red and white panelling just below the neck. The shorts are white, sporting solid blue decorative pieces running from the waist to half way on both legs.

Colchester United

From their entrance into the Football League, Colchester has always employed blue and white as their colours. Apart from one season in the 1970s when a lighter shade was evident, the darker variety has always been favoured. Short colouring has differed but currently blue takes the stage, with a white trim at the bottom. Shirts now have a striped body flanked by solid blue arms which have a snowflake-like decoration at the top.

Coventry City

In 1962, not long after the arrival of forward-looking manager Jimmy Hill, the club's sky blue colours made their first appearance and have stayed around ever since. The 2006–07 season unveiled a solid sky blue strip with a minimal amount of trim, dark blue at shirt cuffs and collar, with similar at mid-mast on the shorts. This is a somewhat subtler blend than the red and green that surfaced briefly in the 1920s. A chocolate away strip from some three decades ago remains legendary.

Crewe Alexandra

For a large part of their existence Alexandra's colours were registered as scarlet and white, although red and white would be what most people would settle on in the present day. The current strip has a red shirt, broken by a white snowflake design at the top of each shoulder and a panel of both black and white running partway down the right of the shirt. The shorts are white with the merest touches of black and red at right hand of the short bottom.

Crystal Palace

Over the decades the Palace management has often seen fit to play around with the club's colours, although the currently favoured red and blue have been around since 1973. From 1905 until 1972, claret and light blue were ostensibly in vogue but always open to invasion by alternative colours. For 2006–07

the shirts had wide red and blue stripes matched with red shorts, carrying blue trim from top to bottom.

Dagenham & Redbridge

The league's newest entrants played their last season in non-league football in red shirts trimmed with blue on the arms, white shorts and red socks, with a change strip of all blue. This reflects the colours of Dagenham FC, one of the teams that merged to form the club in 1992.

Darlington

Black and white have always been a permanent feature of the Darlington strip, which currently features black and white hoops on the body of the shirt, flanked by striped arms. The shorts are white with wide black strips at the sides, running from top to bottom. Hoops (for the first thirty years of the club's existence), stripes and solids have all played their part in the fashion stakes over the years.

Derby County

White shirts with black shorts have long been associated with County but of course Brian Clough saw fit to change the short colouring to blue during his tenure. In 1989 black shorts returned and have been around ever since. The current kit design takes few liberties with a classic strip, for above the solid black shorts the white shirt has only black trim at the collar and thin black panels at the top of the arms to break up its solidity.

Doncaster Rovers

The contemporary Rovers kit of red and white hooped shirts is teamed with red shorts which carry a white band at the top and white trimming at the base of each leg. The teaming of the two colours has been an ever-present factor in the team's kit since 1885. In the previous half-a-dozen years it was blue that caught the eye as the initial kit had a dark blue shirt emblazoned with a bold gold cross, followed by dark blue and white halves.

Everton

Very little modification has taken place to the basic Everton kit of blue shirts and white shorts since its introduction in 1901. The current white collar trim and blue-edged shorts take few liberties with the classic strip. Prior to this century old tradition, the club had dabbled with salmon pink shirts and in 1880–81 had selected an all black ensemble with a red diagonal across the shirt.

Fulham

As Fulham St. Andrews, red and white halved shirts with white shorts had identified the club and as an infant professional outfit, the halving was replaced by solid red with white sleeves, preceding the famous Arsenal design by some years. Since the early part of the twentieth century, the Fulham kit has never strayed very far from the original concept of white shirts and black shorts, apart from the odd splash of red here and there.

Gillingham

From the early 1930s, dark blue took over as the predominant colour in the club's kit. This followed a period of nearly forty years when black and white striped shirts had identified the Kent club. The solid blue shirts and white shorts were more or less around until the mid-1990s when a little design shifting took place, leading to black and blue stripes being adopted for a couple of seasons. Currently Gillingham sport an all blue ensemble with just a hint of white at the shirt neck and sides.

Grimsby Town

Prior to the introduction of black and white stripes in 1910, the Mariners had played in shirts of blue and white hoops, solid white and chocolate teamed with light blue (both quartered and halved). Currently, the shorts are solid black and the shirts of black and white are close to halved but just fall short, as the coloured sleeves encroach on to the body.

Hartlepool United

Even in their days as Hartlepools United (with an s), blue and white have always been the favoured club colours, even if shades and design have constantly been experimented with. Stripes, solids and checks have all previously found their way onto the shirts, until we arrive at today where the body has blue and white halves flanked by a solid white arm to the right and solid blue to the left. The shorts are solid blue.

Hereford United

Black and white have been the Hereford club colours since its formation in 1924, although the black only appeared on the socks at the time. Subsequently, white shirts with black shorts took over with only the odd bow to an all-white kit. The current offering has solid white shirts and white-edged black shorts, as no-nonsense a combination as long-time manager/chairman Graham Turner.

Huddersfield Town

Huddersfield have rarely strayed from their statutory colours of which incorporate blue and white stripes which were introduced in 1913 – albeit that the light blue variety have seen a resurrection in recent seasons. However, for a couple of years now the players have been seen wearing an almost classic club kit of dark blue and white stripes with white shorts decorated with scoops of blue from half way to bottom of leg.

Hull City

The combination of black and amber became associated with Hull back in 1904 and allowing for the unique all-black kit of the 1909–10 season have been tied in with the club ever since. The only exception was for one year in the 1930s and another in the 1940s when light blue shirts and white shorts interrupted the status quo. The current shirts have black and amber stripes and black shorts edged in amber trim running in a downwards direction from half way.

Ipswich Town

Ipswich played in blue and white striped shirts and black shorts up until 1929, when solid blue shirts and white shorts materialised. These became the club colours which have stood the test of time until the present day. The current kit has the shirt broken by an expanding white panel that runs from the arm to the waistband of the shorts, which in turn have a similar blue panel which runs from the waistband across the divided leg.

Leeds United

When Don Revie became manager in 1961 the club's traditional yellow and blue colours were replaced by an all-white strip as a move to emulate the supreme Real Madrid side of the 1950s and early 1960s. One of Revie's players, Trevor Cherry, also adopted all white when manager of Bradford City, but this did not receive widespread approval – hardy surprising given the proximity of the two cities. By 2007, however, the all-white strip seemed to be doing little for Leeds' fortunes though they have latterly revived.

Leicester City

Although royal blue was introduced into the club kit in 1903, it was almost a decade before finally being accepted as an integral part of the club colours, as it had to do battle against a liking in some circles for red. Once established it has never been away as a shirt colouring, presently in solid form touched only by white at the collar and at the shoulders. The solid white shorts have blue edging which runs almost leg length.

Leyton Orient

The club's nickname 'The O's', actually stems from the large white 'O' the club sported on the back of their solid red shirts when playing under the name of Orient in their fledgling days. Red and white took hold in the Clapton Orient days and when becoming Leyton Orient after World War 2, blue and white took a 20-year stint. When reverting to the Orient name in 1966 we also witnessed a return to red and white which, despite the about turn in club name in 1987, have remained as club colours. The current all-red strip has white decoration at the shirt collar and white panels on the body sides which run into the top half of the shorts.

Lincoln City

Since 1885 Lincoln have proudly carried red and white as their colours and to the present day have usually employed them in a striped format on the shirts. The only break with this tradition came at an early juncture in their history when, at the back end of the nineteenth century, Lincoln green shirts were teamed with black shorts. The current stripes have a black trim at collars and cuffs, the shorts are black with red chevrons at the sides.

Liverpool

In the very early years Liverpool could be seen wearing blue, before they opted for red shirts and white shorts. The Shankly era heralded the all-red policy, as the manager believed the solid colour, adopted in 1964, made players look bigger. The period of unprecedented success which followed this move, including their first ever FA Cup win in 1965, probably determined the decision to stick with this kit until the present day, 1980s pinstripes and other minor variations notwithstanding.

Luton Town

Navy blue and pink halved shirts with solid blue shorts were the first striking colours to be unveiled by Luton, not the kind of combination we would expect in the contemporary game. Although hanging around within the basic kit for a further few years, these unlikely bedfellows were eventually dispensed with, as blue and white then black and white bedded in. The preference for the latter remained until the early 1970s, when orange and navy reared its head. After close to three decades of experimentation, the white shirts are back with us, carrying small strips of black and amber running a short distance at the lower arm. The shorts are pure unadulterated black.

Macclesfield Town

The current strip of solid blue from head-to-toe with the barest of yellow trim on shirts and shorts is a departure from the decades-old tradition of blue shirts and white shorts. A similar kit had been employed a few years prior but a return to the status quo in the 2005–06 season had not prepared the fans for the about turn.

Manchester City

The present City kit of light blue-bodied shirts with white arms and light blue shorts with a hint of dark blue decoration at each side satisfies both those demanding a modern looking strip and the traditionalists who would applaud the preponderance of light blue, which was first introduced as a shirt colour way back in 1894.

Manchester United

Whilst their red shirts are as iconic as any club colours in world football, Manchester United have employed a baffling array of second and third strips to avoid clashes at away games, including one or two of indeterminate colouring. As one of the first clubs to appreciate the value of merchandising, it's easy to suggest these alternative options have been intended as a money making ploy. The Newton Heath club which Manchester United sprang from had started their sporting life wearing a fetching combination of green, yellow and blue.

Mansfield Town

The very first Town strip introduced in 1910 was red shirts and white shorts, which after only a season gave way to a black and white combination. This in turn was only a short-term option and by 1919 amber and blue became the established club colours. The latest presentation finds amber shirts carrying blue trim at the neck and blue panels running along the inside of the shirt sleeves and down the sides of the body. The solid blue shorts have vee-shaped decoration of yellow and white at the top on both sides.

Middlesbrough

Since the turn of the twentieth century red and white have been the colours always associated with Middlesbrough, although in recent seasons all red or close to all red has come into favour. The contemporary version sees the red shirt trimmed by white at the neck and arm sides and the shorts have similar side trimming.

Millwall

Millwall's blue and white colours stem from the fact that, in their earliest days as Millwall Rovers, the majority of the players were Scottish. Navy blue was initially the choice but in the mid-1930s the club reverted to royal blue which holds good to the present day. The solid shirts are broken by white panelling running down the sides of the shirts and the white shorts have an eastern-like swirling design from top to bottom on both sides.

MK Dons

Having no history under their present name, little can be said of Milton Keynes Dons' kit, which is basically all white with a dash of red on the shirt and red trimming on shorts and socks. In their first season black and yellow constituted the decoration. It's notable that they have stayed away from the blue of 'traditional' Wimbledon for fear of criticism.

Morecambe

Like Dagenham & Redbridge, with whom they entered the League in 2007, the Shrimps kit themselves in red shirts, white shorts and red socks. (Change kit is blue and white.) Their traditional outlook also extends to their badge which reflects the former Borough of Morecambe and Heysham.

Newcastle

It's difficult to visualise Newcastle United in anything other than black and white vertical stripes as their shirt design, and since 1894 that's as it has always been, combined with statutory black shorts. For a couple of years now the basic kit has sported a grey effect band which runs from collar to half way down the arms, with a similar effect on the sides of the shorts.

Northampton Town

The claret and white colours associated with Northampton Town were chosen in 1899 because they had municipal associations. Originally the shirts were striped and the shorts black, but by 1911 solid claret shirts and white shorts took over. It was not until the 1960s and 1970s before any major changes came about in the clothing department, but if we look at the present day little has altered over the decades, with solid claret shirts having the minimum of trim at the cuffs. The white shorts have a claret vee which edges the bottom of each leg.

Norwich City

Although Norwich City is synonymous with their famous canary yellow shirts, these were not adopted until five years after the club's formation, for initially light blue and white halves were the order of the day. Perhaps surprisingly, in the 1920s dark blue and white became the chosen colours, before a return to yellow, halved with green and supported by black shorts. Post World War 2, solid yellow with green trimming adorned the Norwich players' chests, whilst the shorts stayed the same until the mid 1960s, when a little bit of colour juggling took place. The kit used into the twenty-first century holds true to the fluctuating balance between yellow and green.

Nottingham Forest

In the very early days of the club, the official colours were registered as Garibaldi Red and have never veered too far away from that very clear definition. With allowances for pieces of white or black decoration, the shirts have always been solid red and the shorts, apart from a few years in the 1880s, always white. The current shirts have mere flecks of white decoration at the collar, on the shoulders and at waist level; the shorts sport small red decorative side pieces, both at top and bottom.

Notts County

The current County shirt features a centre panel of black and white stripes flanked by black sleeves with yellow piping, atop black shorts also displaying that piping. This is somewhat in contrast to the styling of the 1870s and 1880s where black and amber hoops, solid amber plus light blue and chocolate halves took their turn as club colours. In 1890, the black and white stripes made their debut and despite the odd disappearance have remained at the heart of the club kit ever since.

Oldham Athletic

Athletic's colours have been blue and white for some years now, the current kit having a blue shirt with white edging to the collar and cuffs and white scoops out of the shoulders. The shorts are blue with thin white decorative lines almost to the sides. This would probably be viewed as a preferable option to the short lived blue and red hoops of the 1990s or the orange shirt/blue short combination utilised from the mid-1960s into the early 1970s.

Peterborough United

Essentially dark blue and white have been the club colours since the late 1930s with the odd nod in the direction of a lighter blue. Originally green and white had been the chosen option but the change came about due to the supporters' club stumping up the cash for a new kit. Currently, the strip is a solid blue with a white swirling panel at the right shoulder.

Plymouth Argyle

Black and green are essentially the colours Argyle have lived with during their lifetime, the combination having local connections with the Borough of Plymouth. The original manifestation of halved shirts was short-lived, as green shirts with black trim and white shorts saw service virtually until the mid 1960s, when years of kit tampering started to take place. In the twenty-first century a much darker green has come into fashion, the current shirt trimmed in white at collar and cuffs. The inner arm is also white, as are the shorts, which have darts of green from waist to side.

Portsmouth

The contemporary club kit has a blue shirt with white panelling on each side of the body and split arms of blue and white; the white shorts carry the club badge. The chosen colours have been with the club since 1911 and have seldom been presented in less than regulation manner. Modern crowds would react with derision if they encountered the original club outfit which had maroon-trimmed salmon pink shirts.

Port Vale

As Burslem Port Vale, the club performed in a number of kits, including claret and light blue stripes and later to be resurrected black and amber stripes. When losing Burslem from the name, red shirts and white shorts took their turn for a period, before, in 1936, white shirts and black shorts secured tenure. The late 1950s and early 1960s witnessed a return to black and amber, which eventually succumbed to what is now an extensive period for black and white. Currently the white shirt has a black left arm which also has amber trimming running from the collar to halfway house. The shorts have amber edging to the bottom and white scoops at waist level on both sides.

Preston

The white shirts and blue shorts of Preston North End were first used when the club joined the Football League in 1888. During the 1970s and 1980s, all-white strips became the fashion before reversion in 1990 to the more traditional look. The current option is for a white solid body with blue sleeves for the shirts and blue shorts carrying white trim at the bottom.

QPR

The blue and white hooped shirts of Queens Park Rangers, which have been used since the late 1920s, have always been combined with white shorts which have frequently carried blue edgings. The hoops may have varied in width over the years but have been ever present, apart from a few years in the 1950s when they were ditched for solid white shirts and blue shorts. The 2006–07 incarnation had a slight deviation by way of a thin red line infilling between the blue and white.

Reading

Reading have never deviated from the use of blue in their kit, right from 1872 when thin navy blue and white hoops were unveiled as the club's first strip. Royal blue and light blue have been the mainstays over the years, the former arriving just before the outbreak of World War 2, again in a hooped pattern on white. Although the hoops have had periods of absence, since 1992 they have been a fixture, reflected in the latest offering where the wide design of the shirt sits atop blue shorts trimmed in white on the left hand side.

Rochdale

The current Rochdale kit is solid blue from top to bottom with the thinnest of blue decoration running from shoulder to armpit on both sides of the shirt. At their foundation the club had played in light blue shirts and white shorts, a combination which existed for fifteen years before giving way to black and white striped shirts teamed with either black or white shorts. Blue has been a mainstay of Rochdale's kit since 1970.

Rotherham

Under the name of Rotherham United the club kicked off with a strip comprised of a yellow

shirt with black vee and solid black shorts, soon to be replaced by a red shirt and white shorts. The latter became established as club colours and despite the obligatory changes in design the overall look has always carried a pleasing balance. The contemporary styling has a red shirt with white panelling at the body sides and arms of red and white split in a curve. The white shorts carry the club badge.

Scunthorpe United

The earliest Scunthorpe teams played in claret and light blue but the colours were jettisoned in the 1960s in favour of blue and white. The all red strip of the 1970s and early 1980s did service until a return to the original colours was deemed desirable. The club have stuck with that decision, with the shirt now having a claret body and light blue arms emblazoned with a claret design, the shorts being solid claret.

Sheffield United

The famous red and white striped shirts of Sheffield United have now been a permanent fixture since 1892, almost the entire length of the club's existence. They had already toyed with the design prior to acceptance, as white shirts and blue shorts had also briefly been an option. Shorts have invariably been black, just occasionally being interrupted by black, blue and red. Currently we have a classic shirt on top of black shorts broken by a band of swirling red, running downwards from the waist across the face of the left leg.

Sheffield Wednesday

Royal blue and white have been Wednesday's colours since the club's foundation with striped shirts invariably being the order of the day. Hoops and solid blue bodies have received short shrift upon introduction but the black shorts have been dispensed with from time to time. For the last couple of years traditionalists can have few complaints at the wide-stripe shirts and solid black shorts.

CLUB FACTS

In October 2006 Shrewsbury Town released a statement that enraged supporters by stating the seats at their 10,000 capacity New Meadow ground would be blue and white. Many supporters favoured a blue and amber colour scheme adopted in the late 1960s which most fans felt is more identifiable with the club. After considerable pressure and a meeting with Shrewsbury Town supporters' groups, a compromise was reached – the seats would be blue in colour with the club's initials (STFC) spelled out in amber.

Shrewsbury Town

The Shrewsbury school colours of blue and white were the club's choice until at the back end of the 1960s, yellow started to be teamed with the blue. Subsequently, whilst white and yellow have vied for inclusion as part of the overall picture, the latter has been winning out in recent years, where a solid yellow panel sits in the centre of the shirt flanked by solid blue. The faintest lines of yellow sit at the front edges of the shorts which are also blue.

CLUB FACTS

Actor Harry Shearer immortalised Shrewsbury Town in film, as his character Derek Smalls wore the blue and amber shirt in the cult rock and roll movie This Is Spinal Tap. The shirt worn in the film is the same one worn by Shrewsbury Town in the early 1980s, and is still available to buy from TOFFS, a company specialising in retro football shirts.

Southampton

The red and white stripes of Southampton shirts have been with us since before the turn of the twentieth century. The teaming with blue shorts disappeared in the late 1930s when black became the norm. It has to be said that stripe width has varied during the ensuing decades but the stripes themselves have been a constant. Widish stripes are currently the thing, with black trim for the collar and arm edges. Shorts are black with red trim down both leg lengths.

Southend United

For the last four seasons Southend have played in an extremely dark all blue kit, the current version only broken by white trim on the shirt collar and cuffs in addition to the club badge. Similarly the shorts only sport the badge. In previous seasons the club had always favoured blue but it had always been of a lighter variety except for one season at the back end of the 1960s.

Stockport County

The current Stockport strip is a blue affair. The shirt has a white collar plus a narrowish white band across the chest, which continues down the length of the sleeve whilst the shorts are a solid blue. This kit is reported as being designed by their own supporters. These colours have dominated the club's lifetime, but for over two decades from 1933, white shirts and black shorts had been worn on the field by County's players.

CLUB FACTS

Which Football League ground is closest to the Mersey? Surprisingly it's Edgeley Park, home to League Two's Stockport County, which stands just over half a mile from the world-famous river as it winds its way through Greater Manchester. Tranmere's Prenton Park is just over a mile from the waterfront, while Goodison Park and Anfield are each almost two miles inland.

Stoke City

Before establishing red and white stripes as their shirt colours in 1908, Stoke had dabbled with all kinds of options including blue and black hoops, yellow and black stripes, blue and red stripes and solid maroon. Now, almost a century down the line it would be difficult to visualise City playing in anything other than a similar kit to the current one, with broad stripes on the body of the shirt flanked by arms carrying thinner stripes. The shorts are white with the thinnest of red lines running close to the sides.

CLUB FACTS

Sunderland's relegation to Division Two at the end of the 1957-58 season marked the end of 68 years (57 seasons) of continuous top flight football for the Black Cats, a record which stood until beaten by Arsenal in the 1980s. Arsenal played their 58th season in the top division in 1983-84, and notched up 69 years amongst the game's elite in 1988.

Sunderland

In the late nineteenth century, Sunderland players were wearing red and white shirts plus black shorts. Move on to the twenty-first century and you will find no change, as apart from short dalliances with both blue and white shorts, the club colours have proudly remained the same for over a century. The sponsor's name may change and the odd trimming may come and go but it is reassuring to know that for some clubs tradition is still paramount.

DAWN COVERS, 27 ASHFIELD ROAD, DAVENPORT, STOCKPORT SK3 8UD

Swansea City

Swansea adopted an all white kit when known as Swansea Town way back in 1912, and allowing for the odd tweak here and there with short colouring or shirt decoration, have remained true to that choice ever since. Essentially the contemporary version sticks to the norm, but the shirt has a black right arm with a white swirling strip at the top, whilst the opposite arm has a similar swirl in black. The white shorts have black edging on both sides.

Swindon Town

Swindon are associated with the colour red and you have to go back to the early twentieth century to find a kit where it doesn't feature. The red shirts and white shorts had been more or less intact until the 1990s, when red shorts crept in. For 2006–07 the club adopted all red, broken by a white panel running from the right shoulder down the shirt, which continues down the shorts. The shirt arms have a smallish token green design.

Tottenham Hotspur

Established in the late nineteenth century, the Tottenham colours of white shirts and blue shorts have remained intact until the present day, allowing for a darkening here and there, plus a few design tweaks. Prior to establishing the status quo, light blue, red and brown had all featured in the club shirts. The most recent offering finds a classic club shirt on top of shorts with white edging.

CLUB FACTS

West Bromwich Albion are the only major team in the West Midlands to play in striped shirts, leading to the name of the Stripes, while the Albion, WBA and West Brom are popular abbreviations of the club's full name.

The Wigan squad for the 1994–95 season display a rare deviation in club colours, with black here replacing half of the better known blue and white striped combination.

Tranmere Rovers

For the last 20 years Rovers have turned out in a kit which favoured white, the latest version being solid shirts with thin blue epaulettes and shorts edged in blue. This basic kit alternated with blue shirts and white shorts throughout most of the twentieth century. The orange and maroon shirts employed from 1889 for five years were undoubtedly more striking.

Walsall

Since 1950, red has been the predominant colour in the Walsall strip, either teamed with white or black. Under the name of Walsall Swifts, red and white stripes had figured but after the Swifts appendage was dropped, the kit went though a number of changes, including the three decades from 1920 when claret and light blue became the norm. For the last two seasons, solid red shirts and white shorts have graced the Bescot Stadium.

Watford

Although Watford have played in either gold and black or red and black since 1959, history shows us that prior to that year, they really had experimented in the colour department. The solid turquoise shirts at the start of the 1930s gave way to solid blue, but in previous years a striking array of colour combinations had been used, including yellow, green and red (hoops), red and yellow stripes and green with red (quarters). The contemporary red-trimmed yellow shirts and yellow-trimmed red shorts look conservative by comparison.

West Bromwich Albion

Since the introduction of blue and white striped shirts in 1895, the club have only once deviated from that design, during World War 2. The current shirts are actually less elaborate than many of their forebears, as the body of the shirt gives way to plain white sleeves and the shorts have small red and blue swirls top and bottom.

West Ham United

West Ham United's claret and light blue shirts came into existence just before the turn of the twentieth century, when they were still known as Thames Ironworks. Although during the 1970s the blue appeared to become more dominant, the claret has always been the major colour on the body of the shirt, with the sleeves invariably blue. The current kit has a combination of both on the sleeve.

Wigan Athletic

Wigan Athletic acquired their blue and white colours by default, due to shortages after World War 2, with a local supplier only able to offer that particular combination. They therefore had to ditch their pre-war red and white in the process. As the club's fortunes have improved dramatically in the last few years the blue has lightened up. The shorts are currently a solid light blue and the shirt displays an almost jigsaw like pattern of blue and white.

The club scarf: essential for many supporters, bringing the colours of the players' kits to the stands.

Wrexham

Since the onset of World War Two, Wrexham have played in red shirts but much earlier strips included tops with black and red hoops, light blue and white stripes and dark blue and white stripes. The solid green of the early twenties was finally replaced by solid blue in the 1930s. Since the introduction of red shirts, white shorts have usually been the contrasting colour, the present kit being no exception, although white can also be found in panels on each side of the shirt.

CLUB FACTS

Yeovil Town have the distinction of being the only non-league club ever to have their team colours issued by Subbuteo.

Wycombe Wanderers

Throughout the life of the club, light and dark blue have been synonymous with the Adams Park residents. For over thirty years the shirts were halved but in 1930 quartering took over, remaining in place to the present day, if you allow for the odd diversion into solid colour. The contemporary shirt has a quartered body, finishing in white panels at the side with striped arms trimmed in white at the wrist. The light blue shorts have white edging at both sides.

Yeovil Town

As far as Yeovil is concerned green is the colour, for during the whole of their existence and those previous playing guises they have never deviated from its use in their kit. Even during the times when white shirts were reverted to, green trimming was in evidence. The latest employment of the colour finds the club reverting to hooped shirts (green and white) plus white shorts edged in green.

Wolverhampton Wanderers

Red and white striped shirts and white shorts were the first colours to be used by Wolverhampton Wanderers before amber and gold was introduced in the 1890s. The first shirt had a two-colour combination, separated on the diagonal, which evolved into stripes, eventually replaced in the 1930s by solid gold with black trim. At the start of the 2006–07 season, the shirts looked barely any different, the black shorts carrying a gold trim reflecting a club with a fine sense of history and tradition.

Chapter 2

Badges of Honour

Badges, or crests if you're posh, have always been both a focus of attention and a bone of contention. Used to differentiate clubs' shirts when only plain colours were worn, they have since appeared on badges, pennants, replica shirts, publications, flags and almost every item of apparel known to the merchandiser.

The arguments have set in when the badge has been changed, usually to make it more contemporary. Focus groups, internet consultations and other sops to the fan never appease the traditionalists, who sometimes threaten to boycott the club shops, though the fuss and bother usually die down.

Here are some examples of how clubs came by their badges, and the historical refinements, sometimes subtle, sometimes not – that followed.

Accrington Stanley

Stanley's badge dates back beyond the club itself. The town of Accrington was granted a coat of arms in 1879, and it is this that makes up the football club's crest. A shuttle represents the local cotton-spinning industry, while the cylinders and calico represent the method of printing on the cotton. A stag represents the Hargreaves family of Broad Oak who were closely connected with these local industries, while the lion is that of the ancient family De Lacy, who held Accrington by grant of Henry VII.

The oak branch at the top of the crest represents the town's name, 'Accrington'. It is bent into the shape of its initial letter; oak (Anglo-Saxon 'ac') expresses the first syllable and the acorns recall the old form of the name, Akerenton. Completing the crest in place of a motto are the initials ASFC.

Arsenal

Arsenal resisted the temptation to try something completely different when they decided to redesign their club crest for the 2002–03 season. After nine months of discussion, the Gunners finally erred on the side of caution by swapping their famous cannon for... a cannon facing the other way! It apparently helped guard against counterfeit goods, hence the following notice appearing on official merchandise: 'The Arsenal crest, Arsenal logotype and cannon are trademarks of Arsenal Football Club Plc and the Arsenal group of companies.'

Brighton & Hove Albion

Brighton & Hove Albion FC's first known crest (used until 1975) was the coat-of-arms of the twin towns of Brighton and Hove. During the 1974–75 season the club became known as 'The Dolphins' and by the beginning of the following season, a new crest had been introduced.

Both nickname and crest proved short-lived, however. The club has been known as 'The Seagulls' since the mid-1970s and the badge was changed once again to represent this. Though the design changed in 1998 following a takeover, a brief return was made to the traditional shields of the former boroughs of Brighton and Hove – now officially one city – during 2001–02, the club's centenary season.

Charlton Athletic

The first known Charlton crest displayed the letters CAF in the shape of a club (from a pack of playing cards) – hence there was no need for the missing letter. After World War 2, a new design was adopted showing a robin on a football in the centre of a quartered shield. A variation included the letters CAFC in the shield's four quarters and was used on shirts worn in the 1946 (but not the 1947) FA Cup Final. This design was revived for use on 'retro' merchandise, but the robin was now facing to the right.

After a spell using the crest of the former metropolitan borough of Greenwich (though never on shirts) a competition was held in

1963 to find a new club crest/badge. The winning entry – showing a hand holding a sword – went on to become the first version of the current club crest. With the robin ditched, the song used to welcome the team on to the pitch changed from 'Red Red Robin' to 'Old Father Thames', but supporters and players lobbied successfully for the song's reinstatement.

Chelsea

In keeping with their lofty ambitions, Chelsea claimed a new badge was intended to represent the club for the next 100 years. It replaced the previous badge, used since 1986, in May 2005. Prior to that, there had been only three official club badges during Chelsea's 100-year history. It was introduced in time for the club's centenary season and a special version of the badge was used during that year. Chief executive Peter Kenyon said:

> **'We are incredibly proud of Chelsea's heritage. The design of this new badge is based on the one from the 1950s and it was a conscious decision to do this. As we approach our centenary year, and the club embarks on a new and very exciting era, it is appropriate that we have a new identity that reflects our tradition and can represent us for the next 100 years.'**

The club lodged the badge with the Government Patent Office and it received the UK Patent Office's Trade Mark 2373227.

Colchester United

The current crest of Colchester United is the club's fifth, having been introduced in 1994. When the club was formed in 1937, they adopted the city coat of arms as an official crest. Featuring the cross of St Helena (said to have been born in Colchester in the third century AD) and the crowns of the three nativity kings, the club used this crest until 1972, when a dispute arose between the Borough Council and Colchester United FC over the use of the borough's arms.

The club's second crest was first to feature the now familiar eagle image, the inspiration coming from the town's long history dating back to the Roman occupation. The badge's current shield shape was adopted in 1994.

Everton

The crest of Everton Football Club, one of the most instantly recognisable in the English leagues, features a tower erect (in heraldic parlance), bordered by two wreaths resplendent. Prince Rupert's Tower, or The Roundhouse, is an old Bridewell or lock-up that is still located on Everton Brow in Netherfield Road. It was built in 1787, and was used to incarcerate wrong-doers until they could be hauled before the magistrate the following day.

Used primarily these days by council workmen to store their tools, the tower itself had fallen into disrepair, but in 1997, then-chairman Peter Johnson announced a plan to spend £15,000 on renovating what was and remains one of Everton FC's most enduring symbols. The club's Megastore has also incorporated the tower design into its facade.

Fulham

Fulham's first crest was a monochrome image of Craven Cottage, introduced in 1931 when it was felt the club needed a new identity. The crest of the London Borough of Hammersmith & Fulham was first used in 1947 and is regarded as the 'traditional' badge thanks partly to its depiction of the River Thames which flows by the ground.

Fulham's earliest crest is here displayed in concrete on a wall outside the ground.

A 'FFC' script logo was worn on shirts between 1972 and 1977, including the FA Cup Final appearance in 1975. The London Borough of Hammersmith & Fulham crest was reintroduced until a new crest was designed after Mohamed Al Fayed's takeover. It was said he did not want to share the club identity with the Borough of Hammersmith & Fulham and wanted something that was unique and copyrightable. The shield of the previous crest was retained but adorned with modern lettering in the club's core colours of black and white. The club claims 'the unique design aims to be much more easily recognisable to football fans around the world and sits nicely when placed side-by-side with the crest of other top British and European clubs.'

CLUB FACTS

The crest of Chester Football Club from 1974 to 1982 featured a pair of seals in reference to their then Sealand Road ground, replacing the more familiar wolves' head crest.

Leyton Orient

Leyton Orient's badge was the result of a competition held in 1976 by the local *Walthamstow Guardian* newspaper, won by Clive Brown and Mark Hodges with similar

entries. The crest was altered slightly in 1987 when the club changed its name back to Leyton Orient from Orient FC, but other than that, the 1976 design is still in use today. Two wyverns represent the mystery of the Orient and the club's history with the area through the Orient Shipping Line. The crest is complemented by the club name and its year of formation. This replaced a short-lived red dragon.

Prior to this, local associations had held sway. The Borough of Leyton's coat of arms, adopted in 1946, was made redundant in the summer of 1965 following the Borough of Leyton's incorporation into the new London Borough of Waltham Forest.

CLUB FACTS

In the early 70s, in common with a number of other league clubs, Crystal Palace decided to give their image a tweak. The strip was revamped and a new club badge introduced in an attempt to give the club a more modern feel. The badge featured a rather fierce-looking bird, originally intended by the designer to represent a phoenix, a reference to the fire in 1936 that had destroyed the glass construction that gave the club its name. Fans, though, saw it as an eagle, so the club gained a new nickname to go with its new image and the former Glaziers became the Eagles.

Manchester United

The Manchester United crest has been altered on a few occasions, but the basic form remains similar. The badge is derived from the crest of the city of Manchester. The devil on the club badge stems from the club's nickname 'The Red Devils', which was adopted in the early 1960s after Sir Matt Busby heard it in reference to the red-shirted Salford rugby league side. By the end of the decade, the devil had started to be included on club programmes and scarves, before it was finally incorporated into the club badge in 1970, holding its unmistakable trident. In 1998, the badge was once again redesigned, this time removing the words Football Club.

Rochdale

The club badge used by Rochdale AFC focuses on a variant of the arms of the former County Borough of Rochdale. A sack of wool and a cotton plant represents the local wool and cotton industries, while eight martlets (birds) are taken from the local Rachdale family coat of arms. Further local industry references include a fleece of wool and the iron centre of an old mill-stone. A Latin motto below the shield reads 'Crede Signo', meaning 'The sign of trust and confidence'. Rochdale Metropolitan Borough Council was formed in 1974 but the football club continues to use the old county borough arms.

Rochdale's crest.

Sheffield Wednesday

The district of Owlerton not only gave Sheffield Wednesday FC its nickname, it also inspired the club's crest. The first version showed an owl perched on a branch, accompanied by the rose of Yorkshire and sheaves taken from the Council's arms. In 1970, the club introduced a 'plain owl' crest which has developed to become the crest used today. Since 1995, a modern image of an owl has been shown sitting on the letters SWFC and the club's year of formation.

Swindon Town

Swindon Town's first crest was a traditional shield with a robin representing the club's nickname, and a train showing Swindon's importance in the rail industry. The motto 'Salubritas et Industria' is that of the town itself. During the 1970s, a new crest had the letters 'S' and 'T' intertwined, with both ends of the 'S' an arrowhead. This second crest was used until the start of the 1986–87 season, when the club reverted to its original crest, after becoming Division Four Champions. Swindon adopted a new crest, their third, in 1991 following the club's major financial problems to give a fresh image. Its diamond shape has the letter 'S' running through it, while a green section reflected a newly introduced trim on the team's home (red and white) shirts.

Wigan Athletic

The Latics' crest is based on the arms of the Metropolitan Borough of Wigan, granted in 1974. The black diamonds on the shield represent the mining industry, the red roses the county of Lancashire. The lion (couchant), crowned lion and castle are all taken from the arms of the County Borough of Wigan, while the Mountain Ash or 'Wiggin Tree' was chosen as a pun. A sparrowhawk is taken from the arms of Leigh and Atherton (two of the 14 districts that came together to form the Metropolitan Borough of Wigan) and originates from the arms of the Atherton family.

Wigan Athletic's first crest was the arms of the now defunct County Borough Council of Wigan, granted in 1922, which included several elements of the current crest. A third crest used in-between these featured the Crown and 'Wiggin Tree' from the original, enclosed by the full club name.

Chapter 3

What's in a Name?

Many football clubs have gone through changes over the years, most not as subtle as the dropping of the 's' from Hartlepool's name, and these have often encountered resistance from die-hards to whom their club's name and identity is understandably sacrosanct.

All aboard as we take a trip on the name train...

CLUB FACTS

United We Stand!
The most common name in use by English and Scottish Football League clubs is United, with 16 teams currently possessed of it, ahead of City (12 teams) and Town (11 teams). The 16 Uniteds currently in top-class football and the year each took their suffix in the following years:

Sheffield	1889
Newcastle	1892
Scunthorpe	1899
West Ham	1900
Manchester	1902
Carlisle	1904
Southend	1906
Hartlepool	1908
Ayr	1910
Leeds	1919
Dundee	1919
Hereford	1924
Rotherham	1925
Peterborough	1934
Colchester	1937
Airdrie	2002

Two more, Torquay (1921) and Boston (1933), left in summer 2007.

Changing Names

Port Vale were originally known as Burslem Port Vale, named after a canal docks in Stoke on Trent. There is a Vale Street close to the erstwhile docks, which may be where the name comes from, though others claim that the club was founded in a pub called the Port Vale, but there is no evidence that such a pub existed in 1876 when the club was formed. The modern Vale Park is actually about a mile away in Burslem proper, but there is no actual place called Port Vale.

Forest Green is a suburb of the Gloucestershire village of Nailsworth, but is far better known for being the name of the tune to 'O little town of Bethlehem', a traditional melody arranged/collected by Vaughan Williams. Forest Green Rovers, who play there, enjoyed a rapid rise up the non-league ladder and reached the FA Trophy Final in 2001 under the management of ex-Aston Villa keeper Nigel Spink. They changed their name to Stroud FC from 1989–91 to try and attract a wider support from a town four miles distant, but the experiment failed.

Eastbourne Borough, a Conference South club in 2007, were founded in 1968 as Langney Sports. They changed identity on entering the Southern League in 2001 despite there being two other clubs, United and Town, with Eastbourne in their name. However, in recognition of the past and continued association with the Langney Sports Club, the club crest and colours were retained. Though it has been mistaken in the past for a sandcastle, and even a Fez, the Eastbourne Borough FC club crest in fact represents a Martello Tower.

Three seasons later they had arrived in the Conference South and only lost out on a place in Conference National after a North/South play-off with Altrincham. In 2005, they reached the first round proper of the FA Cup, losing to Oxford (then a league side). This match was their first against a league side, the first on national television (highlights were shown on BBC's *Match Of The Day*) and the first time home and away supporters had to be segregated due to the huge attendance by non-League standards of 3,770.

Thurrock FC are a football club based in Grays, Essex, and until 2003 were known as Purfleet FC. Purfleet, founded in 1985, moved through the Essex Senior and Isthmian Leagues to qualify for the newly formed Conference South in 2004. In the club's first season in the league, Thurrock qualified for the promotion playoffs but were knocked out by Eastbourne Borough. At the end of the 2000–01 season, the decision was made to change the name of the club from Purfleet to Thurrock in an attempt to attract a wider audience and extra sponsorship by taking on a name that represented the whole borough.

Their example was followed in 2007 by Gravesend & Northfleet FC who took on the name of Ebbsfleet United. The club was formed in 1946 after a merger between Gravesend United (originally formed in 1893) and Northfleet United (originally formed in 1890) with the new club retaining the red and white home colours (and the Stonebridge Road stadium) of Northfleet United.

Ebbsfleet United's new name was chosen in 2007 to better identify the club with its surrounding region of West Kent. The club's crest remains largely unchanged, retaining its powerful visual impact and simple design. The club has also retained its colours and nickname 'The Fleet'.

CLUB FACTS

AFC Bournemouth's name prior to 1971 was Bournemouth and Boscombe Athletic, which was notable as the longest in the football league. A lot of older fans refer to the club as Boscombe, and the chant 'Boscombe, back of the net' can still be heard at matches.

A record in name changes was set by a club that had four names in the space of six years. Originally Emley, they changed their name to Wakefield & Emley, before slightly changing it a season later to Wakefield-Emley, and then simply Wakefield. Running them close was Runcorn, who started life as Runcorn FC at their own ground, then becoming Runcorn FC Halton when they ground shared at Widnes Rugby Club, and then in 2006 reforming as Runorn Linnets and ground sharing at Witton Albion.

When Leicester City were being re-financed and re-homed in 2003, there was a move to revert to the club's original name: Leicester Fosse. The suggestion did not go down too well with the majority of modern day supporters, even though most of them were probably unaware that a fosse is defined in the dictionary as a ditch, moat, trench or canal.

CLUB FACTS

Caledonian Thistle added Inverness to their name at the request of the Scottish FA, who didn't want the name just to contain two words proclaiming Scottishness. They had hoped that fans would use the abbreviation Inverness CT, which could have become Inverness City, as their name. But this hasn't happened…

Leicester fans voted overwhelmingly to keep the name City during a win over Wimbledon. Supporters were given cards showing a C for City on one side or an F for Fosse on the other. At half-time a sea of Cs gave the fans' verdict and the board listened, announcing at the end of the match 'City would stay City forever'. Though the idea was abandoned, the Walkers Stadium does now have a Fosse Kop Stand and the team has an away strip modelled on the one originally worn by Leicester Fosse. Tradition lives on.

Nicknames

Almost all football clubs have a nickname of some sort, even if it's just a shortened form of their official name. The origins of some are fairly obvious, whilst those of others are rather more obscure. A large number of English clubs have nicknames which reflect local industries. Hence Yeovil Town became known as The Glovers, Stoke City – The Potters, Crewe Alexandra – The Railwaymen, and Burton Albion – The Brewers. Sheffield United became The

Blades, Northampton The Cobblers, Barnsley The Colliers (as well as The Tykes) and Grimsby Town became The Mariners.

The local silk industry led to Macclesfield being known as The Silkmen, whilst saddle-making led to Walsall becoming The Saddlers. A furniture-making industry in the Buckinghamshire town of Wycombe meant that Wycombe Wanderers were destined to become The Chairboys, while the rural nature of Suffolk meant that Ipswich Town were doomed to be known as The Tractor Boys. In Yorkshire, Rotherham United are known as The Millers. They used to be known as The Merry Millers, although it is unclear just what they had to be merry about.

Amongst some of the better known nicknames, we have Arsenal as The Gunners (and, more recently, The Gooners). An arsenal is a place for manufacturing and storing guns and other weapons and, before their move to north London, Arsenal FC used to be called Woolwich Arsenal. As well as sometimes being called The Valiants after the name of their ground (The Valley), Charlton Athletic are known as The Addicks. There are two possible reasons for this. One is that the word is a simple corruption of the word 'Athletic', the other that it comes from a local fish merchant who used to shout out 'Haddocks' in a very loud voice. Just why he should have been doing this is of course anybody's guess. It may have been a term of abuse aimed at the players, or he may just have been trying to sell fish to the crowd.

CLUB FACTS

Bristol Rovers were originally known as the Black Arabs. The first part of their name came from the black gowns worn by the schoolteachers who formed them, the second from a rugby team which played on an adjacent pitch known as The Arabs. Their shirts were black with a single yellow diagonal stripe. This unusual name was held for one season only when the name was changed to Eastville Rovers to broaden the base of the club and to encourage players from a much wider area. They kept this name from 1884–1899 before adopting their now familiar handle.

Bolton Wanderers seem to be called The Trotters because the word has a roughly similar meaning to Wanderers, but there is also a suggestion that the nickname came about because, many years ago, players had to trot through pig pens to get their ball back. One hopes this is true. Bristol Rovers are known as The Pirates, due to connections with shipping. Portsmouth have just about the most famous nickname in the country but, apart from there being naval connections, the origins of the word Pompey are obscure. Weymouth are known as The Terras because they play in a terracotta-coloured strip, but nobody seems to know why Exeter City are known as The Grecians.

CLUB FACTS

In 2002, Spice Girl Victoria Beckham moved to stop English Second Division club Peterborough from registering its 68-year-old 'Posh' nickname as a trademark. She claimed her 'Posh Spice' nickname had become globally known and was a well-known trademark. Geoff Davey, the Peterborough United chief executive, warned that the club faced serious financial implications if prevented from using the name on its merchandising, claiming it was part of the club's history and tradition. Mr Davey said: 'I was absolutely stunned when I got the letter yesterday. One reason was that our claim to the use of the name 'Posh' should be challenged. The second reason was that someone as big as Victoria Beckham would want to raise this particular challenge.'

The *San Francisco Examiner* reported in 2003 that Victoria had decided to allow Peterborough United to continue using the nickname. 'A few months ago, she sent them a cease-and-desist letter claiming its use of the name was a trademark violation. But she has apparently had a change of heart, and in the spirit of the new year, decided to drop her lawsuit.'

Everton's nickname, The Toffees or Toffeemen, came from a local product – Everton Toffee – which used to be handed out to supporters by a local shopkeeper. Rather more pleasant than handing out haddock. As to Peterborough United's nickname, rumour has it that a former manager of the club once said he was looking for posh players for a posh team. The nickname 'Posh' has stuck to Peterborough ever since. Presumably Barry Fry was not the manager involved at the time.

Religion plays its part in some nicknames. Lincoln City are called The Imps after the Lincoln Imp statue in the Cathedral, and Chesterfield are nicknamed the Spireites after the famous twisted spire on their nearby church. York City are known as The Minstermen as York Minster can be seen from their ground, while Bury are known as The Shakers. An early Bury chairman is reputed to have said of his team's opponents: 'We'll give 'em a good shaking. In fact, we are the Shakers'. The Shakers are also a Protestant religious organisation founded in the area, so the nickname was probably felt to be appropriate on all fronts. To the north-east of Bury lies Darlington, home of The Quakers. The Quakers, or Religious Society of Friends, have a long association with the Darlington area, so the nickname is appropriate. Woking are known as The Cardinals after their red and white strip.

Some Scottish Nicknames

Scottish clubs have some quite remarkable nicknames, one of the most enigmatic being that of Clyde. Where on earth could the nickname The Bully Wee have come from? In fact, there are three theories. The first refers to the fact that Clyde's support, and many of its players, were drawn from the Bridgeton area. Like many communities on the River Clyde, the people of Bridgeton were renowned for their pugnacious character, and were known as 'wee bullies' – hence the Bully Wee.

The second theory is that some Frenchmen happened to be at Barrowfield around 1900. When a goal was disputed, they cried: 'But il'y, oui?' This translates as: 'Their goal, yes', but sounds very like 'Bully Wee'. The third possibility, and probably the most likely, is that as 'Bully' was a synonym in Victorian times for good or worthy and, as Clyde was a small club, 'Bully Wee Clyde' just rolled off the tongue.

The players of Ayr United are called The Honest Men after a poem by Robert Burns. He wrote as follows: 'Auld Ayr, wa'm ne'er a toon surpasses, for honest men and bonnie lasses'. It's a good job nobody decided to call the team The Bonnie Lasses. Celtic are The Bhoys, but Dumbarton are known as The Sons, and Falkirk as The Bairns. Hopefully, these will all grow up to be honest men too. There seems little hope for Forfar Athletic, as they are known as The Loons.

Rangers are known, not very inventively, as The Gers (an abbreviation of Rangers) and The Light Blues – a little odd as their shirts are a not very pale shade of blue. Almost as strange as The Bully Wee is Cowdenbeath's nickname: The Blue Brazil. It's quite simple really; the team wears blue and the quality of their football is on a par with that of the South American national side. Of course it is. Everybody knows that.

A number of Scottish team nicknames are very obscure in origin, and many have a good bit to do with the vagaries of Scottish pronunciation. Hence we have The Doonhamers (Queen of the South) and the Red Lichties (Arbroath). Stirling Albion are known as The Binos (or Beanos) but are also known as The Yo-Yos because of their habit of gaining promotion the year after suffering relegation, and then being relegated again a season later.

Aberdeen are known as The Dons, probably for two reasons. The city was famous for having two universities, and the River Don flows through it. Meanwhile, there are at least a couple of theories regarding The Pars of Dunfermline Athletic. One is that the side's strip colour resembled a Parr fish, the other that the team played so badly that they were known as the Paralytics.

Animals, Birds and Insects

A quite remarkable number of domestic animals, as well as an assortment of wildlife, has attached itself to football clubs. Hull City are known as The Tigers, due to their black and orange striped strip, but the kings of the jungle are of course The Lions of Millwall. Quite how the nickname came about is uncertain, but it may have been due to giant killing acts in their early days. The club played at the Den from 1910, until moving to the New Den in 1993.

While Sunderland are The Black Cats and Leicester City The Foxes, Wolverhampton Wanderers are, somewhat predictably, known as The Wolves. Less obviously, Derby County are known as The Rams. They have a ram on their club badge, and a ram is the city's mascot. Hereford are The Bulls, because there are still a few of them charging about and looking menacing in the fields of Herefordshire, while Mansfield Town are known as The Stags. Huddersfield Town are known as The Terriers after Yorkshire Terrier dogs, and Shrewsbury Town are The Shrews. A few years ago, Tamworth became famous for escaping pigs, but the football club is not named after porkers. Rather it is known as The Lambs, because the team used to change in a pub called The Lamb. Tamworth still play at The Lamb Ground, but this was in fact once the site of a pig farm.

Robins and Throstles are mentioned elsewhere, but others amongst our feathered friends feature as football club nicknames. Norwich City are known as The Canaries because of the yellow in their shirts (not because they are on the menu in Delia Smith's rather expensive pitchside restaurant) while Cardiff City are known as The Bluebirds. This would seem to be due entirely to their blue strip, but apparently it may be a little more complicated than that. According to one source, the nickname was taken from a children's play written in about 1908 by a Belgian writer called Maurice Maeterlink. The play was entitled L'Oiseau Bleu (The Blue Bird) and it was very popular at the time. Exactly what a play, written by a not terribly famous Belgian, had to do with Cardiff City FC remains an abiding mystery.

Sea birds are also a feature with some coastal teams. Brighton are known as The Seagulls, whilst Torquay United are content to be just plain Gulls. Swansea City is on the coast, but its nickname is an inevitable inland bird: Swansea are The Swans. Sheffield Wednesday are The Owls, but in fact birds of that ilk are not really involved. The nickname comes from the fact that the club's first home was at Owlerton, just outside the city. Crystal Palace, who at one time were known as The

Glaziers because of the connection with the glass of the real Crystal Palace, are now known as The Eagles. Nobody seems to know why, and no-one is really certain why Bradford City are known as The Bantams. One theory is that a bantam (a small chicken) got onto the team bus during 1911 – the year in which City won the FA Cup, and was thereafter considered to be a lucky mascot.

CLUB FACTS

Ask any football fan these days who The Blades are, and they'll tell you it's Sheffield United. But had you asked the same question a century ago, you'd have got a surprisingly different answer – until shortly before the Great War, it was arch-rivals Wednesday who were known as the Blades, while United celebrated the city's steelmaking prowess in their own way, calling themselves The Cutlers. The switch came about after Wednesday player George Robertson presented his side with a mascot in the form of an owl, a reference to the club's home ground being in Owlerton. Wednesday quickly became known as The Owls, while United lost no time in making Wednesday's racier-sounding former nickname their very own.

Back to the coast again, and several clubs, including Southend United and Harwich & Parkeston, are known as The Shrimpers. Southport are known as The Sandgrounders: sandgrounding is what shrimp nets are said to do when they drag along the sand. Morecambe are named after the small edible crustacean itself, and are known as The Shrimps. Presumably, tall centre-halves need not apply for a trial. On the insect front, The Bees of Brentford and Barnet are joined by The Hornets of Watford and The Wasps of Alloa Athletic – kit colour and design once more being the reason. Amateurs Queens Park, reputedly Scotland's oldest club, are known as The Spiders.

Shared Nicknames

It is inevitable that a lot of clubs will share nicknames. Amongst these are Stockport

County and Luton Town, both of which are known as the Hatters: The Stockport area had a substantial hat-making industry in the late nineteenth century, while Luton was famous for the manufacture of straw hats. The odd supporter can still be seen wearing a straw hat today. Berkshire's Maidenhead United share the nickname The Magpies with a rather more illustrious club from the Northeast, Newcastle United, as well as with Notts County. Black and white striped shirts are to blame. Boston United and Plymouth Argyle share The Pilgrims – Boston because the Pilgrim Fathers were at one stage imprisoned in Boston, and Plymouth because that city was the last port of call for said Pilgrim Fathers before they set sail for the New World.

Many teams are known for the colour of their kit. Reds and Blues therefore naturally abound, although such clubs often have an alternative nickname. Fulham, Tottenham Hotspur and Preston North End have at times been known as The Lilywhites, but all have alternative names. Preston were known as The Invincibles or the Old Invincibles in the early days of the Football League, as they were undefeated in the very first season (1888–89) but, although their fortunes may have revived a little in recent years, the Old Invincibles are somewhat less invincible today.

CLUB FACTS

Between August 22nd 1885 and April 26th 1886, Preston North End played 64 games, of which they won 59. During this impressive run, they scored no less than 318 goals, whilst conceding only 60, an average score of almost exactly 5–1 per game! Little wonder they were known as 'The Invincibles'.

There are alternatives to the somewhat boring nickname 'The Reds'. For reasons known only unto themselves, Manchester United are known as the Red Devils, as indeed are Crawley Town. Meanwhile, Bristol City, Cheltenham, Swindon Town and Altrincham are amongst those clubs which proudly display their red breasts, and are consequently known as The Robins. AFC Bournemouth are The Cherries. Shared shirt colours mean that

Blackpool and Dundee United are sometimes called The Tangerines, although both also have other nicknames.

Sometimes the club's official name is adapted to form a nickname so, for example, clubs with the word Athletic in their title are sometimes known by the corrupted form 'The Latics'. Wigan and Oldham Athletic fall into this category. Clubs with the word 'Saint' (St.) in their title, for example St. Albans, St. Johnstone and St. Mirren, will often be known simply as The Saints. Southampton also have this nickname, as the club was originally called Southampton St. Mary's.

Middlesbrough and Newport County have both been known as The Ironsides, while West Ham United are still occasionally referred to as The Irons. The Hammers, as they are more usually called, started life as Thames Ironworks – hence the earlier nickname. Scunthorpe United are known as The Iron because of the local iron industry. All these names sound very hard and industrial, while Brentford and Barnet's nicknames both have a sting in the tail. Well, perhaps not the tail. They share the nickname The Bees, the colour of their kit being responsible in the case of Barnet. In Brentford's case however, the nickname seems to have come from a chant in the 1890s, which featured gentlemen in cloth caps shouting out 'Buck up, Bs'. Well, they would, wouldn't they?

More than one

Many football clubs have more than one nickname, and often one or more of them will fall out of favour, or become irrelevant, over the years.

As well as the Lilywhites, Fulham are, perhaps rather unfortunately, known as The Cottagers. The nickname comes from Craven Cottage, which is still situated in the corner of the attractive Thames-side ground, and serves as offices and changing rooms. There is no truth in the rumour that Fulham supporters are to be seen hanging around in gentlemen's conveniences, when they should be enjoying themselves watching the game. One of the other Lilywhites – Tottenham Hotspur – have sometimes been known as The Cockerels, but113they are more usually called The Spurs. The story goes that Tottenham were called

Tottenham Hotspur after the Shakespearian character Hotspur. The team was at the time playing at Northumberland Park, and Hotspur (also known as Henry Percy) was the son of the Earl of Northumberland. One wonders who thought up the connection, and whether all Tottenham supporters regularly brush up their Shakespeare. It seems a little unlikely.

Leicester City were sometimes known as The Filberts before moving from their Filbert Street ground to the Walkers Stadium. Filberts are of course nuts, but no-one is suggesting that Leicester City supporters are anything other than completely sane. Leicestershire is (or should that be was?) fox-hunting country, so the club is now known as The Foxes and they play stirring and defiant fox-hunting music over the Tannoy before games.

Sunderland also moved to a new location, making the nickname Rokerites (after their Roker Park ground) redundant. No matter – they still have another two: The Black Cats came from the Black Cat battery gun on the banks of the River Wear, while The Mackems came about because Sunderland was a ship-building area. Originally, Mackems was probably a term of abuse, coined by Geordies. They said that the ships built in Sunderland were never properly finished, so they were taken to Newcastle to be completed. Hence 'They make them, we take them' or, in Geordie-speak: 'they mack 'em, we tack 'em'. Abuse or not, Sunderland folk seem now to be quite happy to be known as Mackems.

CLUB FACTS

Rothwell Town are known as 'The Bones' after a collection of bones, located in the town's parish church. It is thought that these may be from soldiers killed at the nearby Battle of Naseby.

Chelsea are known as The Blues or The Pensioners. The latter nickname comes from the Royal Hospital, Chelsea, whose inmates are known as the Chelsea Pensioners. Some of these elderly ex-servicemen can at times be seen in their bright red uniforms at Stamford Bridge games. Presumably chairman Roman Abramovich continues the tradition of letting

them in for nothing. Because of the billionaire Russian, Chelsea are also currently known as Chelski. Fulham supporters have yet more nicknames for the Stamford Bridge club, but these are not printable.

Reading, the Premiership's newest club, used to be nicknamed The Biscuitmen after Huntley and Palmer's, a local firm of biscuit makers. They are now known as The Royals, after the Royal County of Berkshire in which Reading is situated. West Bromwich Albion have a couple of nicknames: They were known as The Throstles, a Brummie name for the thrushes which used to fly in and out of the hawthorn bushes surrounding the ground. This name has largely gone out of fashion,

but West Brom are still known as The Baggies. The origin of the second nickname is either the baggy clothing once worn by supporters or, rather more likely, the excessively baggy shorts once worn by the players. As well as being called The Tangerines, Blackpool are known as The Seasiders, while the other Tangerines, Dundee United, are also known as The Terrors and the Arabs. The Arabs nickname appears to have come from a time in the 1960s, when the pitch at Tannadice was heavily sanded.

Amongst other Scottish clubs with more than one nickname, we have Heart of Midlothian, the Edinburgh club known as Hearts and occasionally as The Jam Tarts and Celtic, who are known as The Hoops, The Celts and The Bhoys. The latter is an Irish pronunciation of 'Boys' and reflects the fact that the Glasgow club was founded by Irish immigrants to Scotland. Motherwell are known as The Well and also The Steelmen, in honour of a steelworks near the ground, while Inverness Caledonian Thistle are both Caley Thistle and Caley Jags – thistles having jagged edges. Berwick Rangers, the English club which plays in the Scottish League, has two nicknames: The Wee Rangers, because the club is somewhat smaller than the Rangers from Glasgow, and The Borderers.

Home Turf: Stadium names

Have you ever wondered who christened your club's ground and why? Here are a few clues from history as we ask, what's in a name?

Football may be putting many of its traditions behind it, but back in the latter part of the nineteenth century when the Football and Scottish Leagues began, many clubs chose to name their grounds after the districts, roads or streets in which they were situated. Examples of such grounds include Old Trafford (Manchester United), Anfield (Liverpool), Bloomfield Road (Blackpool), Elland Road (Leeds United), Filbert Street (Leicester City) and Love Street (St. Mirren).

There are, of course, many more. In some cases the historical significance of these place or street names is lost in the mists of time, but sometimes it is possible to trace them back to a person of note who lived several hundred years ago, to a geographical feature, or to the previous use of the land. One wonders exactly what went on in Love Street.

England still has quite a lot of lanes, but lanes were almost as numerous as streets or roads a century ago. It is hardly surprising therefore, that clubs like Sheffield United, Bury, Notts County and later Wimbledon, made their homes at Bramall Lane, Gigg Lane, Meadow Lane and Plough Lane respectively.

Football's founding fathers were probably too busy making money and getting their clubs set up to worry too much about the name of the ground. When in doubt, they tended to call it a park, which was reasonable enough in the circumstances. Parks have always been popular, and they were particularly so in the grime ridden industrial towns in which many professional football clubs were founded. And so we have, or had, Ayresome Park (Middlesbrough), Villa Park (Aston Villa), Brunton Park (Carlisle), Boothferry Park (Hull City), Boundary Park (Oldham), Edgeley Park (Stockport County) and a host of others.

The good Saint James was responsible for two football parks: the homes of Newcastle United in the north-east, and of Exeter City in the south-west, both being called St James' Park. In Scotland, the vast majority of league grounds still have 'Park' in their name.

The origins of many other names are fairly obvious. Rotherham was surrounded by mills and moors, hence the football club made its home at Millmoor, while Millwall's ground in Cold Blow Lane was named The Den as it was the home of 'The Lions'. Southampton's former home, The Dell, was, in the 1890s, a deep hollow surrounded by trees: in other words it was a dell, except that this particular dell also featured a pond which had to be drained before a football pitch could be laid.

Quite a few football pitches were laid on the site of former rubbish dumps. Hartlepool United's Victoria Ground was one such, located as it was near to the town docks. Constructed in 1886, it was named after Queen Victoria, in honour of the Golden Jubilee which the ageing monarch celebrated a year later. The ground was originally used for rugby, but soccer was played there from 1890 and Hartlepool(s) United occupied it from 1908. Lincoln City's Sincil Bank ground was not built on a rubbish dump, but it was named after a drain. Fortunately for the club's supporters, this is not an open sewer but a conduit which runs along the side of the ground from the nearby River Witham, to remove excess water. The conduit is entirely wholesome and really rather attractive in its way.

Amusement parks and other leisure areas were also popular places for the provision of early stadia. Scunthorpe United's home until 1988 was the Old Show Ground. As its name implies, this piece of land was once an old show ground. A variety of events took place there a hundred or more years ago, notably the Scunthorpe Show. Aston Villa's ground stands on the site of the mid Victorian Aston Lower Grounds Amusement Park, Wrexham's Racecourse Ground – having previously had a reputation as a place of drunken debauchery – had later been a site for charity shows and other decorous entertainments, while Wolverhampton Wanderers' Molineux once had pleasure gardens, a boating lake and a cycle and athletics track.

Wolves' ground was named after a local family, whilst the Pittodrie Stadium, the home of Aberdeen, was named in honour of a local worthy who lived in the village of Pittodrie,

some 20 miles north-west of the city. Supporters of Aberdeen will tell you that there is no truth in the rumour that in the ancient Celtic language pittodrie meant a 'place of manure'.

There was probably little going on in the way of entertainment at Swansea City's Vetch Field in the nineteenth century (Cardiff supporters will probably tell you that there hasn't been much going on since, either). Vetch is in fact a species of plant, which is also known as tare. It obviously grew where Swansea's ground now stands, but Vetch Field was also known as the Old Town Ditch Field. The ground at which West Bromwich Albion play, the Hawthorns, seems to have fostered plants of a more spiky nature, whilst Shrewsbury Town's Gay Meadow, which closed in 2007, was so named because, before the advent of the football club, the field was a favourite spot for fun and games. It just goes to show how the English language evolves. On the east coast of Scotland, Arbroath's Gayfield perhaps had similar origins.

The 'cosier' St. James' Park, home to Exeter City.

Spotland was a township which became part of Rochdale Borough in 1856, hence the name of Rochdale's home. Sheffield Wednesday's Hillsborough ground was originally known as Owlerton, and the club still bears the nickname 'The Owls'. When the ground was constructed, it was well outside the city boundaries but, by 1914, the area was very much a part of a burgeoning metropolis and had become a part of the parliamentary constituency of Hillsborough. The name of the ground was changed accordingly, but even so the club, known in those days as The Wednesday, did not change its name to Sheffield Wednesday until 1929.

CLUB FACTS

Anyone who has followed football over the past 40 years will recognise Coventry City as one of the game's great escape artists. For much of their 34-year stay in the top flight, Coventry seemed to be fighting a rearguard action to avoid relegation, the closest escape being in 1997, when only Middlesbrough's three-point penalty for cancelling a match at short notice earlier in the season kept the Sky Blues up. In retrospect, Coventry's first season in the league, 1919–20, can be seen as a sneak preview – they lost their first game, at home to Tottenham, 5-0, failed to win at all until Christmas Day, and avoided relegation in dramatic fashion on the final day of the season. Plus ça change, as the French would say.

Grimsby Town used to be called Grimsby Pelham and they played at Clee Park. However, they soon moved to Blundell Park which, as every football fan knows, is in Cleethorpes rather than in Grimsby. The ground was named after one Peter Blundell, who left money to Sidney Sussex College in 1616. The college later purchased land which encompassed the site for a football ground which was to be built almost 300 years later. Grimsby plan to move but their new ground will still be in the constituency of Cleethorpes.

A number of clubs have homes which were, at one time, used only for rugby football but

Derby County's former home, the Baseball Ground, was indeed once used for baseball. Francis Ley, a local industrialist, laid out the ground during the 1880s for the use of the workers. Mr Ley later visited the United States and returned full of the joys of baseball. He encouraged the American game in Derby and he had some success – the club had its own baseball team for a time – but in the end football prevailed.

AFC Bournemouth, Walsall and Cardiff City all had grounds named after their benefactors. Cooper Dean let some wasteland to Boscombe FC in 1910 and two years later Bournemouth and Boscombe Athletic became a professional club. Bournemouth still play at Dean Court, even though it is now known as the Fitness First Stadium. Walsall's former ground, Fellows Park, was named in honour of HL Fellows, a club chairman who had ensured Walsall's survival during times of great difficulty, while Cardiff's Ninian Park was so called after the delightfully named Lord Ninian Crichton Stuart. His Lordship had secured the lease on what was going to be called Sloper Park, and the name of the ground was duly altered.

Tottenham Hotspur had a somewhat less likely benefactor in the shape of a pub landlord. The brewery firm of Charringtons owned the land upon which Tottenham's White Hart Lane pitch was eventually built. The landlord of the nearby White Hart pub was keen that a football pitch be constructed on the site and, thinking of the profits to be made from thirsty supporters, he apparently talked the Tottenham directors into approaching the brewery about providing such an amenity. Charringtons had intended to build houses on the site, but they agreed instead to rent it out to the football club.

Other London grounds have interesting origins, and none is perhaps more unusual than Fulham's Craven Cottage. The original Craven Cottage, built in 1780 by the sixth Baron Craven, stood on land which had once formed part of Anne Boleyn's hunting grounds. It was used as a hunting lodge by George IV and Edward Bulwer-Lytton wrote his famous tome *The Last Days of Pompeii* within its walls. The original cottage burned down in 1888 and when Fulham Football Club took

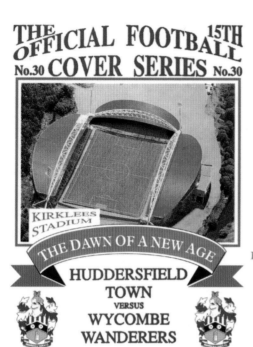

THE OFFICIAL FOOTBALL COVER SERIES No.30 No.30 15TH

KIRKLEES STADIUM

THE DAWN OF A NEW AGE

HUDDERSFIELD TOWN
VERSUS
WYCOMBE WANDERERS

FIRST LEAGUE MATCH AT KIRKLEES STADIUM
HUDDERSFIELD TOWN VERSUS WYCOMBE WANDERERS HUDDERSFIELD
20 AUG 94

MATCH RESULT

HUDDERSFIELD T 0   WYCOMBE W.   1
                                   Garner

The Huddersfield Daily **Examiner**   HUDDERSFIELD TOWN AFC
                                        KIRKLEES STADIUM
                                        HUDDERSFIELD

over the site in the mid 1890s it was overgrown and thoroughly neglected.

Although West Ham's home is usually known as Upton Park, its official name is The Boleyn Ground. The name was taken from a nearby house, built in 1544, and because it had turrets it was known as Boleyn Castle, after Anne Boleyn. The Addicks' ground, meanwhile, is known as The Valley because it was originally a derelict chalk pit, which looked like a valley after excavations to turn it into a football field had been completed.

New Stadia

There is a recent vogue, which some people dislike intensely, for naming stadia after a club's main sponsor. It is the way of the commercial world and supporters will probably just have to get used to it. We now have, amongst others, Bolton Wanderers' Reebok Stadium, Leicester City's Walkers Stadium (a crisp name if ever there was one), Dumbarton's Strathclyde Homes Stadium and

Bradford City's Bradford and Bingley Stadium. The latter is of course named after the building society, but it does at least have the merit of sounding like a proper local name, as indeed does Southampton's St. Mary's. The club's magnificent new arena was officially called the Friends Provident St. Mary's Stadium until the five-year £1.2 million deal ended in 2006.

During planning and construction, Huddersfield's new ground was referred to as the Kirklees Stadium after the borough in which it is situated. Built in 1994 on the site of a disused chemical refuse tip and originally sponsored by Alfred McAlpine, it was awarded the RIBA Stirling Prize for architecture in 1995. Huddersfield Town currently play at the Galpharm Stadium, the pharmaceutical company having taken on the naming rights in 2004, and share it with Huddersfield Giants RLFC. It is also a regular venue for international rugby league, hosting Bradford Bulls' World Club Challenge matches along with several semi-finals of the Challenge Cup.

The previously mentioned Fitness First Stadium, home to AFC Bournemouth, may perhaps serve to inspire the team during training sessions and, just possibly, Hull City's players will coordinate their on-field activities with more precision at their Kingston Communications Stadium. Some clubs content themselves with naming stands or other specific areas of the ground after their modern day benefactors. Blackburn Rovers have their Jack Walker Stand, named after the man who put millions into the club, but Scunthorpe United very nearly deserve a prize for cramming in as many sponsors as possible: All four of their seating areas bear sponsors' names – County Chef, Scunthorpe Evening Telegraph, Don Cass Community and Caparo Merchant Bar stands now grace the stadium at Glanford Park.

A few new grounds have escaped the names of builders, banks, and building societies. Having spent eighty years at Maine Road, where a crowd of 83,260 once watched a league game, Manchester City's new ground is known simply, and elegantly, as the City of Manchester Stadium. Known at first as Eastlands, the stadium was built for the 2002 Commonwealth Games, City moving in during August 2003. Sunderland's Stadium of Light may not, as names go, sound very original, but it does convey a degree of much needed hope for the future. The name was also chosen for a good reason. The ground is built on the site of the former Monkwearmouth Colliery and its gates bear the legend 'Into the light'. These words formerly appeared on a sign at the top of the colliery, so the stadium, which also features a giant miners' lamp, honours the former pit workers.

Northampton Town's Sixfields Stadium, to which they moved from the County Ground in 1994, and Middlesbrough's Riverside Stadium are nice and straightforward, but some Scottish clubs are even more down to earth: Hamilton Academical used to play at Douglas Park, but they now play at New Douglas Park.

In February 2001, Third Division Hull City FC and their Boothferry Park ground were separated as David Lloyd, of tennis and health-club fame, sold the club but retained the ground. The club went close to going out

of business before Harrogate-based dotcom millionaires Adam Pearson and Peter Wilkinson stepped in and wiped out debts. They were then clever enough to get into bed with Kingston Communications, the formerly council-owned telephone company which, having floated on the stock market, was cash-rich. The Kingston Communications Stadium with seating for over 21,000 allowed them to entertain dreams of giving the city, the biggest never to have experienced top-flight football, their dream.

Other grounds, while not bearing the name of a sponsor, simply bear the name of their owner or chairman. Hence, Reading's magnificent Madejski Stadium, conveniently situated just off the M4 Motorway and named after chairman John Madejski and Oxford United's Kassam Stadium, named after the club's former owner Firoz Kassam. Dave Whelan did not name Wigan's ground after himself when he became chairman. Well, not quite. Having made his fortune with JJB sports shops, he decided to call Wigan's new home the JJB Stadium.

When Darlington moved from their Feethams home in 2003, their new Arena was named after then-chairman George Reynolds. But the club went into administration in December that year, Reynolds blaming the Quakers' problems on difficulties putting their new stadium to non-football uses. 'We've tried very hard, built the stadium and worked untold hours. If you look at other stadiums, they are allowed to do car boot sales, markets, and computer and antique fairs – but we're not. We're not allowed to make any money.' 15,000 people had attended the first game, but the Quakers lost 4–1, suggesting that you can have a top ground or a top team but not both. On the departure of Mr Reynolds, the ground changed name to the 96.6 TFM Darlington Arena, sponsored by a radio station.

Chapter 4

Club Mascots

The role of mascots on the periphery of the game has not been without controversy. The form the mascot takes usually has some connection with the club's history, but the human inside the costume has often caused the club's reputation to be brought into disrepute.

Mascots these days tend to incorporate the club's colours and/or wear the obligatory replica shirt, and this has occasionally led to confusion: at least one has been ruled offside and subsequently banned from the touchline.

Mascots usually operate only on home turf: it's when there has been a visiting mascot threatening to steal the home mascot's thunder that problems have often arisen. In 2001, Cyril the Swan and Zampa the Lion did battle off the pitch as Swansea and Millwall competed on it.

The competitive spirit between mascots has been harnessed to more creative effect in the annual mascot grand national, which sees the mascots compete in a hurdles race, of which more elsewhere. In 2003, an attempted £10,000 betting coup using a Commonwealth Games gold medallist as Sedge the Field Mouse failed when one of the rodent's feet fell off!

The origins and history of the mascots differ greatly. Some seem to have been plucked out of thin air, while others have roots in events and tradition. The Hereford Bull, paraded around Edgar Street on big occasions, is clearly a local reference, but another animal mascot, H'angus the Monkey from Hartlepool owes its name to the strange piece of local history: townsfolk once famously hanged a shipwrecked monkey, believing him to be a French spy.

In 2003, the man inside the suit, former call centre manager Stuart Drummond, 28, was elected as Mayor of Hartlepool and found himself in charge of a council budget of more than £1 million. The monkey mayor, who lives with his mum, pocketed a £53,000 a year salary. He ran on a manifesto of giving free bananas to Hartlepool's schoolchildren. At his first council meeting the simian first citizen was confronted by a troop of grunting reporters dressed in gorilla suits.

Cardiff City also paid heed to tradition when in the 1980s they dubbed their bluebird mascot Bartley. It was the suggestion of Jacques Aviles, an eight-year-old supporter from Cardiff Bay, and has a nice alliterative ring to it, as all mascots should. Jacques had come up with the name because he'd read somewhere that a man called Bartley Wilson had founded Cardiff City back in 1899...

AFC Wimbledon's womble mascot makes a new friend.

Mascot names

Arsenal ....Gunnersaurus Rex

Aston Villa......................Hercules Lion

Birmingham City..............Beau Brummie Bear

Blackburn Rovers............Roar Lion

Bolton Wanderers ....Lofty Lion

Chelsea..........................Stamford the Lion

Derby County ....Rammie Ram

Everton ....Mr Toffee

Fulham...........................Billy the Badger
(New)

Manchester City..............Moonchester

Manchester United..........Fred the Red

Middlesbrough................Roary Lion

Newcastle United............Monty Magpie

Portsmouth ....Frogmore the Frog
(New)/Nelson the
Dog

Reading..........................Kingsley the Lion

Sunderland.....................Samson

Tottenham Hotspur ....Chirpy Cockerel

West Ham United............Herbie the Hammer

Wigan Athletic.................JJ

CLUB FACTS

Everton was first described as 'the School of Science' by Steve Bloomer of Derby County and England in the late Twenties. It was in 1928, so legend has it, that Bloomer said of Everton: 'They always manage to serve up football of the highest scientific order' and 'worship at the shrine of craft and science.' His words stuck, and Goodison Park duly became the School of Science. Skill and ability have always been hugely prized by Everton fans who will to this day break into spontaneous and prolonged applause to acknowledge a touch of individual or collective skill. The way in which the term has stuck with Everton is puzzling, however, as the occasions on which the team has deserved this accolade have been rare.

Championship

Barnsley.........................Toby Tyke

Blackpool ....Bloomfield the Bear

Bristol City......................Scrumpy the Robin
(New)/Lady & City
Cat

Burnley..........................Bertie Bee/Bumble
Bee

Cardiff City ....Bartley the Bluebird

Charlton Athletic ....Floyd and Harvey

Coventry City ....Sky Blue Sam

Colchester United ....Eddie the Eagle

Crystal Palace ....Alice the Eagle/
Pete the Eagle

Hull City ....Roary the Tiger

Ipswich...........................Tractor Boy

Leicester City.................Filbert Fox

Norwich..........................Splat the Cat
(New)/Captain &
Camilla Canary

Plymouth Argyle ....Pilgrim Pete

Preston North End ....Deepdale Duck

Queens Park Rangers......Jude the Cat

Scunthorpe.....................Scunny Bunny

Sheffield United..............Captain Blade

Sheffield Wednesday.......Barney the Owl
(New)/Bazz-Ollie-
Ozzie

Southampton..................Super Saint

Stoke City ....Pottermus Hippo

Watford ....Harry and Harriet
Hornet

West Bromwich Albion.....Baggie Bird/Jr

Wolves ....Wolfie & Wendy

League One

Bournemouth..................Cherry Bear

Bristol Rovers ....Captain Gas

Carlisle United ....Olga the Fox

Crewe Alexandra.............Gresty the Lion

Doncaster Rovers ....Donny the Dog

Gillingham ....Tommy Trublew

Hartlepool United............H'Angus the Monkey

Huddersfield	Trisha
Leeds United	Lucas the Kop Cat
Leyton Orient	Theo the Wyvern
Luton Town	Harry the Hatter
Millwall	Zampa the Lion
Northampton Town	Clarence the Dragon
Nottingham Forest	Sherwood Bear
Oldham Athletic	Chaddy the Owl
Port Vale	Boomer the Dog
Southend United	Sammy the Shrimp/Elvis J Eel
Swansea City	Cyril the Swan
Swindon Town	Rockin' Robin
Walsall	Swifty
Yeovil Town	Mark the Jolly Green Giant

League Two

Accrington Stanley	Fraser the Eagle (New)/Stan the Monkey
Bradford City	Billy Bantam/ City Gent
Brentford	Buzz Bee
Bury	Robbie the Bobbie
Cheltenham Town	Whaddney the Robin
Chester City	Centurian
Chesterfield	Chester Field Mouse
Dagenham & Redbridge	No Mascot
Grimsby Town	Mighty Mariner
Hereford United	Billy the Bull
Lincoln City	Poacher Imp
Macclesfield Town	Roary
Mansfield Town	Sammy the Stag
Milton Keynes Dons	Mooie & Donny
Morecambe	No Mascot
Notts County	Mr and Mrs Magpie
Peterborough United	Mr Posh/ Peter Burrow
Rochdale	Desmond the Dragon
Rotherham United	Dusty Miller Man
Shrewsbury Town	Lenny the Lion/ Mrs Lenny
Stockport County	Vernon
Wrexham	Rockin' Robin
Wycombe Wanderers	Bodger

The Mascot Grand National

The Mascot Grand National was first held in 1999 at Huntingdon Racecourse when 17 mascots competed over 220 yards and six hurdles. Beau Brummie Bear of Birmingham City Football Club won the inaugural event.

By 2000, the numbers had swelled to 49, Watford's Harry the Hornet pipping a ruffled Cyril the Swan at the post. In 2001, a huge field of top-flight mascots were left in the wake of Freddie the Fox who turned out to be an Olympic athlete! He was disqualified and Dazzler the Lion of Rushden & Diamonds FC proclaimed the new winner.

CLUB FACTS

In the 1933–34 season, Newcastle United were relegated for the first time in their history, but they went down fighting – in the space of one remarkable week, they beat Liverpool 9–2 and Everton 7–3, scoring almost a quarter of their season's tally of 68 goals in just two games.

2002 saw Oldham's Chaddy the Owl fly to victory thanks to a vigorous training routine that enabled him to wing it easily. He was to win for the second successive year, but only after several of his rivals were sent off course by a scantily-clad lady distracting them!

Graham the Gorilla, mascot of local football club Finedon Volta FC, sent the crowd bananas in 2004, and much was expected when previous champions Chaddy the Owl and Graham Gorilla went head to head. However, it was *The Sun* newspaper's Scoop 6 Squirrel who became the Mascot Grand National Champion of 2005. He was followed by Kick For Life mascot Mickey the Monkey in 2006, but by then the silver trophy had become the preserve of non-footballing figures.

Auto Windscreens, best known for their shield, were also Bristol City's shirt sponsors in the 1990s.

Chapter 5

Club Associations and Traditions

In a world where Reading are no longer the Biscuitmen but the Royals, Chelsea the Blues and not the Pensioners and Fulham seldom the Cottagers, image is everything. But there have been outbreaks of random behaviour that have resulted in the clubs being associated with objects they appear to have no logical link with. It's almost like finding a crop circle around your centre spot! Here are a few with the best explanation that can be offered.

Bananas/Inflatables – Manchester City

The introduction of inflatables to football grounds is generally credited to City fan Frank Newton who borrowed a five-foot banana from a friend and thought it should accompany him to Maine Road for the first home game of the season in August 1987.

The visiting Plymouth Argyle players could not have helped notice the latest fan accessory, as the fans delighted in its presence. Frank took off his City shirt and placed it over the banana, which had soon acquired a drawn face and hat.

So started a craze which the blues supporters embraced whole-heartedly, with an inflatable plane, a toucan and a golf club joining what had now become a host of bananas. Frank himself graduated to a six-foot crocodile.

The range of inflatables became even more impressive and other clubs' supporters soon picked up on the idea. On a famous Boxing Day at Stoke, the City players took the initiative and threw five-foot bananas into the crowd. The fad was perhaps not likely to last very long, as a number of clubs started to ban these alien bodies from the terracing, citing safety issues and spectators having their view blocked as their main reason for the bans.

Breakfast cereal – Bristol Rovers

The story behind Weetabix appearing whenever Rovers play Shrewsbury stems from events prior to a league match at Gay Meadow some years ago. A few Rovers fans, or Gasheads as they are known, banded together and raised some money for the trip up to Shrewsbury. They hired a coach for the day after which about £300 was left in the kitty, so it was decided to go to the pub before the game where £200 was stuck behind the bar to pay for drinks. After a while a few Gasheads started to feel hungry but unfortunately the pub didn't serve food.

The helpful landlord directed them to a nearby supermarket, telling them to bring the food back to the pub and eat it there. A lone Gashead was then despatched to fetch appropriate provisions, with £75 in his pocket after taking out £25 owed to the coach driver. By this point the individual concerned was slightly the worse for drink and returned to the pub armed with £75 worth of Weetabix.

The following day they took all the cereal into the ground and, noticing some birds on the pitch, decided to feed the entire Weetabix hoard to the fortunate feathered spectators. Liberally coating the pitch in Weetabix, the Bristol Rovers fans managed to turn the penalty area in front of the away section from green to brown, as well as littering the terracing.

A few years later Rovers played Shrewsbury again and the same group were seen wearing T-shirts saying 'Weetabix Invasion of Gay Meadow' and of course throwing plenty of Weetabix around. Unfortunately, whenever Rovers now play Shrewsbury the police have been instructed to confiscate all forms of breakfast cereal.

Bull – Hereford

With Hereford cattle much revered in beef circles and the bull in particular being such a magnificent creature, it is slightly strange that it was not until the 1971–72 season, when the club was elevated to the Football League, that the Herefordshire Bull found itself as part of the club crest. Since then, although some alterations have been made, the creature sits proudly at its centre. One of the club nicknames is The Bulls, the club programme carries the name Bullseye and appropriately the fanzine is called *Talking Bull*. Quite a lot of Bull, then.

Celery – Chelsea

Chelsea's associations with this vegetable goes back a couple of decades, supposedly to when a single supporter started singing an obscene four-line ditty entitled 'Celery' which makes reference to touching a lady's backside with a stick of celery. This was taken up by the vociferous hordes and immediately became a celebratory song, accompanied by celery throwing. This may seem a fairly innocuous article to throw around, but things came to a head during the 2007 Carling Cup Final when Arsenal players were targeted and Cesc Fabregas took a direct hit.

Consequently, the Chelsea authorities banned celery from Stamford Bridge, announcing that anyone found trying to enter the ground with the odd stick or two would be turned away and anyone found in possession on the premises would face a ban. This was not well received by those who had a penchant for vegetable-tossing who felt that they were in some way being denied an inalienable rite. Of the many books written about the club, a fairly recent addition was a substantial work carrying the title *Celery! – Representing Chelsea in the 1980s.*

Sweets – Everton

Known as The Toffees or the The Toffeemen, Everton have had an association with confectionery since they moved to Goodison Park in 1892. The nickname(s) appears to have come via a number of sources, the frequently documented one being the close proximity to the ground of Mother Noblett's Toffee Shop which sold Everton mints, leading in turn to a girl walking round the pitch throwing them into the crowd. Another 'toffee' connection can be traced to 'Ye Anciente Everton Toffee House' which stood near to the Queen's Head hotel, a regular venue for club meetings in those early days. It should also be noted that the legion of Irishman resident in Liverpool at the end of the

nineteenth century were referred to as 'Toffeemen' who favoured Everton rather than their rivals Liverpool.

Sing When You're Winning:

Musical Associations

The terrace choir all but became a thing of the past when the Taylor Report outlawed standing at top football grounds. Yet musical links have been established that will never be broken, emanating both from songs sung by supporters and the music used by the club to welcome their side to the pitch. Both have earned a place in folklore. Here are some of the most famous examples.

Bristol Rovers – Goodnight Irene

'Goodnight Irene' was originally associated with the legendary blues and folk singer Leadbelly and became a smash hit in the United States for the Weavers in 1950. The version by the Five Smith Brothers was regularly played at Rovers' old Eastville ground and the fans always sung along with it, hence the tune became synonymous with the club. The supporters seem to have particularly identified with the line 'sometimes I have a great notion, to jump in the river and drown', for the River Frome ran alongside Eastville.

Celtic – You'll Never Walk Alone

Since the 1960s, there has been constant debate has to whether Celtic or Liverpool were the first to use the song as a club anthem and, whilst no concrete proof exists, the latter club seem to be most likely. At Celtic Park, the Rodgers and Hammerstein song has to rub shoulders with both the Irish National Anthem and songs of a republican nature.

Chelsea – The Liquidator

One of three teams associated with 'The Liquidator', Chelsea could have well been the first club to introduce it as a regular match day feature. It seems to have been played at Stamford Bridge ever since its release, when the occupiers of 'The Shed' (now long gone) would clap along to its repetitive lines. In 1997, a special 7" remix was issued via the Billie Bluebeat label which found favour with the Blues faithful and it has cropped up on more than one compilation devoted to the club's associated music. Abramovich and Avram Grant may constitute the present but 'The Liquidator' conjures up memories of Osgood and Co.

Crystal Palace – Glad All Over

As part of the celebrations at Palace reaching the 1990 FA Cup Final, the playing squad went into the recording studios where they laid down two tracks, one of which was 'Glad All Over'. The tune had originally been a Number 1 chart hit for the Dave Clark Five back in January 1964 when the Londoners ousted the Beatles from the top spot, and had been heard regularly at the ground thereafter. The club's bid for Cup glory eventually ended in failure but the song has stayed around as very much a part of each home game. It is played before kick-off, every time Palace score and also if they win.

Everton – Z Cars Theme

The Z Cars theme came from the popular BBC police drama which made its first appearance in 1962. The tune is based upon a folk song called Johnny Todd and was especially arranged for the series by Fritz Spiegl. The Everton fans could easily associate with the programme, supposedly set in an area close to Goodison Park and consequently took up the melody as their own. One story runs that the very first playing of the tune at a game celebrated the presence of cast members at Goodison. From the 1960s onwards, the theme has been played at virtually all home games as the players take to the field.

Liverpool – You'll Never Walk Alone

The song is from the Rodgers and Hammerstein musical *Carousel* but has been recorded by such diverse talents as Frank Sinatra, Mario Lanza, Elvis Presley and Patti Labelle and the Blue Belles. Most famously it became a hit in 1963 when Gerry Marsden with his group the Pacemakers took it to Number 1 in the charts. Gerry has sung the song before games at Anfield, where he delivered an emotionally charged version and also at Celtic Park (Celtic also claim the song as their anthem) prior to a UEFA cup tie

between the Scottish club and Liverpool.

Why did Liverpool fans adopt the song? One theory, is the simple explanation that it had been played a number of times before matches, then one Saturday it failed to get a play over the PA system but the Kop started singing it anyway. From then on it became *de rigueur* for the Kop to perform the song before each home game.

The words You'll Never Walk Alone also became part of the club's crest.

Stoke City – Delilah

'Delilah' seems a strange song for the fans of a Midlands football club to adopt as their own given its associations with Tom Jones and, in latter years, Welsh rugby. Although it's difficult to ascertain exactly when the tune became part of Stoke folklore, there is no doubting the supporters' enthusiasm for its rousing verses. Many a report is on record as to how a rendition from Stoke fans has raised the roof at grounds up and down the country, particularly when their team are performing well. When a CD entitled 'Play Up Stoke –The Songs of Stoke City' was released in 2002, a version was inevitably included.

West Ham – I'm Forever Blowing Bubbles

In 1927, a famous advertisement campaign for soap featured a young child blowing bubbles. The similarity between the child and a current West Ham player was seized upon by the fans, who quickly took up 'Bubbles' as the club song, which has stuck around ever since. The lyrics have been tweaked a little but essentially it remains the original song. Before all home games the 1980 version using the original lyrics is played over the PA system and taken up by the assembled throng. 1980 was of course an FA Cup winning year for the club and punk-rockers Cockney Rejects issued their own version of the tune in celebration.

Wolverhampton Wanderers – The Liquidator

The playing of reggae instrumental 'The Liquidator' at Wanderers home games became something of an issue when the local police put a ban on the playing of the tune, which

Gerry and the Pacemakers, whose rendition of 'You'll Never Walk Alone' became an anthem of both Liverpool and, later, Celtic.

they felt could contribute to violent behaviour between rival fans. This also affected local rivals West Bromwich Albion who also had a penchant for the 1960s Ska classic. Recent years have seen supporters clamouring for its permanent reintroduction. Various claims have been put forward as to who originally instigated its use, for Chelsea are also associated with the Harry J Allstars favourite.

Local Derbies and Tribal Loyalties

The origin of the term 'local derby' to refer to a match between two clubs from the same town or region seems to stem from the annual Shrove Tuesday football match in the Derbyshire village of Ashbourne, which started in the Middle Ages and lives on to this day. The whole town participates, and a good time is had by all... so long as all the windows are boarded up!

The game is played every Shrove Tuesday and Ash Wednesday, and consists of two teams, one from anyone born to the North of the River Henmore, and one from people born South of the river, known as Up'ards and Down'ards.

We haven't included that one in our list of local hotspots, but as with all derby games there's always much more than mere league points at stake. Bragging rights at school and the workplace are all important and even if the influx of foreign players may have diluted the fervour on the pitch, there's never any lack of passion off it.

Portsmouth – Southampton

The competition for ascendancy on the South Coast precedes the footballing age by some centuries, for history tells us that the cities' rivalry was initially based on commercial issues rather than less important sporting prowess. This is of little consideration to football supporters, however, and the animosity between the two sets of fans (Scummers and Skates to the opposition) is as fierce as any in the country. Portsmouth were the senior club in their late-1940s heyday, though Saints' FA Cup win in 1976 preceded a spell in the top flight which their neighbours would only reach in 1988.

CLUB FACTS

Southampton's 1982 side included no less than seven former, contemporary and future England captains – Mick Channon, Alan Ball, Kevin Keegan, Mick Mills, Peter Shilton, Dave Watson and Mark Wright.

Amazingly, in the last 30 years the clubs have only played league fixtures against each other for three seasons. In 2004–05, they also faced each other in the FA Cup, where Southampton came away triumphant, although the Fratton Park faithful would have relished the 4–1 home victory towards the end of a season which witnessed The Saints – managed at that time by former Pompey boss Harry Redknapp – exit the Premier league.

Ipswich – Norwich

East Anglia is somewhat limited for those looking for major football action, so it is no wonder that any clash between Ipswich and Norwich is regarded as of significant importance. Although fixtures are regarded as local derbies, the clubs play approximately forty miles apart, so for visiting fans there is the away-day element to look forward to as they journey into a foreign county.

Neither club has had much to crow about in recent years for not since 1962 (when the Canaries won the League Cup and Ipswich won the Championship) have both claimed a major prize in the same season. Both sides were desperate to climb out of the Coca-Cola Championship in 2007–08, and 25,461 attended a 2–2 draw at Carrow Road in November, but Norwich's sole aim that season was survival.

Celtic – Rangers

Ignoring the religious issues surrounding the Old Firm rivalry, there is every likelihood that the passionate feelings held by respective supporters would have existed anyway given the need for football supremacy in any city and the fact that both clubs are always looked at as contenders for major honours at the start of each season. Certainly a fixture no true fan would ever miss, the Glasgow derby has been responsible for club record crowds at both grounds; in January 1938, 92,000 crammed into Celtic Park and a year later, a staggering total of 118,567 souls had Ibrox bursting at the seams.

This is never an easy fixture to predict, whatever the form of either side, as was underlined by Rangers' shock win in a league fixture in March 2007 when Celtic were romping away with the title and Rangers struggled in a distant second place.

Aston Villa – Birmingham City

In one of the more significant recent meetings between these two clubs, towards the back end of the 2005–06 season, at Villa Park victory was a 3–1 victory for the home team, which completed the league double over their rivals and helped consign the visitors to relegation – double satisfaction for the Villa faithful and

Match programmes for just two of the many 'Old Firm' derbies to have been played down the years. Matches between Celtic and Rangers have always been hard-fought affairs, with passions often spilling over both on and off the pitch.

deep humiliation for Blues fans. Of course Villa have always aspired to and often achieved greater success than City, who have to go back to 1963 when they won the League Cup for their greatest triumph. Birmingham's promotion in 2007 put the second city derby very much back on the Midlands' footballing agenda.

WBA – Aston Villa

Although the Villa and Birmingham derby may be the most eagerly contested in the Midlands, Villa versus Albion fixtures probably come a very close second, given the Hawthorns' closer proximity to Villa Park than St Andrews. West Brom tumbled into the Coca-Cola Championship at the back end of season 2005–06, so this particular derby was put on hold for a while. Neither club has won anything worthwhile for over ten years, so come the 2007–08 season, Albion were desperate to at least regain league parity with their still underperforming neighbours.

Everton – Liverpool

For a Merseyside supporter, the day on which Everton and Liverpool meet exists in limbo; other events in the universe and beyond have no relevance during the build-up to the game and for its duration. Passions run high and the result is as important to the Merseyside factions as they are for the committed hordes of Glasgow during Celtic/Rangers clashes. This derby has been played out since 1894 and, whilst having the atmosphere of all local matches, restraint is generally the byword for devoted supporters. Everton have been looking for a trophy since 1995 and must covet the glory Liverpool has acquired in the twenty-first century. In the meantime the Toffees will just have to settle for the four points they took from the two league fixtures in 2006–07.

Arsenal – Tottenham

Arsenal, whose success of recent years has given them ascendancy in North London, have dominated the derby fixtures during the last few seasons. Prior to January 2007, when the Gunners ran out comfortable winners by three goals to nil, we have to go back as far as November 1999 for the last time a Spurs victory was recorded, whether it be in the league or either cup competition.

Given Arsenal's recent move to the 60,000 plus capacity Emirates Stadium, a little local jealousy is understandable from their closest competition who are desperate to achieve success on a par with their neighbours. Though it wasn't a derby game, the sequence of events one Saturday afternoon in May 2006 which saw Arsenal claim a Champions League place, consigning Tottenham to a UEFA Cup slot, left a particularly bitter taste – especially as a number of Spurs players had come down with food poisoning before their game at West Ham. Sour grapes? Forensics are still investigating!

Chelsea – Fulham

Fulham have always existed as the poor relations to their rivals down the road. Even when Mohamed Al Fayed's millions arrived at Craven Cottage to change the club's fortunes in 1997, the even richer Roman Abramovich moved into Stamford Bridge a few years later and totally upstaged the Harrods boss.

Fixtures between the clubs were sporadic for a number of years but in recent times Premiership status for both sides has meant a regular coming-together with Chelsea invariably holding the upper hand in both league and cup. Wins such as that in March 2006 have been greeted ecstatically by Fulham's faithful, to the point of pitch invasion, but that had no effect on the blue juggernaut's drive to a second title.

Manchester United – Manchester City

If animosity exists towards Manchester United in other parts of the country, this is nothing to that which emanates from the supporters of their city rivals. The success of United in all competitions during the 1990s, which carried on into the twenty-first century, has been a bitter pill to take for City supporters whose team has not won anything of significance for over 30 years.

United have the lion's share of victories in these derby matches which go back to 1891 but City have had a modicum of success in recent seasons, the 4–1 league victory in March 2004 being a most significant result to rank alongside the 5–1 win after promotion to the top flight in 1989. In the 2005–06

Once upon a time, local derbies were commonly held on Boxing Day, a measure designed to boost crowds at a time of year when visiting fans were thought unlikely to attend if forced to travel any great distance.

campaign, City claimed four points from the two fixtures, small consolation for a woeful campaign.

Liverpool – Manchester Utd

There is no bigger inter-city clash in Premiership football as when Liverpool and Manchester United confront each other, whatever may be at stake. The rivalry between these giants, separated by the East Lancs Road, not only revolves around city pride but the need to outdo each other in all the major home and European competitions, taking into account that either side is capable of carrying off silverware at the

drop of a hat. It has certainly, in the last decade, overshadowed the more local affairs with Everton and City respectively as both teams have cemented their Champions League qualification year on year.

In these more recent seasons Liverpool have struggled when faced by United, having failed to win any of their last six league clashes, their FA Cup victory in February 2006 a welcome sequence-breaker. In 2007 the clubs looked as though they could be on for a confrontation in the Champions League, but AC Milan ensured it was not to be.

Hearts – Hibernian

These two Edinburgh clubs have been going head to head since 1875 and, though split by religious beliefs (Hibs are traditionally Catholic, Hearts Protestant), encounters between the clubs have always emphasised sporting rather than sectarian differences. Hearts have always tended to be the more successful of the two, having won the Scottish Cup as recently as 2006 (beating Hibs 4–0 en route), but both clubs have always tended to operate in the shadow of their more illustrious Glasgow counterparts.

The teams ply their trade in the Scottish Premier League, so meetings come round pretty quickly with Hearts having notched up an impressive three victories and a draw in their league fixtures in 2006–07.

CLUB FACTS

During the 1982 season, Bristol City were in dire financial straits that caused their main players to tear up their contracts and play for free to save the club. Thus the club was reincorporated as Bristol City 1982 plc. As part of the rivalry that exists between the two clubs, Rovers fans enjoy taunting City supporters about this and hence often refer to them as City '82.

Bristol City – Bristol Rovers

When the Bristol clubs met in the LDV Vans Trophy in 2002, won 3–0 by City, this brought their derby meetings to a round one hundred. City has always been regarded as the more successful of the two, although neither has ever won anything of significance. City last made a few minor waves in 1989 when they reached the semi-final of the League Cup and a year later Rovers sparked briefly when they won the Third Division title.

As the 2006–07 was reaching its climax, City gained an automatic promotion place from League One while Rovers won in the play-offs to win elevation from League Two. While these events brought joy to the city, it ensured they would continue to be kept a division apart. The clubs had, however, played a derby in the Johnstone's Paint Trophy semi-final in 2007, a single Rovers goal sending them through to the Millennium Stadium despite their underdog status. The two legs had been well attended by five-figure crowds, proving the appetite for football in Bristol.

Nottingham Forest – Notts County

When Forest and County first met each other in 1866, albeit in a friendly game, they could well have established the oldest derby fixture in world football (though this is generally said to have been the game between Sheffield FC and Hallam FC some years earlier). It was not until 1878 that the clubs confronted each other in true competition when they played out an FA Cup tie, won 3–1 by Forest.

Up to 1994, when the sides last clashed, there had been 139 meetings between the clubs with Forest holding a majority of 52 victories. As the 2006–07 season came to its conclusion it became apparent that these league fixtures were not to be revived in the foreseeable future. It has been said that Forest, who have graced the top flight more often than their rivals in recent history and won two European Cups under Brian Clough, chose their name instead of City as County was larger. But that was back in the 1860s.

Newcastle – Sunderland

Neither Newcastle nor Sunderland have won anything of note for some considerable time, so given those circumstances, local pride has become even more important for both clubs. Newcastle have flattered to deceive on numerous occasions in the last few years and Sunderland are far from happy in being the slightly poorer relations. The ascent of Middlesbrough, less than 40 miles distant, has also increased the importance of resuming top-flight status (which Newcastle have enjoyed since 1993) and the corresponding derby fixture(s).

It's a long time since the Wearsiders inflicted Newcastle's biggest home defeat of 9–1 back in 1908. Their last meeting in 2005–06 saw the Magpies produce two victories which contributed to the big drop for the Black Cats but all indications were that an immediate return to the Premiership was on the cards for the latter (as indeed proved to be the case). The most memorable recent Sunderland win was the Mackems' 2–1 triumph at St James' Park in 1999 which ensured the sacking of Ruud Gullit. Since the Dutchman had benched local hero Alan Shearer, the Geordie fans probably didn't mind too much.

Darlington – Hartlepool

It may technically be a lesser Northeast derby, but games between Darlington and Hartlepool are still fiercely contested. The two clubs have traditionally slugged it out in the bottom division, but the Pools' aspirations have been increased by major investment from Norwegian owners, while Darlington have left Feethams behind to play in a 25,000 all-seater stadium.

The pair met in the 2000 play-off semi-finals, where Darlo triumphed, while Andy Toman played for both clubs and comments: 'Hartlepool fans hate Darlington and the other way round. The fans are passionate and they won't accept second best.'

Manager Danny Wilson's good work at Hartlepool ensured promotion to League One in 2006–07, a season in which they took four points from their neighbours, while the Quakers also have a good manager in Dave Penney who might well put this fixture back on the list – if Hartlepool can stay up this time.

Stoke – Port Vale

Stoke City and Port Vale (then Burslem Port Vale) first met on a football pitch in 1887 for an FA Cup tie but it was not until the 1920s that their meetings established themselves as regular affairs. Subsequently, there have been substantial periods of time when this Potteries derby has been put on hold due to division differences, particularly throughout the 1960s, 70s and most of the 80s.

Stoke have always carried an edge with regard to status but honours remain reasonably even when reviewing match statistics. The two sides have not met since the 2001–02 season when Vale lifted four points from the games, which do not look like being renewed in the very near future.

West Ham – Millwall

The rivalry between these two clubs goes back to the time when they both played in the East End of London, Millwall putting a couple of further miles between the sides when they moved south of the Thames in 1910. There have been sizeable periods of time when the clubs didn't meet but the Football League Championship witnessed impassioned clashes between the two sides from 2003 to 2005 when Millwall clearly took the honours with a couple of wins plus two draws. Since then, West Ham's position in the Premiership and their rivals' slump to League One has meant a cessation of hostilities.

Cardiff – Swansea

It is almost accepted that, when these two clubs meet, violence on or off the pitch is inevitable.

Due to Cardiff's superiority they tended to avoid each other for many years until 1980 when 'the troubles' really started, culminating in a riot at Ninian Park in 1993 which led to a five-year ban on Swansea supporters (known as Jacks) visiting the ground.

CLUB FACTS

Swansea Town hold the unenviable record for the furthest distance travelled between consecutive matches – on Good Friday 1936, the Swans played, and won 2–1, at Plymouth, but for the following day's fixture had to travel to Newcastle, 417 miles away, to face the Magpies. Unsurprisingly, Newcastle ran out 2–1 winners.

Although South Wales Police would probably prefer that the clubs never encountered each other again, as things stand only a set of poor or outstanding results from one side or the other could mean a resumption of hostilities as Cardiff inhabit the Championship, though the Swans lost a League One promotion play-off in 2006.

Blackburn Rovers – Burnley

With Blackburn a *bona fide* Premiership side and Burnley struggling to make an impact somewhat lower down the league structure, it is easy to forget that these two towns have a rivalry going back some decades. Both have a long history and were in fact founder members of the Football League.

They have not been face to face in the same division since 1982, although two hard-fought FA Cup ties in 2005, producing an eventual win for Rovers, showed there was no love lost between the clubs or their fans. Burnley have a desperate desire to close the gap between themselves and Rovers, exaggerated by the latter's 1995 Premiership title win and 2002 League Cup victory.

Wolves – West Bromwich Albion

Albion and Wanderers first started competing against each other in the 1880s and were still battling it out together in the Coca-Cola Championship in the 2006–07 season with both clubs desperate to return to the upper

Local derbies are passionate affairs, and frequently prove to be volatile too. This courteous handshake before kick-off at the derby game between Wolverhampton Wanderers and West Bromwich Albion is about as cordial as proceedings are likely to get!

echelons. Honours in the league were shared in the last-mentioned season with a league victory each but Baggies fans delighted in a 3–0 FA Cup victory at Molineux.

In over 150 meetings, Albion have enjoyed the most victories, although not overwhelmingly so; the biggest margin ever in this derby came in March 1963 when Wolves coasted to a 7–0 home win. In 2007, two legs of the promotion play-offs saw West Bromwich prevail 4–2 on aggregate, though they were not to attain their ultimate goal when beaten by Derby in the final.

Derby – Nottingham Forest

For a period in the 1970s both County and Forest tasted big time success thanks to Brian Clough, County lifting two League titles and Forest taking the League, two League Cups and two European Cups. Forest further distinguished themselves in the 1980s and even as late as 1990 put their name on the League Cup again. Since then it has been a bit of a struggle for both clubs who feel aggrieved at their respective positions in the lower divisions.

The last time the Midlands pair met was in season 2004–05 when Derby drew away and

CLUB FACTS

Aston Villa owed their formation to cricket and religion. Players of the summer game associated with Villa Cross Wesleyan chapel in Aston, Birmingham, decided they wanted something to do in the winter and formed the club in 1874. Unfortunately, local opposition was thin on the ground, so their first game against Aston Brook St Mary's Rugby Club saw them swap codes at half time! Ten years on, they would be one of Britain's leading clubs, a change of gear attributed to Scottish player and captain George Ramsay, who joined them in 1876.

won at home, repeating the previous campaign's results. Both clubs see themselves as big-time performers but of the two it is Derby who proved Premiership material by winning through the play-offs in 2007, while Forest slumped in the semi-final of League One.

Dundee Utd – Dundee

The Dundee rivals have both been European Cup semi-finalists in the past and United made the final of the UEFA Cup in 1987, the last time the city made the football world sit up. Their respective grounds, Tannadice and Dens Park, are within a couple of minutes' walking distance of each other with postcodes one letter different but they operate a league apart, with United struggling to compete against their more illustrious opponents in the Scottish Premiership and Dundee FC desperate to join them. The Premiership campaign of 2004–05, when they last fought out league games, had Dundee winning a couple to United's one, sharing the spoils in the fourth fixture.

Brentford – QPR

Queens Park Rangers have always viewed Chelsea and Fulham as the yardstick by which their own results are measured but in terms of true West London rivalry, Brentford, who reside just three miles away, are their main protagonists. The two clubs have met a total of 62 times in the league but the future does

not look as though it includes a reappearance for this most competitive of derbies, as Rangers look safely entrenched in the Championship while Brentford appear in freefall in League Two. The prospect of the clubs merging in 1967, QPR taking over Griffin Park, has never been forgotten by Bees fans.

Sheffield Wednesday – Sheffield United

The Sheffield clubs first met in the 1890s and have played each other in every subsequent decade. In well over 100 matches the Blades hold the greatest number of victories. Fortunes for both teams have fluctuated over the years with both boardrooms desperate for any kind of silverware, Wednesday's 1991 League Cup victory the last time either club won anything.

Season 2005–06 saw United promoted to the Premiership. Wednesday supporters would have been doubly choked, for they had seen their side lose both league fixtures as well. Thereafter United battled gallantly but failed to maintain their much-valued position while Wednesday wallowed in Championship mid-table obscurity. The 2007–08 season saw Steel City hostilities renewed.

Lincoln – Boston United

This rivalry flourished but briefly as Boston gained league status in 2002 and then fell back into the Conference five years later. The Imps, 33 miles distant, had been a league team since 1892 but had lost League status in 1908 to Tottenham (they were re-elected after a season) plus two single seasons, 1911–12 and most recently 1987–88, when they bounced back from exile in the Conference. The roll of honour between the sides in the Football League now reads three wins apiece, in addition to four draws, and will remain so for a while as Boston were demoted two levels after going into administration.

Different Shaped Balls – Playing Other Sports

Football and rugby have always enjoyed a close relationship – one that began in 1823 when William Webb Ellis's legendary dash with the ball eventually gave rise to the oval-ball

Turf is cut at Fulham's Craven Cottage ground, home for some years to both the well-known football club and a sister rugby league side, as can be seen from the sign on the stand at the rear of the picture.

game. Since then the two codes – three, if you count Rugby League and Union as different – have co-existed in varying degrees of amity. Indeed, some football clubs directly owe their existence to rugby clubs.

One is Bradford City, who came into existence when Manningham Rugby Club needed to attract additional revenue – other ventures had included an archery competition! Having decided to form a sister club in 1903 to share their Valley Parade ground, they sent a delegation to London to apply for admission to the Football League and the infant club was accepted without having played a single match!

In a dramatic shift, the committee of Manningham RFC then proposed to abandon rugby altogether in favour of association football. The motion was eventually carried by a 2–1 majority and Bradford City was born.

For the first few months of their inaugural season, City wore the claret and amber hooped jerseys of the rugby team (of the Prince of Wales' Own West Yorkshire Regiment) before their new vertically striped shirts were delivered. The claret and amber colours were unique in the league.

Ironically, Bradford City lodged temporarily with their rugby league neighbours at the Odsal Stadium while their home was repaired following the 1985 fire at Valley Parade.

Rugby clubs have been frequent lodgers at football grounds, most notably at a time when the Rugby League was seeking to gain a foothold in the south (Fulham's team of the 1980s became the London Broncos, then Harlequins RL) and more recently with the Rugby Union's Premiership requiring more advanced facilities than most clubs could afford. Hence London Irish playing at the Madejski, Wasps buzzing between Loftus Road and Adams Park, Wycombe, and Rotherham playing at Millmoor in 2003–04, having the previous session been denied entry into the elite due to supposed ground inadequacies.

In the North, football clubs have often been the latecomers, competing against the long established Rugby League code. Horwich RMI decided in 1995 that if you couldn't beat them, you could join them. They relocated to Hilton Park, home of rugby league club Leigh Centurions. Once agreement had been reached to share the 10,000 capacity stadium, Horwich officially changed their name to Leigh RMI to reflect their new surroundings. Hilton Park is nicknamed The Coliseum for Rugby fixtures in view of the 'Centurions' nickname of the rugby league team.

Five years after this move, Leigh RMI reached the Conference, the highest level of non-league football. With Leigh being known as a rugby league town, the football club averages attendances of less than 200. The club is planning to relocate to a new purpose-built stadium in Leigh, at which they will continue to ground-share with the Centurions.

The best example of football and rugby living in harmony is surely the magnificent JJB Stadium in Wigan. Built with both codes in mind, it is home to both Wigan Athletic and Wigan Warriors.

PART III: The Modern Game

Chapter 1

Sponsorship – A Necessary Evil

It's impossible now for most of us to remember a football shirt without a sponsor's name emblazoned across the chest, but the past three decades have seen first shirts and then other areas of the game (including the League Cup) take on strange associations. Some sponsorship deals, like Liverpool's with Carlsberg, have lasted decades rather than years, while others come and go. Manchester United's 2006–07 link with insurance firm AIG led to wags claiming it stood for Alex Is God, or, later, Almost In Greece!

It's certain, however, that clubs now bank on sponsors' money, lavished for anything from exposure on shirts to the naming rights of a stadium, to help them meet the ever-increasing costs of being a success in football. Here are some groundbreaking examples.

Clubs

Southport

Southport were bought by the Vulcan Motor company and in 1918 were known, for one year only, as Southport Vulcan. This is probably the earliest example of a club being named after a sponsor/owner.

Kettering Town

Non-leaguers Kettering were the first British club to carry a sponsor's name on their shirts when they did so in a Southern League fixture against Bath in January 1976. Kettering Tyres had done a deal with the then manager Derek Dougan which totally flouted FA sponsorship rules that were in place at the time. The football authorities acted swiftly, demanding that the name be removed from the shirts immediately.

Never one to accept situations on face value, Dougan had the lettering changed to 'Kettering T' which he claimed had validity as the 'T' obviously stood for Town. This threw the FA for a few weeks before eventually they reiterated their request which also carried the threat of a fine if the order was ignored.

At this point the club waved a white flag and complied. But that was not the end of the matter for, with the help of Bolton Wanderers and Derby County, Kettering made an official request to the FA, asking that they review the whole matter of shirt sponsorship, and in 1977, the rules were finally relaxed. Ironically, by this time the Northants club had difficulty in finding a new sponsor.

Llansantffraid

In 1996, Llansantffraid FC won the Welsh Cup, consequently qualifying for a first-time entry into the European Cup Winners Cup. Local computer company Total Network Solutions offered them a £250,000 sponsorship deal if they would agree to incorporate the company name into that of the club. This was the first instance in the UK of a football club renaming itself using a sponsor's name. Although the new club title of Total Network Solutions Llansantffraid FC was ridiculously unwieldy, the injection of cash did wonders for a side that now were able to employ a full-time playing staff (at the time the only club in the League of Wales to have such a luxury). A year later Llansantffraid disappeared totally from the club name and in 2003 they merged with Oswestry Town.

In 2006, Total Network Solutions became part of British Telecom and their commitment to the club sadly had to come to an end. A new name had to be found and The New Saints FC was eventually arrived at after much deliberation. This had the advantage of retaining the club's abbreviated form.

Coventry City

Once shirt sponsorship became the norm for football clubs it was perhaps inevitable that one club or another would fall foul of the BBC's strict rules on advertising products. Coventry City's infamous early 1980s strip heavily incorporated the Talbot logo which was totally unacceptable to the highly sensitive Beeb who announced they would not show any more City fixtures until a substitute strip could be used for any broadcast games. Prior to the kit controversy, managing director Jimmy Hill had pursued the possibility of changing City's name to Coventry/Talbot, which received short shrift from the vast majority of all those involved with the club.

West Bromwich Albion

One of the most bizarre and yet very socially responsible sponsorship deals came about in 1984 when a large 'No Smoking' logo was emblazoned on the front of West Bromwich Albion's traditional navy and white striped shirt. The deal was a result of an initiative launched with the West Midlands Health Authority and also naturally involved the Baggies players promoting a non-smoking lifestyle, often accompanied by the strapline: 'Be like Albion – kick the smoking habit'.

The Old Firm

Because of the fierce rivalry between Celtic and Rangers it has become the norm for both Glasgow clubs to be sponsored by the same company, therefore eliminating the possibility of a brand or product being shunned by 'the other side'. From the 2003–04 season, both clubs carried the Carling logo on their shirts, after a deal had been finalised which promised close to £12 million. Previously the clubs had inked a joint deal with NTL, the communications giant.

This kind of high profile business arrangement suits all parties concerned, summed up by a Coors/Carling spokesman at the time, who was quoted as saying: 'Both Rangers and Celtic are known the world over, so with Carling's heritage in football and its availability in over 20 countries this is a great chance for three major names to work together to the benefit of Scottish football in general.'

CLUB FACTS

In the middle of the 2005–06 season, Charlton Athletic's shirt sponsor, all:sports, went into administration. This meant that Charlton had to find a new sponsor in the middle of the season – the first time a top-level club has had to do this. Eventually Llanera, a Spanish property company, agreed to become their new shirt sponsor.

Venues

Emirates Stadium

Originally the Emirates Stadium was to be named after its Ashburton Grove location, but this all changed in October 2004 when Arsenal struck a sponsorship deal with Emirates Airlines worth £100 million. This did not sit well with a number of supporters who objected to this blatant use of corporate sponsorship in this manner, but in a modern footballing world few if any clubs could have refused the deal on offer.

Under the terms of the agreement the Stadium must retain its present name for at least 15 years and the club shirts must carry the Emirates name for eight years.

The official opening of the stadium was carried out by The Duke of Edinburgh in October 2006, although by then Arsenal were well ensconced in their new home which sports a capacity of over 60,000, way above the Highbury figure of less than 39,000.

On the face of it, this places Arsenal in a perfect situation for forthcoming campaigns both home and abroad. They have the second highest capacity club stadium in the country which is producing a substantial increase in revenue and a solid sponsorship deal that is the envy of all but a handful of clubs.

Reebok Stadium

In 1987, when Bolton Wanderers found themselves languishing in the old Fourth Division, many at the club must have viewed the future with grave misgivings, little realising that ten years later their fortunes would have gone full circle and the team would be running out at a brand new facility known as the Reebok Stadium.

Reebok had already been sponsoring the club's shirts since 1990 (as they do to the present day) so the association between sportswear giant and football club has become one of the game's most enduring tie-ups. When the Reebok company were taken over by Adidas in 2005, questions were asked as to future implications but to date the status quo has been maintained.

The Reebok, with its close to 28,000 capacity, quickly became much more than a football ground, as it incorporates a hotel and offices inhabited by the Reebok company themselves. Concerts and boxing matches have been held there regularly. This is a thoroughly modern facility which has

helped pay for itself via means other than football.

Walkers Stadium

Leicester City's move to the Walkers Stadium has not been a truly happy one, for the club's fortunes have not been the best since taking up residence at the ground.

Yet things looked promising when Gary Lineker officially opened the stadium, only a couple of hundred yards away from their old Filbert Street stamping ground, in July 2002. Fans had managed to put a stop to the original idea of calling it the Walkers Bowl and looked forward to the future in their 32,500 all-seater ground. The food giant Walkers had previously been associated with Leicester shirt sponsorship before stumping up a reported seven-figure sum for ten years of naming rights in respect of the new venue.

A combination of relegation from the Premiership and the multi-million pound bill for the new stadium took its toll on the club, leading to receivership and a bailing-out operation led by Lineker. The club's yo-yo existence between the Premiership and the next tier down has contributed little to financial

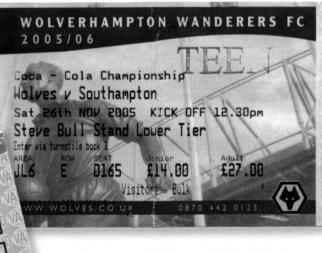

Tickets from Hereford and Wolverhampton Wanderers, showing the once common habit of naming areas of the stadium after club legends – in this case, Len Weston and Steve Bull respectively. These days, the name of a sponsor is much more likely!

stability, although the arrival of Milan Mandaric as Chairman and owner in March 2007 could steady the ship. New homes do not necessarily supply all the answers in the unforgiving sporting world.

Friends Provident St. Mary's Stadium

Opened in 2001, this stadium located about a mile and a half from Southampton's old ground, The Dell, only witnessed Premiership football for four seasons before the club were relegated to the Championship. Although, this was a disappointment, Southampton had clearly made the right move for their former home's capacity had been reduced to something in the region of 15,000.
The £32 million spent on this impressive structure gave them the flexibility to offer a lot more than just football to the public, which is in keeping with the policies of all new club stadia.

Friends Provident had started their sponsorship of Southampton in 1999 and extended the agreement until 2006. For a five year period they attained naming rights for the new stadium which cost them something over £1 million. When FP chose to opt out, budget airline Flybe stepped into the breach, taking up shirt sponsorship but declining ground naming rights. Hence, the ground simply became the St. Mary's Stadium, which fans had always favoured due to its historic reference to the club's church-based past.

McAlpine/Galpharm Stadium

At the commencement of the 1994–95 season Huddersfield Town moved into the sparkling new Alfred McAlpine Stadium having vacated their historic Leeds Road ground. This edifice cost around £40 million to build and proved to be an architectural triumph which won the RIBA Building Of The Year Award in 1995.

McAlpine retained the naming rights to the

Stadium sponsorship can be a big affair – here the sponsor's name completely dwarfs that of the ground's occupants, Portsmouth Football Club!

An example of the lengths to which sponsorship can be taken: even Forest Green's fixture board is sponsored – by the company that made the sign in the first place!

stadium until 2004, although ownership was shared by Kirklees Metropolitan Council, the football club and Huddersfield Giants Rugby League Club who share the ground. When McAlpine's sponsorship lapsed, Galpharm Healthware took up the reins and the stadium name altered accordingly. Quite correctly, all publicity for the stadium describes it as a multi-purpose venue with its regular menu of two football codes and playing host to a number of high profile pop concerts.

CLUB FACTS

Accrington Stanley's Fraser Eagle Stadium, with a maximum capacity of 5,057, is the smallest stadium in the Football League. Dagenham's ground the Glyn Hopkin Stadium (Victoria Road) has a capacity of 6,078 while Morecambe's Christie Park can accommodate 6,400.

Ricoh Arena

The Ricoh Arena is more than just a football ground but is currently home to Coventry City who were the initial movers for the project. Originally Jaguar Cars had acquired the naming rights but after they pulled out of the much-delayed venture very late in 2004, electronics company Ricoh stepped into the breach with a £10 million deal. Much of the money for the Arena's construction had come from the local council and the Alan Edward Higgs Charity.

It became home for Coventry City in the 2005–06 season but not on the basis they had hoped. Due to a mixture of ill luck and financial difficulties, partly brought on by relegation from the top flight, the club's dream of owning the ground had evaporated and having to cough up rent for the privilege of using the facility must stick in a few gullets.

An example of how clubs attempt to gain sponsorship

Sponsorship At Southampton Football Club

Your company can benefit from a wide range of sponsorship opportunities at Southampton Football Club to develop wide brand exposure, drive marketing and promotional activities and to motivate and entertain your staff, customers and clients.

We will work with your company to build a fully integrated sponsorship package, offering high-level advertising, branding and marketing options that meet your business's objectives and budget.

Why sponsorship with Southampton Football Club could benefit your business:

- Football offers a global audience of over 1.3 billion people – one sixth of the world's population
- The Southampton Football Club brand is the most recognised and established brand in the South
- Southampton Football Club featured in 9 live matches during season 2005/06, attracting an average audience of approximately 450,000 people per match*
- Commercial partnerships have been formed with national and local media groups including: Sky Sports, BBC, ITV, Southern Daily Echo
- We have our very own radio station broadcasting across Hants and Dorset, reaching over 100,000 people per month*
- We can boast a 74% ABC1 audience, with 48% of our fans earning over £30,000 pa – a substantial increase on the 39% FAPL average*

A number of tangible and intangible sponsorship rights are on offer, including:

- Pitch-side perimeter boards
- Website advertising
- Matchday programme advertising
- Big screen advertising
- Disabled block advertising
- Access to players for promotional or motivational purposes
- Hospitality and ticket benefits
- Access to signed merchandise
- Controlled access to the Southampton Football Club database (for direct marketing purposes)
- Product sampling/leaflet distribution opportunities

Breeze Volkswagen's first season with Southampton Football Club has enabled us to generate wide brand awareness and enhance our profile in the local community. Our sponsorship with the Club allows us to use a range of communication channels to directly market to thousands of Saints fans and corporate clients.

Tim Treweeks,
Breeze Volkswagen.

* Research sourced from: TNS – Taylor Nelson Sofres, SMS – Sports Marketing Surveys, The FA Premier League, The Football League, SFC Internal, Connexus Media.

Chapter 2

Foreign Ownership

The money-making potential of British football has been noted around the world. So just as players from overseas have been attracted as moths to a flame, so investors have started circling the Premiership. It had long been obvious that the standard football club board of 'butchers, bakers and candlestick makers' would struggle to keep top-flight clubs competitive and some money has flowed into the game from outside national borders to make up the shortfall.

Why should the establishment and/or the fans fear foreign money – especially with the cosmopolitan nature of the playing staff these days? The answer probably lies in the fact that these 'incomers' lack the roots and connections that local owners of the past had. By summer 2007, eight English Premiership clubs and one Scottish Premiership club had been bought by 'foreign' investors, with Arsenal the likely next target.

Arsenal

In April 2007 American entrepreneur Stan Kroenke, who owns several major sports franchises in the United States, completed the purchase of a 9.99 percent shareholding in Arsenal from ITV. He also secured a 50 percent stake in Arsenal Broadband Ltd for a combined total of £65 million. Arsenal appeared to be going down the road of fellow English Premier League clubs Manchester United, Liverpool and Aston Villa, who are all already in American hands. Kroenke owns Major League Soccer club Colorado Rapids, the National Basketball Association's Denver Nuggets and Colorado Avalanche from the National Hockey League.

Meanwhile manager Arsene Wenger maintained it is the quintessential feeling within the club which makes Arsenal so special. 'It is just somebody who has bought shares. You have to wait in the future to see what his intentions are,' he said. 'At the

A wealthy, celebrity patron, but Elton John had supported Watford since his childhood. Can the same be said of today's billionaire owners?

moment, 60 percent of shares are in the hands of three people and he has just put 10 percent, so that means nothing will change for us. It is important Arsenal maintains its values because they are what makes the club so popular and that is beyond any investment. The values are a bit of human class, distinction, respect for people and ambition to have a certain class in what you do.'

David Dein, a director between 1983 and 2007 and the man behind Wenger's appointment, sold his 14.5% shareholding in the club to Red & White, an investment vehicle of Russian metal billionaire Alisher Usmanov and his business partner Farhad Moshiri. Dein was appointed as chairman of Red & White, the largest shareholder in the club outside of the board of directors. So one way or another, it seemed likely Arsenal's future lay in foreign hands.

Aston Villa

Aston Villa were owned by Randy Lerner, a US magnate who ended the long reign of previous owner Doug Ellis with a £62.6m takeover in August 2006. Lerner, 44, has an estimated

$1.2 billion fortune and is chairman of the credit-card company MBNA. Business magazine *Forbes* ranked his Cleveland Browns NFL franchise as the seventh most valuable in North America at $892 million. His bid was preferred to the other contender, lifelong Villa fan Michael Neville, who headed a rival consortium.

Lerner graduated from Columbia University in 1984, spending 1983 at Clare College in Cambridge. During his time at Cambridge he followed English football, taking an interest in Arsenal, Fulham and Villa. He followed Malcolm Glazer into the Premiership and was followed by Liverpool's owners, Messrs Gillett and Hicks.

CLUB FACTS

Charlton became the first Premiership club to establish a formal youth academy in the United States; the club opened an academy in Tucson, Arizona in May 2005. This scheme was discontinued in August 2006 due to limited success. Charlton already operated youth academies in Spain and South Africa, as well as in the vicinity of its London home.

Chelsea

The owner of Chelsea Football Club, Roman Abramovich, tops any football 'Rich List' as far as overall personal wealth is concerned. A remarkably young billionaire, he initially made his money in oil (aluminium and meat processing were also involved) during the economic chaos which afflicted Russia following the fall of communism, and is reputed to be worth £3.8 billion, although estimates do vary and the figure could be considerably higher. In the year 2000 Abramovich was elected Governor of the province of Chukotka in north-east Russia, and has since poured money into the region. He has put quite a bit into Chelsea, too. It cost him about £150 million to buy the club, and he has spent in excess of £250 million in his four years in charge.

Former chairman/owner Ken Bates took the £18 million made from the sale of his shares to Abramovich to Leeds United, but appears to have the Midas touch in reverse.

CLUB FACTS

After Everton cruised to the League title in 1963 having splashed out £100,000 on players, they were dubbed 'the chequebook champions'. It all seems a far cry from the multi-million pound industry football has become in the last twenty years or so...

Fulham

The exact origins of Mohamed Al Fayed's millions are shrouded in a certain amount of mystery, but Fulham's Egyptian born chairman, who will be 80 in 2009, has put a good many of them into the football club. His business interests include the ownership of Harrods and the Paris Ritz, luxury apartments in London and Kurt Geiger shoe retailers. He also owns an estate in Scotland and a very large property in Surrey. In common with many rich men, he also has a number of charitable interests. Fayed's fortune is probably in excess of £500 million, and he has put anything up to £200 million into Fulham Football Club over ten years. Recent times have seen him rein back his outgoings, managers tending to have to sell to buy rather than being furnished with seemingly unlimited funds as Jean Tigana, but his financial commitment to the club remains undoubted.

Hearts

Controversial Lithuanian Vladimir Romanov bought control of Heart of Midlothian Football Club in January 2005 after attempts to acquire other Scottish clubs (Dundee United, Dundee and Dunfermline) were rejected. He took full control in October but in that month sacked George Burley as manager, then sacked his chief executive, and saw his chairman resign in protest. Romanov replaced both of them with his son, Roman.

The players were unhappy with Romanov Sr's hands-on approach to the team under Graham Rix's management, and he responded by replacing him with former FBK Kaunas coach Valdas Ivanauskas. He took Hearts to second place in the Scottish Premier League and victory in the Scottish Cup, but players continued to report 'significant unrest in the Hearts dressing room' following Romanov's

Fulham's Egyptian-born owner, Mohammed Al-fayed (inset) and (main picture) walking along the touchline of fierce rivals Chelsea – ironically also owned by a foreign billionaire, Russian Roman Abramovich.

comments regarding selling players if Hearts failed to beat Dunfermline.

While Romanov has saved Hearts from the consequences of their £20m debt and enabled them to keep a stadium that has, in the past, been earmarked for housing, their long-term future under him remains unclear and potentially controversial.

Liverpool

The American duo of George Gillett and Tom Hicks gained unconditional control of the club in March 2007. Gillett owned the Montreal Canadiens ice hockey club, and had interests in motor racing, while Hicks controlled the Dallas Stars (ice hockey) and Texas Rangers (baseball) teams. The pair's £450million total investment completed a four-sport franchise they intended to market around the globe, especially the Far East.

Gillett said: 'Liverpool is the number one brand in Europe. If you go to the Far East, where Manchester United has historically been the number one brand, Chelsea has recently become quite popular. They have a global branding concept which involves playing a number of games in the Far East. In that part of the world, Liverpool is number two and growing. We have had conversations with management in the last several months and I believe you will see Liverpool playing some friendlies in Asia. I think you'll see Japan first in this coming year and then others beyond that.'

Interestingly Liverpool had previously been in talks with the Dubai government.

Liverpool fans would merely hope that Rafael Benitez would be given a war chest to enable them to rival Manchester United and Chelsea on the domestic scene. Player Jamie Carragher: 'Being able to compete in the transfer market with United would be good enough, and being able to sign players of the calibre they've managed in the last ten years would make a big difference.'

Manchester City

City initially sought American money like their Manchester rivals but ended up courting Thailand's former Prime Minister, Thaksin Shinawatra, who in 2004 had been revealed to be interested in buying a stake in Liverpool. They even sacked manager Stuart Pearce in readiness for the takeover but lost his first choice replacement Claudio Ranieri who opted to stay in Italy rather than risk being left in managerial limbo. A counter offer from a consortium headed by former player Ray Ranson was rejected and Shinawatra's £81 million bid for a majority shareholding accepted in June 2007.

Chairman John Wardle told the City AGM of late 2006: 'The board is aware that we need further investment to maintain our challenge in an increasingly competitive and high-finance Premier League.' Wardle and David Makin were the football club's major shareholders, each owning nearly 30% of the shares. Shinawatra's problems at home, where he is accused of corruption and many of his assets were frozen, seemed to be no impediment to his football ambitions as far as the Premier League was concerned.

Manchester United

Born in Rochester, New York in 1928, Malcolm Glazer's self-made wealth was estimated to be $1 billion in 2004 – a far cry from when, in 1943, he took over the running of his late father's shop. He began investing money in mobile home parks during the 1970s, but the 1980s brought failed bids for businesses such as Harley-Davidson, although he did successfully buy the virtually bankrupt oil company Zapata, founded by former President of the US George Bush Sr.

Three of his sons run the Tampa Bay Buccaneers which he bought for $192 million, but after winning the Super Bowl in 2003, the team's worth soared and it took $8 million to hire coach Jon Gruden. Since 2003, Glazer had been building up a sizeable stake in United, but fans were hostile to his interests in the club. Glazer installed his sons Joel, Avram and Bryan on the board. Oldest son Avram is credited with formulating his father's £790 million takeover of United after previous owners the Edwards family had sold out and the club floated on the stock exchange.

Portsmouth

Milan Mandaric breathed new life into Portsmouth when he took the helm at Fratton Park in 1998, funding Harry Redknapp to create a team capable of winning promotion from the Championship and establishing themselves in the Premiership.

In 2006, the Serbian business tycoon, 69, sold his remaining stake in the club to joint-owner Alexandre Gaydamak for around £32m. The younger Russian had arrived at Fratton Park in January as co-owner and invested around £20m, which enabled manager Redknapp to make a host of signings to help save the club from relegation. Gaydamak was quick to praise the work of his predecessor and told the club's website: 'What Milan has done for this club is priceless. Milan's vision, belief, hard work and compassion has laid the foundation for all that we started to do in January. Following in these footsteps is not easy.'

Mandaric took over at ailing Leicester City, intending to repeat the promotion process.

West Ham United

Icelandic magnate Eggert Magnusson took control of West Ham in November 2006 with an £85m takeover bid for the club. The former owner of a import/export and bread and biscuit manufacturing company, Magnusson was also former president of Valur Reykjavik and had been president of the Icelandic FA since 1989. He had been on Uefa's executive committee since 2002.

Magnusson said he would consider moving the club from Upton Park to London's Olympic Stadium. 'In terms of the club's location we are buying what we see, which is West Ham at Upton Park,' he explained. 'But if there were an opportunity to discuss a long-term move to the Olympic Stadium I would explore that.'

Magnusson's consortium was backed by Bjorgolfur Gudmundsson, a financier worth $1bn and chairman of Icelandic bank Landsbanki. He showed decisiveness by sacking boss Alan Pardew and escaping relegation, but Magnusson left the club in December 2007, selling his five per cent shareholding to Gudmundsson.

Chapter 3

Hall of Shame – Clubs in Trouble

Administration, bankruptcy, bungs, fines and points deductions are far from recent phenomena. The history of the game is littered with clubs that strayed from the path of righteousness in the pursuit of glory: some, like Leeds United, have come unstuck more than once, albeit many decades apart. Here is the roll of shame – is there a skeleton in your club's closet?

'Every fan you ask will say he wants to see lively, open football. But what the fan really wants to see is his team win.'

This observation, made by Arsenal director Dennis Hill-Wood a few yeas ago, hits the nail squarely on the head. It's all about results, about winning, about being the best. These days, there are phenomenal rewards available to the game's most successful clubs, but even years ago, when the money to be made from football was insignificant by today's standards, the drive to succeed was just as powerful.

When the FA was founded in 1863, the game was essentially upper-class, dominated by the public schools, the Old Boys' sides and a few others that had their origins in the country's cricket clubs. It was seen as a gentleman's sport, played for the love of the game on a purely amateur basis, and its new governing body was made up of like-minded individuals drawn from the upper echelons of society. For some years, this was the basis on which the game was played, and all the time the game remained the preserve of the privileged few, the status quo was easy to maintain.

By the early 1880s, however, there was a shift in the balance of power, at least on the pitch. While the FA continued to be run by members of the upper classes, whose idea of the way the game should be played was based on the public school ethic, the game itself was increasingly finding favour amongst working-class men, particularly in the North of England. The likes of Darwen, Nottingham Forest, Notts County and Aston Villa began to make their mark, and impressive results soon led to them being able to attract equally impressive crowds.

Maintaining the momentum became increasingly important, and by the middle of the decade, many of the more successful Northern clubs were making illicit payments to retain and motivate their players. Even the mighty Preston North End were disqualified from one FA Cup competition for making payments to their players. Professionalism was now a reality, even if the game's governing body initially refused to countenance its existence.

The turning point came in 1885, when the FA finally bowed to the inevitable and sanctioned payments to players, but it was a grudging acceptance of the way things were, and the game's founding fathers placed severe restrictions on the payments clubs were allowed to make. As a result, illicit payments continued as clubs found different ways to reward the best players – 'boot money' being a particularly common method, whereby a cash sum would be placed in a player's boots prior to each game.

Other, less obvious means were developed, one favourite being to find the player a job with a sympathetic local firm, often one run by a club dignitary. No-one would care whether the chap could do the job he was paid to do, as long as he 'did the job' on the pitch on Saturday afternoon. There were 'bonuses', 'benefits' and a multitude of other roundabout methods of boosting a player's income, rendering the FA's attempts to level the playing field with a maximum wage rule totally ineffective.

The FA also brought in a system of player registration, another attempt to retain control over the game they clearly felt was slipping away from them. Professionalism might have arrived, but the FA were going to do everything they could to maintain their grip on things. Not only were payments to players to be strictly regulated, but the FA would be able to dictate who could play, and against whom, by insisting players were registered and approved before being eligible to take to the field.

J. E. Doig, Sunderland.
Photo by Thiele, London.

Ned Doig, who was lured from Arbroath to Sunderland, only for his new club to incur a points deduction as punishment for fielding the player before his registration had been finalised, the first such punishment ever meted out.

No surprise, then, that clubs sometimes got caught out. Sunderland suffered a two-point penalty as early as the 1890–91 season, after fielding goalkeeper Ned Doig in a match against West Bromwich Albion in the opening weeks of the campaign. Doig had been attracted south of the border from Arbroath, but his registration had not been approved before the game, and Sunderland incurred the league's first points deduction.

While ineligible players seem to figure only occasionally during the first few League seasons, the spectre of illegal payments was far more prominent. Sunderland made headlines for all the wrong reasons at the beginning of 1904, after the FA launched an enquiry into a payment made to right back Andrew McCombie prior to the start of the 1903–04 season.

Sunderland's directors had given McCombie the considerable sum of £100, intended to allow the player to start up a business, and in the expectation that the sum would be repaid from the receipts of a future benefit game. McCombie, however, refused to pay the money back, claiming that it had been a gift, and Sunderland decided to pursue the matter in the courts. When the scandal broke in January 1904, McCombie took the opportunity to sign with bitter local rivals Newcastle United, becoming an important member of the Magpies side that enjoyed considerable success in the years that followed.

Meanwhile, the FA investigation got under way. Although the courts ruled that the money was, indeed, a loan, and ordered it to be repaid, the FA decided that it had been a gift – a bonus payment for re-signing with the club for the 1903–04 season – and thus in contravention of Football Association rules. Declaring Sunderland's books to be inaccurate, the FA fined the club £250, handed down lengthy suspensions for six of its directors, and suspended manager Alex Mackie for three months.

While Sunderland were suffering, Manchester City were enjoying success in the FA Cup, winning the 1904 final against Bolton Wanderers by a single goal scored by the legendary Billy Meredith. Meredith was described by one contemporary writer as 'the finest right winger living, an awkward customer to tackle, as slippery as an eel with shooting powers extraordinary'. The 'Welsh Wizard' was perhaps the greatest player of his time but in 1905 he received an 18-month suspension for attempting to bribe City's opponents into throwing matches. There's no doubt that

Manchester City were not only well aware of what was happening but also supported it, but when the storm broke they distanced themselves from both Meredith and his actions.

Understandably, Meredith was none too pleased – and City were soon made to pay a heavy price for abandoning their star to his fate. Meredith became the game's first 'whistle-blower' (leaving aside referees!), and reported his employers to the FA for a number of irregularities including illegal signing-on payments to players, persistent breaches of the maximum wage and player bonus rulings, and repeated attempts to bribe opponents and fix matches. The FA imposed the most severe penalties yet seen in English football – every member of the 1904 FA Cup-winning side was suspended from the game and banned from playing for Manchester City in the future, several club directors were banned from the game indefinitely, and the very survival of the club was in severe doubt for a while.

Meredith served his ban and then joined arch-rivals Manchester United. His experiences had understandably left a bitter taste in the mouth and led to him having a far greater impact on the game than just his achievements on the field. In 1907, Meredith became instrumental in the formation of the players' union, the PFA. His fellow professionals embraced the idea enthusiastically, seeing a measure of security in numbers and an opportunity to improve the player's lot in the face of the FA's continued tight control over earnings and bonuses.

Obviously, the pursuit of success wasn't the only reason clubs might make irregular

Billy Meredith, who was banned from football for accepting illegal payments from Manchester City, though he later returned to the game in the service of City's arch-rivals, Manchester United!

payments to their players. Survival could also provide a powerful incentive, and it was just such a fight that led to Chesterfield Town becoming embroiled in another scandal in 1909. What became known as the Parsonage Affair highlighted the difficulties faced by clubs and players in the lower reaches of the Football League, where job security was non-existent, and players relied on illegal payments to make ends meet.

In 1909, players were generally given only one-year contracts, running from August to April, and even those staying at the same club had to re-sign prior to each season. The FA rules allowed for a signing-on fee of up to £10, and a maximum wage of £4 per week, which was a good salary by comparison with most manual workers at the time. Chesterfield were struggling in the lower reaches of Division Two, and desperate to avoid having to apply for re-election at the end of the 1908–09 season. In an attempt to strengthen their squad, Chesterfield approached Fulham with a view to signing their half-back George Parsonage.

Parsonage, by all accounts, wasn't keen on the move, but eventually agreed to discuss the idea with George Swift, Chesterfield Town's manager. Swift duly offered Parsonage a signing-on fee of £10, and a weekly sum of £4, the maximum he could offer under FA rules. Parsonage replied that unless Swift made the signing-on fee £50, he would not agree to the transfer. Swift immediately terminated negotiations, told Fulham's officials that no agreement had been reached, but made mention of Parsonage's demands in passing. Swift seemed unconcerned by the player's comments, but Fulham immediately demanded that Chesterfield report Parsonage to the FA, twisting their arm by adding that if Chesterfield didn't report Parsonage, they would report both Parsonage *and* Chesterfield Town to the authorities. Left with little alternative, Chesterfield duly reported Parsonage for demanding an illegal payment.

An FA enquiry found Parsonage guilty, and banned him from any involvement in football for life. It was an extremely harsh sentence, designed to make an example of Parsonage and so discourage demands for, and the provision of, illegal bonuses and payments to players. The FA, still being run by the old guard who had so resented the advent of professionalism twenty years before, were desperate to stamp out illegal payments and Parsonage had provided them with the ideal whipping-boy.

For his part, Parsonage claimed at the hearing that the comment had been made in jest. Perhaps it had, but the case highlighted a serious issue for players – £10 was a large sum of money compared to the average weekly wage at the time, but nowhere near enough to encourage a man to relocate his entire family in order to play for a club where job security was almost non-existent. Viewed in those terms, a demand for £50 was not unreasonable. There is also the question of why Parsonage might have felt able to make such a demand; the game was awash with rumours of illegal payments, and it's more than likely that it was a serious attempt to engineer himself the sort of payment commonly being made to secure players at the time. Perhaps Chesterfield had a reputation as one of the clubs who might involve themselves in such a deal, or perhaps Parsonage was just chancing his arm.

Whatever the truth of the matter, Parsonage paid the price, although he appears to have been on Oldham Athletic's books as a coach a few years later, so his ban must have been lifted at some point. Chesterfield, too, suffered for their part in the affair – despite having been innocent of any wrong-doing, they were guilty by association, and found themselves voted out of the league after finishing last but one in Division Two at the

end of the season. The club was disbanded at the beginning of World War 1, and a new Chesterfield FC was formed in its place. Incredibly, the new club lasted only a couple of years before history repeated itself – an FA enquiry into illegal payments forced it out of business after the board, the players and the manager were all banned from further footballing activities!

Despite these high-profile cases, the practice of making illegal payments continued unabated, and even during World War 1, when domestic football was severely curtailed, and clubs were prevented from paying players at all, many carried on regardless. As the first peacetime season got under way in the autumn of 1919, the most famous footballing scandal of the 20th Century was about to unfold.

CLUB FACTS

Both Scunthorpe United (then known as Scunthorpe and Lindsey United) and Shrewsbury Town, joined the Football League at the beginning of the 1950–51 season, when the Third Division (North) was extended to 24 teams. Scunthorpe and Shrewsbury were due to play each other in their first fixture, and an excited crowd numbering nearly 13,000 packed the Old Show Ground in eager anticipation of an exciting game. The result was a goalless draw, and attendances rather tended to drop after that.

Leeds City were a modestly successful side, formed in the early 1900s, whose entire career had been spent in Division Two. The years leading up to World War 1 had been the club's most successful – in 1914, under the guidance of the legendary Herbert Chapman, Leeds City finished 4th in the league – and there was every reason to suppose a breakthrough might be on the cards. The war put an end to any hopes of top-flight football for a few years, but when normal service was resumed, City fans were looking forward to their team picking up where they left off. Nothing could have prepared them for what happened next...

In fact, the club was in serious trouble even before the new season got under way. In 1914, Herbert Chapman had left Leeds City to help with the war effort, suggesting that his assistant, George Cripps, should take care of the administration of the club in his absence. Chapman had been a strong manager and had built a sense of unity throughout the club as well as improving matters on the field. With Chapman gone, internal disagreements began to surface, the most significant being between Cripps and Joseph Connor, one of the club's directors.

Connor had no confidence in Cripps, and made it abundantly clear. There's some evidence that his fears were well-founded, because by the time Cripps was relieved of his administrative duties in 1917 the value of the club's assets had fallen considerably. In the year that followed, the Board seriously considered winding the club up, but the Football League persuaded them to carry on, and unwittingly denied City a dignified, if unspectacular, demise.

Cripps, meanwhile, was put in charge of managing the team, but he proved as unpopular with the players as he had with some of the directors, and this only added to the club's woes. At one point, the players threatened to strike if Cripps were allowed to travel to an away game with them, although Connor managed to persuade them that this would threaten the club's very existence and the strike was averted. Leeds City continued to lurch from one crisis to another...

Even the return of Herbert Chapman as manager in 1918 failed to stop the rot. With Chapman back in harness, Cripps was offered his old job as assistant manager, but he was having none of it and threatened legal action against the club for wrongful dismissal. Cripps engaged James Bromley, a former club director, as his solicitor. Bromley would play a significant part in the events that followed.

Cripps sought compensation from the club – the sum of £400 is recorded – and made Bromley aware of a number of illegal payments the club had made to players during the war. Bromley saw this as an opportunity to broker a deal, and in January 1919, Leeds City's Board came to an agreement with Bromley whereby Cripps would give a written guarantee not to disclose any aspect of the club's dealings and would hand over to the club a number of incriminating documents, including cheque books and correspondence, that he had in his possession. In return, he would be compensated for losing his job as manager, although the eventual sum of £55 was appreciably less than his original demand. Bromley also, according to Joseph Connor, gave his word that he would not reveal any of the impropriety that had come to light.

If the Leeds City directors thought that was the end of the affair, they were sadly mistaken. As the club began to build a team for the forthcoming season, contracts were drawn up with players in the time-honoured manner, and amongst them was one Charlie Copeland, a full-back whose association with the club stretched back to 1912. Copeland had been an occasional first-team player in the years leading up to the war, earning £3 a week, with a £1 bonus for each appearance in the first team. During the war, he'd become a regular, and City now offered him a new contract at £3 10s. (£3.50) a week, with bonus payments for first-team appearances, or a free transfer if the new terms were unacceptable.

Copeland stunned the Board by demanding £6 a week, adding that if this was not forthcoming he would report the club to the FA and the Football League for making illegal payments to players during the war. The Board decided to ignore Copeland's threats, and released him on a free transfer to Coventry City, but in July 1919 Copeland decided to make his allegations to the footballing authorities, and the FA and the Football League had no option but to set up an enquiry.

Perhaps it was a coincidence that James Bromley was also Copeland's solicitor, but the City Board strongly suspected that Bromley had secretly provided Copeland with the ammunition to make his devastating claims. Whatever the truth of the matter, Leeds City were now in deep trouble. The enquiry demanded to see City's books but City refused to produce them, prompting the FA to deliver an ultimatum – produce the required documents by October 6th or face the consequences.

The documents were not forthcoming, and it seems clear that City's board must have been bracing themselves for whatever punishment the FA might hand down. No one could have predicted what happened next. Announcing their decision, Football League Chairman John McKenna said: 'The authorities of the game intend to keep it absolutely clean. We will have no nonsense. The football stable must be cleaned and further breakages of the law regarding payments will be dealt with in such a severe manner that I now give warning that clubs and players must not expect the slightest leniency.'

With eight games of the new season completed, Leeds City were expelled from the Football League, and the FA closed the club down. Five City officials received life bans from football, four of the directors including Joseph Connor, and, rather surprisingly, manager Herbert Chapman. After providing evidence that the alleged payments had been made while he was away from the club, Chapman managed to get his ban rescinded, and went on to find sustained success as manager of Huddersfield in the 1920s and Arsenal in the 1930s.

The club's assets, including the players, were auctioned off, and the Leeds City story was complete. Never before had a club making illegal payments been so harshly punished, and City's fate stood as a stark warning to others in the years to come. Despite the risks, clubs still resorted to underhand tactics to achieve success. Take Stockport County, champions of Division Three (North) in 1937. Stockport finished the season three points clear of Lincoln City, who missed out on elevation to Division Two because only one team from each of the regional Division Three competitions was promoted.

Stockport found life in Division Two hard, but as they struggled to survive, allegations that bribery had played a part in the previous season's championship win surfaced. An FA Commission sat to hear the evidence, and County director George Worsley was duly found guilty of having made payments to Carlisle United players in return for a win against Lincoln. Ironically, by the time the verdict had been reached, Stockport were already relegated to Division Three (North) and,

although the club were held partially responsible for Worsley's actions, no further punishment was handed down.

CLUB FACTS

The first substitute fielded by Northampton Town was... future Leeds City, Huddersfield and Arsenal manager Herbert Chapman! In a friendly match against Port Vale during the 1904–05 season, Northampton's Len Benbow sustained an injury, and his side sought permission to bring Chapman on to replace him. Chapman went on to become the Cobblers' first manager, bringing them the Southern League championship in 1909, before moving on to Leeds City in 1912. Later, of course, Chapman achieved legendary status after steering first Huddersfield, and then Arsenal to championship glory.

Sunderland found themselves embroiled in another row over illegal fees in 1957, when it became clear that the club had been making huge under-the-counter payments for years. Senior club officials found themselves suspended or fined, the chairman and manager were summarily removed, and once again the issue of the maximum wage was thrust back into the limelight. Sunderland were the last big club to be hauled over the coals for making illegal payments to players – in 1961, the maximum wage was abolished, and with it the need for any financial sweeteners.

As is often the way, one development leads to another, and the abolition of the maximum wage inevitably brought agents into the game. Players were often from working-class backgrounds, many of them poorly-educated, and clearly needed professional assistance in securing the best deal. Agents quickly assumed the role of go-between in transfer deals, and a new form of illicit payment began to become a major part of the game – the 'bung'.

In fact, agents were not officially sanctioned by the FA until 1995 and all earlier dealings with them were, effectively, illegal. Clubs broke the rules every time they dealt with an agent, so the introduction of a 'bung' into the equation was simply part of an already illegal process. As time went by, some managers were also tempted to accept a slice of an increasingly lucrative transfer market, and although only one manager, Arsenal's George Graham, has ever been found guilty of taking bungs, it's acknowledged that the practice was widespread during the 1980s and beyond.

There are, of course, other ways clubs can get themselves into hot water. Match-fixing has been alleged on many occasions, although it can be difficult to prove. One such, unsubstantiated, claim resulted in a fundamental change to the game as we know it today.

When a new Division Two was introduced in 1892, the Football League decided that a system of play-off matches, known as Test Matches, would be used to determine who, if anyone, should be promoted and relegated. Initially, the top Division Two clubs played the bottom Division One clubs, and the winner of each match would be in Division One the following season. By 1898, the format had changed, and the bottom two clubs in Division One played the top two clubs in Division Two in an end-of season mini-league, with two points for a win and one for a draw as in the main league competition. In the final game of the season, Stoke played Burnley, but the game was rendered meaningless after both sides realised that a goalless draw would see them both in Division One the following term.

Predictably, they engineered a 0–0 draw, and although the match had clearly been fixed the FA felt there was insufficient evidence to take any action against either club. They did, however, review the Test Match system, and from the 1898–99 season onwards, promotion and relegation became automatic.

After Manchester United and Liverpool played each other on April 2nd 1915, an FA Commission decided the result, a 2–0 win to United, had been fixed. The two points United gained meant that they finished in 18th place, one point ahead of Chelsea, and one place above the relegation zone. Perhaps because there were more pressing matters to consider, the result was allowed to stand, and no action was taken against either club.

Sometimes, matches are fixed for personal gain, as was the case with Mansfield Town players in the 1960s. In May 1963, a Sunday newspaper printed allegations of match-fixing at Mansfield, and went as far as singling out club captain Brian Phillips. Mansfield immediately suspended Phillips, who missed the last few games of the club's promotion-winning season. Further allegations followed, and towards the end of the following campaign, five more Mansfield players were accused of having made payments to ensure a win at Hartlepools in the run-up to the previous year's promotion. Jimmy Gauld was identified as the instigator of the match-fixing activities, which he subsequently admitted had taken place over almost 18 months from November 1961 to April 1963. During this time, it was later revealed that Gauld had been making around £1,000 a week from betting on the fixed matches, and in January 1965 he was finally convicted of fraud and sentenced to four years' imprisonment.

CLUB FACTS

When Stoke City brought forward 'Archie' Maxwell to the potteries from Darwen in February 1896, the transfer 'fee' was a set of wrought-iron gates for the Lancashire side's ground. Just over two years later, Stoke were involved in another bizarre transfer deal – player-secretary William Rowley transferred himself to Leicester Fosse, agreeing his own signing-on fee in the process. The football authorities were predictably unhappy with the deal, and Rowley was duly suspended.

Two other Mansfield players also received prison sentences for their part in the scam – Brian Phillips a 15-month term, and Sammy Chapman, Phillips' replacement as club captain, six months. Seven players from other clubs were also convicted and given custodial sentences in what the *People* newspaper called 'the biggest soccer scandal of the century.'

Swindon Town became the focus of another betting scandal during the 1989–90 season. Allegations were made that club chairman Brian Hillier and then-manager Lou Macari had made an illegal bet against their team in an FA Cup tie against Newcastle United in January 1988. In February 1990, Hillier and Macari were found guilty, Hillier was banned for six months, and both men received fines. Macari, by then manager of West Ham United, stood down from his new job. In May, Hillier and Macari were arrested on suspicion of tax offences, along with club captain Colin Calderwood and chief accountant Vince Farrar. Calderwood was quickly cleared, but the other three were charged and released on bail.

Meanwhile, Swindon Town successfully negotiated the old Second Division play-offs and won a place in the top flight for the first time in their existence under Glenn Hoddle. But the dream was shattered in June with the news that the club had been found guilty on 34 counts of financial irregularities, and would be relegated to Division Three as a punishment. The club immediately launched an appeal, and early in July managed to have the decision overturned. They did, however, lose their promotion to Division One, which went to defeated play-off finalists Sunderland.

As investigations continued, more people connected with the club had been implicated – in the end, Brian Hillier was given a jail term, and Vince Farrar and former club secretary Dave King received suspended sentences. Lou Macari, to the relief of Swindon fans who still regarded him as a hero, was found not guilty on all counts.

The Football League and the Premiership routinely deal with minor breaches of the rules by imposing fines on clubs or individuals, or by points deductions. Some of these are token slaps on the wrist that have little real effect on the clubs involved, but sometimes points are deducted to achieve a specific result, as Peterborough United found out after the 1967–68 season. With 50 points from their 46 Division Three matches, Peterborough finished the season in ninth position, only seven points behind champions Oxford United.

Unfortunately, an FA investigation into allegations of illegal bonus payments to players during the previous 18 months found the club guilty, and a 19-point penalty was imposed. This placed Peterborough at the foot of the table, and meant that they started the following season in Division Four. Ironically,

one of the games for which the FA found that Peterborough had made illegal bonus payments to players was the Fourth Round FA Cup tie against Sunderland in January 1967 – ironic, because Posh lost the tie 7–1!

CLUB FACTS

In February 1956, Portsmouth were the first club to host a Football League match played under floodlights, when they lost 2–0 against Newcastle at Fratton Park.

Chesterfield were the victims of another tactical points deduction following the 2000–01 season, when they were found guilty of financial irregularities and had nine points wiped from their Division Three total. This denied them an automatic promotion place, although they were still successful in winning promotion via the play-offs.

Coventry City (who had avoided relegation in 1920 through a later discovered match-fixing schedule) benefited from a controversial points deduction at the end of the 1996–97 season. In one of the tightest Premiership relegation dogfights, the Sky Blues ended the campaign level on 41 points with Southampton, but their inferior goal difference meant that they faced relegation after 31 years on top-flight football.

Middlesbrough were one of two clubs that finished one point above them, but the club's decision to pull out of a fixture at Blackburn on December 21st was to cost them their Premiership place. A combination of injuries and illness had meant Boro were unable to field eleven fit players for the Blackburn match, but the Premier League took a dim view of their last-minute withdrawal and imposed a three-point penalty. Middlesbrough found themselves on 39 points, in 19th position and out of the Premiership for the 1997–98 season.

In May 2004, the Football League introduced an automatic 10-point penalty for any club entering financial administration, a move which has attracted much criticism and not a little consternation. Blame Leicester City, who took the opportunity to write off a large proportion of their debts during the 2002–03 season by entering into a Creditor's Voluntary Agreement, and then used the cash freed up by the move to strengthen their squad and win promotion to the Premiership. Whilst there was nothing illegal in what Leicester had done, the Football League clearly felt they had to take steps to prevent the dozens of other clubs in financial peril from using the same tactic, hence the introduction of the points penalty.

At the end of the 2004–05 season, the new ruling saved MK Dons from relegation to League Two, after Wrexham went into administration and lost 10 points as a result. The club's argument that it would be all the more difficult to get out of administration if the club suffered relegation is understandable, but fell on deaf ears. Cambridge United also entered administration in the final days of the season but had already been relegated to the Conference, so the points deduction made no difference apart from putting Cambridge in last position rather than last but one.

In 2006–07, two more clubs followed Cambridge's example. Leeds United chose to go into administration with one game still to play. As a result, the 10-point deduction was made from the 2006–07 season's tally, and since Leeds were already relegated, it served no purpose whatsoever. A further 15-point penalty was levied for 2007–08.

Boston United took brinkmanship to the limits, entering administration in the final minutes of the last game of the season, and in the wake of the outcry against both clubs, there's little doubt that the authorities will have to amend the rules to prevent others from taking advantage of this loophole in the future. Boston were, in the end, relegated two steps into the Conference North.

The 2006–07 season saw League Two's Bury thrown out of the FA Cup for fielding an ineligible player, while non-League AFC Wimbledon suffered a worse fate for a similar offence in the FA Trophy. The Isthmian League club were expelled from the competition, docked 18 points – reduced to three on appeal – and fined £400.

The most costly and controversial contravention of footballing rules and regulations, however, took place in 2006 when the Argentine pair of Carlos Tevez and Javier Mascherano signed for West Ham.

The problem arose because their contracts were owned not by Corinthians, the club they'd last played for, but by MSI, a sports management company, in contravention of the rules. The Hammers were found guilty of acting improperly and withholding vital documentation over the duo's ownership.

Tevez's goals effectively saved West Ham from relegation, but the sanction against them for transgressing was a £5.5 million fine rather than a points deduction. Given the supposed £50 million benefit of Premiership membership, this was small beer, and Sheffield United – the team relegated in their place – threatened to take their protest all the way to the European Court of Justice.

Ironically, Bryan Robson, Middlesbrough manager when they were relegated from the Premiership in 1997 thanks to a three-point deduction, was now the new manager of Sheffield United.

The independent disciplinary commission that belatedly made the initial 'Tevezgate' judgement in April 2007 controversially observed that a points sanction at this late stage of the season (the delay in addressing the issue has never been adequately explained) would have condemned West Ham to certain relegation. The commission added that a different decision may well have been taken if the hearing had been in January as a points deduction with four months of the season remaining 'would have been somewhat easier to bear'.

APPENDICES

Appendix I: English Football

English Football League Champions

The highest tier of the English Football League has, at different times, been known as the Premiership, Division One or simply the Football League. The following list of champions, arranged chronologically, is divided into sections reflecting these changes in name, though in all instances the lists indicate status as champions of the top tier of English football – i.e., Champions of the English Football League itself!

Premiership Champions

Year	Club	Year	Club
2007	Manchester United	1999	Manchester United
2006	Chelsea	1998	Arsenal
2005	Chelsea	1997	Manchester United
2004	Arsenal	1996	Manchester United
2003	Manchester United	1995	Blackburn Rovers
2002	Arsenal	1994	Manchester United
2001	Manchester United	1993	Manchester United
2000	Manchester United		

Football League Champions

Year	Club	Year	Club
1992	Leeds United	1972	Derby County
1991	Arsenal	1971	Arsenal
1990	Liverpool	1970	Everton
1989	Arsenal	1969	Leeds United
1988	Liverpool	1968	Manchester City
1987	Everton	1967	Manchester United
1986	Liverpool	1966	Liverpool
1985	Everton	1965	Manchester United
1984	Liverpool	1964	Liverpool
1983	Liverpool	1963	Everton
1982	Liverpool	1962	Ipswich Town
1981	Aston Villa	1961	Tottenham Hotspur
1980	Liverpool	1960	Burnley
1979	Liverpool	1959	Wolverhampton Wanderers
1978	Nottingham Forest	1958	Wolverhampton Wanderers
1977	Liverpool	1957	Manchester United
1976	Liverpool	1956	Manchester United
1975	Derby County	1955	Chelsea
1974	Leeds United	1954	Wolverhampton Wanderers
1973	Liverpool	1953	Arsenal

1952	Manchester United
1951	Tottenham Hotspur
1950	Portsmouth
1949	Portsmouth
1948	Arsenal
1947	Liverpool
1946	World War 2
1945	World War 2
1944	World War 2
1943	World War 2
1942	World War 2
1941	World War 2
1940	World War 2
1939	Everton
1938	Arsenal
1937	Manchester City
1936	Sunderland
1935	Arsenal
1934	Arsenal
1933	Arsenal
1932	Everton
1931	Arsenal
1930	Sheffield Wednesday
1929	Sheffield Wednesday
1928	Everton
1927	Newcastle United
1926	Huddersfield Town
1925	Huddersfield Town
1924	Huddersfield Town
1923	Liverpool
1922	Liverpool
1921	Burnley
1920	West Bromwich Albion
1919	World War 1
1918	World War 1
1917	World War 1
1916	World War 1
1915	Everton
1914	Blackburn Rovers
1913	Sunderland
1912	Blackburn Rovers
1911	Manchester United
1910	Aston Villa
1909	Newcastle United
1908	Manchester United
1907	Newcastle United
1906	Liverpool
1905	Newcastle United
1904	Sheffield Wednesday
1903	Sheffield Wednesday
1902	Sunderland
1901	Liverpool
1900	Aston Villa
1899	Aston Villa
1898	Sheffield United
1897	Aston Villa
1896	Aston Villa
1895	Sunderland
1894	Aston Villa
1893	Sunderland
1892	Sunderland
1891	Everton
1890	Preston North End
1889	Preston North End

CLUB FACTS

If there was an award for closest runners-up in football's top flight, it would surely go to Cardiff City, who finished the 1923–24 Division One season tied at the top with Huddersfield on 57 points. In those days, such things were decided by goal average rather than goal difference – and Cardiff's goal average was just 0.024 worse than Huddersfield's, giving the Yorkshire side the first of their three consecutive League titles. Worse still, a win on the final day of the season would have secured the championship for the Bluebirds, but they could only manage a 0–0 draw against Birmingham, and to add insult to injury Len Davies missed from the penalty spot.

If the rules in place today had applied then, the Welshmen would have edged it – both clubs had the same goal difference, but Cardiff had scored just one more goal during the campaign than Huddersfield, so the championship trophy would have gone across the border for the first, and only, time.

In the lower divisions, the award would have to go to Manchester City, who finished third behind Middlesbrough and Portsmouth to miss out on promotion from Division Two in 1927 by just 0.005 of a goal. City topped the table themselves the following year, but had to wait rather longer to exact their revenge on the south coast side – in 1985, City pipped Pompey to a Division Two promotion spot on goal difference.

English League Championship Success

Position	Club	Division One	Premiership	Total
1	Liverpool	18	–	18
2	Manchester United	7	9	16
3	Arsenal	10	3	13
4	Everton	9	–	9
5	Aston Villa	7	–	7
6	Sunderland	6	–	6
7	Newcastle	4	–	4
8=	Chelsea	1	2	3
8=	Blackburn Rovers	2	1	3
8=	Leeds United	3	–	3
8=	Wolverhampton Wanderers	3	–	3
8=	Huddersfield Town	3	–	3
13=	Derby County	2	–	2
13=	Manchester City	2	–	2
13=	Tottenham Hotspur	2	–	2
13=	Burnley	2	–	2
13=	Portsmouth	2	–	2
13=	Preston North End	2	–	2
19=	Nottingham Forest	1	–	1
19=	Ipswich Town	1	–	1
19=	West Bromwich Albion	1	–	1
19=	Sheffield United	1	–	1

Surprisingly, only 22 clubs in just over a century have shown the consistency to win English football's top prize. The concentration of honours has been even more marked since the arrival of the Premiership in 1992, though it is surprising that Liverpool, who top the chart, have yet to lift the newer trophy.

CLUB FACTS

Arsenal are the only team to score in every game in a Premiership season, doing so on their way to the title in 2002. This sequence formed part of another record-breaking run, in which Arsenal scored in 55 consecutive League games between May 19th 2001 and November 30th 2002.

Of the clubs to have won the title once, two – Nottingham Forest (1978) and Ipswich Town (1962) – enjoyed the inspiration of great managers in Brian Clough and Alf Ramsey. The other 'one-off' winners, Sheffield United and West Bromwich Albion, won much earlier on, in 1898 and 1920 respectively.

Nottingham Forest and Leeds United are now in the third tier of English football along with Huddersfield Town, while 13 of the 22 clubs here enjoyed Premiership status in 2007–08.

Only four managers have led their teams to the title in the first decade and a half of the Premiership – Sir Alex Ferguson, Kenny Dalglish, Arsene Wenger and Jose Mourinho. None are English.

Only seven clubs have remained ever-present for those 15 years – Aston Villa, Arsenal, Chelsea, Everton, Liverpool, Manchester United and Tottenham.

Only five clubs have taken the (pre-Premiership) First Division title immediately after winning promotion to the top flight.

Liverpool 1905–06
Everton...1931–32
Tottenham Hotspur 1950–51
Ipswich Town 1961–62
Nottingham Forest 1977–78

Tier Two Champions

The second tier of the English Football League has, at different times, been known as the Championship, Division One and (prior to the introduction of the Premiership) Division Two. The following list of champions, arranged chronologically, is divided into sections reflecting these changes in name, though in all instances the lists indicate status as champions of the second tier of English football.

The Championship (Tier Two) Champions

2007 ....Sunderland
2006 ....Reading
2005 ....Sunderland

Division One (Tier Two) Champions

2004...Norwich City
2003...Portsmouth
2002 ....Manchester City
2001 ....Fulham
2000...................................Charlton Athletic
1999 ....Sunderland
1998...............................Nottingham Forest
1997 ....Bolton Wanderers
1996 ....Sunderland
1995 ....Middlesbrough
1994...Crystal Palace
1993 ....Newcastle United

Division Two (Tier Two) Champions

1992...Ipswich Town
1991....................................Oldham Athletic
1990.......................................Leeds United
1989 ....Chelsea
1988 ....Millwall
1987....................................Derby County
1986.......................................Norwich City
1985 ....Oxford United
1984 ....Chelsea
1983 ....Queen's Park Rangers
1982 ....Luton Town
1981 ....West Ham United
1980 ....Leicester City
1979....................................Crystal Palace
1978...................................Bolton Wanderers

CLUB FACTS

When Reading gained promotion to the Premiership, on 25th March 2006, they achieved elevation to the top flight earlier in the season than any other post-war side.

1977.....................Wolverhampton Wanderers
1976 ....Sunderland
1975 ....Manchester United
1974 ....Middlesbrough
1973 ....Burnley
1972.......................................Norwich City
1971 ....Leicester City
1970 ....Huddersfield Town
1969...Derby County
1968...Ipswich Town
1967...Coventry City
1966 ....Manchester City
1965 ....Newcastle United
1964.......................................Leeds United
1963 ....Stoke City
1962.......................................Liverpool
1961 ....Ipswich
1960 ....Aston Villa
1959 ....Sheffield Wednesday
1958 ....West Ham United
1957 ....Leicester City
1956 ....Sheffield Wednesday
1955 ....Birmingham City
1954 ....Leicester City
1953 ....Sheffield United
1952 ....Sheffield Wednesday
1951...................................Preston North End

CLUB FACTS

Aston Villa were runaway League champions in 1897, finishing eleven points ahead of their nearest rivals, Sheffield United. This was a winning margin that would remain unbeaten in the League for over 90 years, until Chelsea took the Division Two title in 1989 by 17 points. When Bolton were promoted to the Premier League in 1997, they went one better, finishing 18 points ahead of second-placed Barnsley, and in the same division two seasons later, Sunderland repeated the feat ahead of Bradford City. In 2000, Manchester United beat Arsenal into second place by the same margin to set a new record for the top flight.

1950...Tottenham
1949 ....Fulham
1948 ....Birmingham City
1947 ....Manchester City
1939 ....Blackburn Rovers

CLUB FACTS

Bristol is the largest city in England never to have produced a league championship side. In championship terms, Liverpool is far and away the country's most successful footballing city, Liverpool and Everton having topped the league on no less than 27 occasions between them. Liverpool is arguably only England's sixth city, with London, Birmingham, Manchester, Leeds and Sheffield all able to claim a superior population (if not footballing record!).

1938 ....Aston Villa
1937 ....Leicester City
1936 ....Manchester United
1935 ....Brentford
1934..Grimsby Town
1933 ....Stoke City
1932....................Wolverhampton Wanderers
1931..Everton
1930..Blackpool
1929 ....Middlesbrough
1928 ....Manchester City
1927 ....Middlesbrough
1926 ....Sheffield Wednesday
1925 ....Leicester City
1924..Leeds United
1923...Nottts County

CLUB FACTS

On 28th April, 1923, the ten Division One matches played produced just ten goals in total, an all-time low for a full programme of top-flight games, and not one of them was scored by an away side. By way of contrast, the 44 League games played on 1st February 1936 produced a record 209 goals, 23 of them in just 2 Division Three (North) matches – Chester City's 12–0 rout of York City, and Chesterfield's remarkable 6–5 away win at Crewe Alexandra.

1922 ....Nottingham Forest
1921 ....Birmingham City
1920 ....Tottenham Hotspur
1915...Derby County
1914 ....Notts County
1913.................................Preston North End
1912...Derby County
1911 ....West Bromwich Albion
1910 ....Manchester City
1909.................................Bolton Wanderers
1908 ....Bradford City
1907 ....Nottingham Forest
1906 ....Bristol City
1905 ....Liverpool
1904...............................Preston North End
1903 ....Manchester City
1902 ....West Bromwich Albion
1901...Grimsby Town
1900 ....Sheffield Wednesday
1899 ....Manchester City
1898 ....Burnley
1897 ....Notts County
1896 ....Liverpool
1895 ....Bury
1894...Liverpool
1893...............Small Heath (Birmingham City)

Tier Three Champions

The third tier of the English Football League has, at different times, been known as League One, Division Two or (prior to the introduction of the Premiership) Division Three. The following list of champions, arranged chronologically, is divided into sections reflecting these changes in name, though in all instances the lists indicate status as champions of the third tier of English football.

League One (Tier Three) Champions
2007 ....Scunthorpe
2006 ....Southend United
2005 ....Luton Town

Division Two (Tier Three) Champions
2004...Plymouth Argyle
2003 ....Wigan Athletic
2002 ....Brighton & Hove Albion
2001 ....Millwall
2000.................................Preston North End
1999 ....Fulham
1998...Watford

1997	Bury
1996	Swindon Town
1995	Birmingham City
1994	Reading
1993	Stoke City

CLUB FACTS

Bury have spent a total of 39 seasons in the second tier of English football, during which time they scored 2,396 goals – and conceded 2,396 goals.

Division Three (Tier Three) Champions

1992	Brentford
1991	Cambridge United
1990	Bristol Rovers
1989	Wolverhampton Wanderers
1988	Sunderland
1987	AFC Bournemouth
1986	Reading
1985	Bradford City
1984	Oxford United
1983	Portsmouth
1982	Burnley
1981	Rotherham United
1980	Grimsby Town
1979	Shrewsbury Town
1978	Wrexham
1977	Mansfield Town
1976	Hereford United
1975	Blackburn Rovers
1974	Oldham Athletic
1973	Bolton Wanderers
1972	Aston Villa
1971	Preston North End
1970	Leyton Orient
1969	Watford
1968	Oxford United
1967	Queen's Park Rangers
1966	Hull City
1965	Carlisle United
1964	Coventry
1963	Northampton Town
1962	Portsmouth
1961	Bury
1960	Southampton
1959	Plymouth Argyle

Division Three (North) Champions

1958	Scunthorpe
1957	Derby County
1956	Grimsby Town
1955	Barnsley
1954	Port Vale
1953	Oldham Athletic
1952	Lincoln City
1951	Rotherham United
1950	Doncaster Rovers
1949	Hull City
1948	Lincoln City
1947	Doncaster Rovers
1939	Barnsley
1938	Tranmere Rovers

CLUB FACTS

Coventry City hold the distinction of being the only club to have played in the Premiership, the old Divisions One, Two, Three and Four, and both Division Three (North) and Division Three (South).

1937	Stockport County
1936	Chesterfield
1935	Doncaster Rovers
1934	Barnsley
1933	Hull City
1932	Lincoln City
1931	Chesterfield
1930	Port Vale
1929	Bradford City
1928	Bradford Park Avenue
1927	Stoke City
1926	Grimsby Town
1925	Darlington
1924	Wolverhampton Wanderers
1923	Nelson
1922	Stockport County

Division Three (South) Champions

1958	Brighton & Hove Albion
1957	Ipswich Town
1956	Leyton Orient
1955	Bristol City
1954	Ipswich Town
1953	Bristol Rovers
1952	Plymouth Argyle
1951	Nottingham Forest
1950	Notts County

The Oldham Athletic team of 1953 – Champions of Division Three (North).

CLUB FACTS

In the 1929–30 season, Brentford set a record that can never be broken, nor has it ever been equalled. The side won all 21 of their home fixtures in that season's Division Three (South) campaign, but poor away form meant they missed out on promotion to Division Two. It was the start of a golden era for the Bees, who went on to spend four seasons in the top flight in the years leading up to World War 2. In the 1935–36 season, they finished as London's top team, 5th in Division One, and one place above the mighty Arsenal. But the glory years were brief, and relegation at the end of the first post-war season marked the end of Brentford's time with the game's elite.

Tier Four Champions

The fourth tier of the English Football League has, at different times, been known as League Two, Division Three or (prior to the introduction of the Premiership) Division Four. The following list of champions, arranged chronologically, is divided into sections reflecting these changes in name, though in all instances the lists indicate status as champions of the fourth tier of English football.

League Two (Tier Four) Champions

2007 ....Walsall
2006 ....Carlisle United
2005 ....Yeovil Town

CLUB FACTS

AFC Bournemouth (formerly Bournemouth & Boscombe Athletic) hold the record for the longest continuous membership of Division Three – 47 years, from their successful application to join Division Three (South) in 1923, until relegation at the end of the 1969–70 season. In all, the South Coast side have spent only 11 seasons since 1923 outside the third tier of the League.

Division Three (Tier Four) Champions

2004...................................Doncaster Rovers
2003.............................Rushden & Diamonds
2002.................................Plymouth Argyle
2001 ....Brighton & Hove Albion
2000 ....Swansea City
1999 ....Brentford
1998..Notts County
1997 ....Wigan Athletic
1996................................Preston North End
1995 ....Carlisle United
1994 ....Shrewsbury Town
1993...Cardiff City

Division Four (Tier Four) Champions

1992 ....Burnley
1991 ....Darlington
1990 ....Exeter City
1989 ....Rotherham United
1988.....................Wolverhampton Wanderers
1987 ....Northampton Town
1986 ....Swindon Town
1985...Chesterfield
1984 ....York City
1983..Wimbledon
1982 ....Sheffield United
1981..Southend
1980 ....Huddersfield Town
1979 ....Reading
1978..Watford
1977 ....Cambridge United
1976 ....Lincoln City
1975 ....Mansfield Town
1974 ....Peterborough
1973 ....Southport
1972.....................................Grimsby Town
1971 ....Notts County
1970 ....Chesterfield

CLUB FACTS

The 1996–97 season saw all four English divisions won by teams from Lancashire – Manchester United took the Premiership title, Bolton topped Division One, Bury won Division Two, and Wigan secured top spot in Division Three. It wasn't the first time Lancashire clubs had hogged the limelight – the 1972–73 season ended with Liverpool, Burnley, Bolton and Southport as divisional champions.

1969...................................Doncaster Rovers
1968 ....Luton Town
1967..................................Stockport County
1966 ....Doncaster Rovers
1965 ....Brighton & Hove Albion
1964...Gillingham
1963 ....Brentford
1962 ....Millwall
1961 ....Peterborough
1960 ....Walsall
1959..Port Vale

FA Cup Winners

The following is a list, arranged chronologically, of the FA Cup Winners for every year since the tournament's inception.

2007	Chelsea
2006	Liverpool
2005	Arsenal
2004	Manchester United
2003	Arsenal
2002	Arsenal
2001	Liverpool
2000	Chelsea
1999	Manchester United
1998	Arsenal
1997	Chelsea
1996	Manchester United
1995	Everton
1994	Manchester United
1993	Arsenal
1992	Liverpool
1991	Tottenham Hotspur

CLUB FACTS

Wolves were the first of only two clubs to win all four divisions. They achieved the feat in 1989, and were followed three years later by Burnley.

Division One	1954, 1958, 1959
Division Two	1932, 1977
Division Three	1989
Division Four	1988

(Also Third Division North in 1924)

Burnley

Division One	1921, 1960
Division Two	1973, 1898
Division Three	1982
Division Four	1992

Former Conference clubs now in The Football League

Club	Years in the Conference National
Accrington Stanley	2003–2006
Barnet	1979–1991; 2001–2005
Carlisle United	2004–2005
Cheltenham Town	1985–1992; 1997–1999
Chester City	1999–2004
Colchester United	1990–1992
Darlington	1989–1990
Doncaster Rovers	1998–2003
Hereford United	1997–2006
Lincoln City	1987–1988
Macclesfield Town	1987–1997
Shrewsbury Town	2003–2004
Wycombe Wanderers	1985–1986; 1987–1993
Yeovil Town	1979–1985; 1988–1995; 1997–2003

Of the former Conference clubs now in the Football League, Colchester United is the most successful, having reached the Championship in 2006 – 14 years after being Conference champions. Accrington Stanley have yet to progress beyond the league's basement division, as have Barnet, Chester City and Hereford United – although they did progress to the third tier of the league in their first spells of Football League membership.

1990	Manchester United
1989	Liverpool
1988	Wimbledon
1987	Coventry City
1986	Liverpool
1985	Manchester United
1984	Everton
1983	Manchester United
1982	Tottenham Hotspur
1981	Tottenham Hotspur
1980	West Ham United
1979	Arsenal
1978	Ipswich Town
1977	Manchester United
1976	Southampton
1975	West Ham United
1974	Liverpool
1973	Sunderland
1972	Leeds United
1971	Arsenal
1970	Chelsea
1969	Manchester City
1968	West Bromwich Albion
1967	Tottenham Hotspur
1966	Everton
1965	Liverpool
1964	West Ham United
1963	Manchester United
1962	Tottenham Hotspur
1961	Tottenham Hotspur
1960	Wolverhampton Wanderers
1959	Nottingham Forest
1958	Bolton Wanderers
1957	Aston Villa
1956	Manchester City
1955	Newcastle United
1954	West Bromwich Albion
1953	Blackpool
1952	Newcastle United
1951	Newcastle United
1950	Arsenal
1949	Wolverhampton Wanderers
1948	Manchester United
1947	Charlton Athletic
1946	Derby County
1945	World War 2
1944	World War 2
1943	World War 2
1942	World War 2
1941	World War 2
1940	World War 2
1939	Portsmouth

1938	Preston North End
1937	Sunderland
1936	Arsenal
1935	Sheffield Wednesday
1934	Manchester City
1933	Everton
1932	Newcastle United
1931	West Bromwich Albion
1930	Arsenal
1929	Bolton Wanderers
1928	Blackburn Rovers
1927	Cardiff City
1926	Bolton Wanderers
1925	Sheffield United
1924	Newcastle United
1923	Bolton Wanderers
1922	Huddersfield Town
1921	Tottenham Hotspur
1920	Aston Villa
1919	World War 1
1918	World War 1
1917	World War 1
1916	World War 1
1915	Sheffield United
1914	Burnley
1913	Aston Villa
1912	Barnsley

CLUB FACTS

The present FA Cup trophy was first competed for in the 1910–11 season. Weighing almost 11lb (5kg), and standing 19ins (48cm) high, it was made by Fattorini and Sons of Bradford, and appropriately, if curiously, Bradford City were its first holders. Curiously, because 1911 remains the only time in the competition's history that a Bradford side has got anywhere near the final.

1911	Bradford City
1910	Newcastle United
1909	Manchester United
1908	Wolverhampton Wanderers
1907	Sheffield Wednesday
1906	Everton
1905	Aston Villa
1904	Manchester City
1903	Bury
1902	Sheffield United
1901	Tottenham Hotspur

CLUB FACTS

Three clubs have appeared in the FA Cup final after losing a match in an earlier round – Oxford University contested the 1872 final despite having lost to Glasgow club Queen's Park in the semi-final. Queen's Park, however, couldn't afford to travel to London for the final, and so withdrew from the tournament, leaving Oxford University to face Wanderers. Wanderers won 2–0, although Oxford University turned the tables in the 1873 competition, beating the holders at the quarter-final stage on their way to winning the trophy.

In 1890, Sheffield Wednesday (then known simply as The Wednesday) reached the final after a farcical quarter-final encounter with Notts County. Wednesday beat the Magpies 5–0, but the game was replayed after County protested. County won the rematch 3–2, but this time Wednesday protested and forced a third meeting. Wednesday finally triumphed 2–1, and went on to play Blackburn Rovers in the final – where they lost 6–1.

The only team to achieve this distinction in the modern era is Charlton in the 1946 competition. League football had yet to resume after World War 2, so the FA decided that the best way to give the fans more football while things were sorted out was to organise an FA Cup competition in which each round, up to and including the quarter-finals, would be played over two legs. In the Third Round, Charlton lost 2–1 to Fulham at Craven Cottage, but beat them 3–1 at the Valley, before disposing of Wolves, Preston, Brentford and Bolton on their way to Wembley. Like Oxford University and The Wednesday before them, Charlton could only finish as runners-up, losing 4–1 to Derby County.

1900	Bury
1899	Sheffield United
1898	Nottingham Forest
1897	Aston Villa
1896	Sheffield Wednesday
1895	Aston Villa
1894	Notts County
1893	Wolverhampton Wanderers
1892	West Bromwich Albion
1891	Blackburn Rovers
1890	Blackburn Rovers
1889	Preston North End
1888	West Bromwich Albion
1887	Aston Villa
1886	Blackburn Rovers
1885	Blackburn Rovers
1884	Blackburn Rovers
1883	Blackburn Olympic
1882	Old Etonians
1881	Old Carthusians
1880	Clapham Rovers

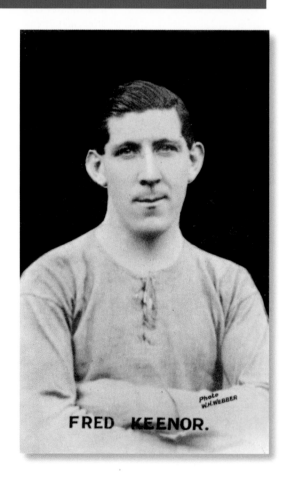

FRED KEENOR.

Fred Keenor, who captained Cardiff City to victory in the 1927 FA Cup final. The victory remains the only occasion on which a non-English club has lifted the trophy.

CLUB FACTS

Amazingly, the 2007 FA Cup final is only the third to feature the two sides that finished first and second in the top division. The previous occasions were in 1986, when Liverpool played Everton, and more than 70 years earlier in 1913, when Sunderland met Aston Villa in front of English football's second biggest crowd ever, officially recorded as 120,081, at Crystal Palace.

1879	Old Etonians
1878	The Wanderers
1877	The Wanderers
1876	The Wanderers
1875	Royal Engineers
1874	Oxford University
1873	The Wanderers
1872	The Wanderers

FA Cup Runners-up

The following is a list, arranged chronologically, of the teams to finish runner-up in the FA Cup for every year since the tournament's inception.

2007	Manchester United
2006	West Ham
2005	Manchester United
2004	Millwall
2003	Southampton
2002	Chelsea
2001	Arsenal
2000	Aston Villa
1999	Newcastle
1998	Newcastle
1997	Middlesbrough
1996	Liverpool
1995	Manchester United
1994	Chelsea
1993	Sheffield Wednesday
1992	Sunderland
1991	Nottingham Forest
1990	Crystal Palace
1989	Everton
1988	Liverpool
1987	Tottenham Hotspur
1986	Everton
1985	Everton
1984	Watford
1983	Brighton & Hove Albion
1982	Queen's Park Rangers
1981	Manchester City
1980	Arsenal
1979	Manchester United
1978	Arsenal
1977	Liverpool
1976	Manchester United
1975	Fulham
1974	Newcastle United
1973	Leeds United
1972	Arsenal
1971	Liverpool
1970	Leeds United
1969	Leicester City
1968	Everton
1967	Chelsea
1966	Sheffield Wednesday
1965	Leeds United
1964	Preston North End
1963	Leicester City
1962	Burnley
1961	Leicester City
1960	Blackburn Rovers
1959	Luton Town
1958	Manchester United
1957	Manchester United
1956	Birmingham City
1955	Manchester City
1954	Preston North End
1953	Bolton Wanderers
1952	Arsenal
1951	Blackpool
1950	Liverpool
1949	Leicester City
1948	Blackpool
1947	Burnley
1946	Charlton Athletic
1945	World War 2
1944	World War 2
1943	World War 2

CLUB FACTS

In the 1920–21 season, one famous name was missing from the FA Cup. Birmingham City took no part in the competition, but their failure to appear was unintentional – club secretary Sam Richards simply forgot to send in the entry form!

1942	World War 2
1941	World War 2
1940	World War 2
1939	Wolverhampton Wanderers
1938	Huddersfield Town
1937	Preston North End
1936	Sheffield United
1935	West Bromwich Albion
1934	Portsmouth
1933	Manchester City
1932	Arsenal
1931	Birmingham City
1930	Huddersfield Town
1929	Portsmouth
1928	Huddersfield Town
1927	Arsenal
1926	Manchester City
1925	Cardiff City
1924	Aston Villa
1929	West Ham United
1922	Preston North End
1921	Wolverhampton Wanderers
1920	Huddersfield Town
1915	Chelsea
1914	Liverpool
1913	Sunderland
1912	West Bromwich Albion
1911	Newcastle United
1910	Barnsley
1909	Bristol City
1908	Newcastle United
1907	Everton
1906	Newcastle United
1905	Newcastle United
1904	Bolton Wanderers
1903	Derby County
1902	Southampton
1901	Sheffield United
1900	Southampton
1899	Derby County
1898	Derby County
1897	Everton
1896	Wolverhampton Wanderers
1895	West Bromwich Albion
1894	Bolton Wanderers
1893	Everton
1892	Aston Villa
1891	Notts County
1890	Sheffield Wednesday
1889	Wolverhampton Wanderers
1888	Preston North End
1887	West Bromwich Albion
1886	West Bromwich Albion
1885	Queen's Park (Glasgow)
1884	Queen's Park (Glasgow)
1883	Old Etonians
1882	Blackburn Rovers
1881	Old Etonians
1880	Oxford University
1879	Clapham Rovers
1878	Royal Engineers
1877	Oxford University
1876	Old Etonians
1875	Old Etonians
1874	Royal Engineers
1873	Oxford University
1872	Royal Engineers

League Cup Winners

The following is a list, arranged chronologically, of the League Cup Winners for every year since the tournament's inception. The League Cup has changed name several times over the years, largely due to sponsorship, and the list is divided accordingly.

Carling Cup

2007	Chelsea
2006	Manchester United
2005	Chelsea
2004	Middlesbrough

Worthington Cup

2003	Liverpool
2002	Blackburn Rovers
2001	Liverpool
2000	Leicester City
1999	Tottenham Hotspur

CLUB FACTS

There was an avalanche of goals in the first round of the 1890–91 FA Cup – first prize goes to Nottingham Forest, whose 14–0 away win at Clapton remains the highest away victory in an English first-class fixture. In the same round, Darwen thrashed Kidderminster 13–0, Aston Villa trounced Casuals 13–1, and The Wednesday brushed Halliwell aside 12–0. It was a good day for the two Nottingham clubs – Notts County, also playing away from home, trounced Sheffield United 9–1.

Coca-Cola Cup

1998	Chelsea
1997	Leicester City
1996	Aston Villa
1995	Liverpool
1994	Aston Villa
1993	Arsenal

Rumbelows Cup

1992	Manchester United
1991	Sheffield Wednesday

Littlewoods Cup

1990	Nottingham Forest
1989	Nottingham Forest
1988	Luton Town
1987	Arsenal

Milk Cup

1986	Oxford United
1985	Norwich City
1984	Liverpool
1983	Liverpool
1982	Liverpool

League Cup

1981	Liverpool
1980	Wolverhampton Wanderers
1979	Nottingham Forest
1978	Nottingham Forest
1977	Aston Villa
1976	Manchester City
1975	Aston Villa
1974	Wolverhampton Wanderers
1973	Tottenham Hotspur
1972	Stoke City
1971	Tottenham Hotspur
1970	Manchester City
1969	Swindon Town
1968	Leeds United
1967	Queen's Park Rangers
1966	West Bromwich Albion
1965	Chelsea
1964	Leicester City
1963	Birmingham City
1962	Norwich City
1961	Aston Villa

League Cup Runners-Up

The following is a list, arranged chronologically, of those teams to have finished as runner-up in the League Cup for every year since the tournament's inception. The League Cup has changed name several times over the years, largely due to sponsorship, and the list is divided accordingly.

Carling Cup

2007	Arsenal
2006	Wigan
2005	Liverpool
2004	Bolton Wanderers

Worthington Cup

2003	Manchester United
2002	Tottenham Hotspur

FA Cup Final Success

Two points for winning, one point for being runners-up.
Clubs on the same number of points are ranked in order of the number of wins.

Position	Club	Total Apps.	Winners	Runners-Up	Points
1	Manchester United	17	11	7	29
2	Arsenal	17	10	7	27
3	Liverpool	13	7	6	20
4	Newcastle United	13	6	7	19
5	Tottenham Hotspur	9	8	1	17
6	Aston Villa	10	7	3	17
7	Everton	12	5	7	17
8	West Bromwich Albion	10	5	5	15
9	Blackburn Rovers	8	6	2	14
10=	Chelsea	8	4	4	12
10=	Manchester City	8	4	4	12
10=	Wolverhampton Wanderers	8	4	4	12
13	Bolton Wanderers	7	4	3	11
14	The Wanderers	5	5	–	10
15	Sheffield United	6	4	2	10
16	Sheffield Wednesday	6	3	3	9
17	Preston North End	7	2	5	9
18	West Ham United	5	3	2	8
19	Sunderland	4	2	2	6
20	Huddersfield Town	5	1	4	6
21	Nottingham Forest	3	2	1	5
22=	Southampton	4	1	3	5
22=	Derby County	4	1	3	5
22=	Leeds United	4	1	3	5
22=	Oxford University	4	1	3	5
26=	Bury	2	2	–	4
26=	Old Etonians	2	2	–	4
28=	Portsmouth	3	1	2	4
28=	Burnley	3	1	2	4
28=	Royal Engineers	3	1	2	4
31=	Leicester City	4	–	4	4
31=	Old Etonians	4	–	4	4
33=	Barnsley	2	1	1	3
33=	Cardiff City	2	1	1	3
33=	Charlton Athletic	2	1	1	3
33=	Clapham Rovers	2	1	1	3
33=	Notts County	2	1	1	3
38=	Blackburn Olympic	1	1	–	2
38=	Blackpool	1	1	–	2
38=	Bradford City	1	1	–	2
38=	Coventry City	1	1	–	2
38=	Ipswich Town	1	1	–	2
38=	Old Carthusians	1	1	–	2
38=	Wimbledon	1	1	–	2

FA Cup Final Success (continued)

Position	Club	Total Apps.	Winners	Runners-Up	Points
45=	Birmingham City	2	–	2	2
45=	Blackpool	2	–	2	2
45=	Queen's Park (Glasgow)	2	–	2	2
48=	Brighton & Hove Albion	1	–	1	1
48=	Bristol City	1	–	1	1
48=	Crystal Palace	1	–	1	1
48=	Fulham	1	–	1	1
48=	Luton Town	1	–	1	1
48=	Middlesbrough	1	–	1	1
48=	Millwall	1	–	1	1
48=	Queen's Park Rangers	1	–	1	1
48=	Watford	1	–	1	1

Taking into account the clubs that no longer exist, fewer than half the country's clubs have given their supporters a day out at Wembley. In Millwall's case, it was Cardiff!

2001 ....Birmingham City
2000 ....Tranmere Rovers
1999 ....Leicester City

Coca-Cola Cup

1998 ....Middlesbrough
1997 ....Middlesbrough
1996...Leeds United
1995.....................................Bolton Wanderers
1994 ....Manchester United
1993 ....Sheffield Wednesday

Rumbelows Cup

1992...................................Nottingham Forest
1991 ....Manchester United

Littlewoods Cup

1990......................................Oldham Athletic
1989 ....Luton Town

1988 ....Arsenal
1987 ....Liverpool

Milk Cup

1986 ....Queen's Park Rangers
1985 ....Sunderland
1984...Everton
1983 ....Manchester United
1982................................Tottenham Hotspur

League Cup

1981 ....West Ham United
1980 ....Nottingham Forest
1979 ....Southampton
1978..Liverpool
1977...Everton
1976 ....Newcastle United
1975..Norwich City
1974 ....Manchester City

CLUB FACTS

How names and numbers relate in the FA Cup draw:

The League One and Two teams are numbered 1–48 when the first round draw for the FA Cup is made, 1 being the first in alphabetical order and 48 the last. The total is made up with the Non-League clubs that make it through the fourth qualifying round.

The third round sees the Premiership and Championship sides in the fray. They will join the draw alphabetically taking up the places of the teams that have been knocked out. Therefore Arsenal will be number 1 only if the previous Number 1 did not survive.

From the fourth round onwards, teams retain their numbers. So a team that is Number 1 in the fourth round draw will remain Number 1 until it is knocked out.

League Cup Final Success

Two points for winning, one point for being runners-up.
Clubs on the same number of points are ranked in order of the number of wins.

Position	Club	Total Apps.	Winners	Runners-Up	Points
1	Liverpool	10	7	3	17
2	Aston Villa	7	5	2	12
3	Nottingham Forest	6	4	2	10
4	Chelsea	5	4	1	9
5=	Leicester City	5	3	2	8
5=	Tottenham Hotspur	5	3	2	8
7=	Arsenal	6	2	4	8
7=	Manchester United	6	2	4	8
9	Norwich City	4	2	2	6
10	Manchester City	3	2	1	5
11	Wolverhampton Wanderers	2	2	–	4
12=	Middlesbrough	3	1	2	4
12=	West Bromwich Albion	3	1	2	4
14=	Birmingham City	2	1	1	3
14=	Leeds United	2	1	1	3
14=	Luton Town	2	1	1	3
14=	Queen's Park Rangers	2	1	1	3
14=	Sheffield Wednesday	2	1	1	3
14=	Stoke City	2	1	1	3
20=	Blackburn Rovers	1	1	–	2
20=	Oxford United	1	1	–	2
20=	Swindon Town	1	1	–	2
23=	Everton	2	–	2	2
23=	West Ham United	2	–	2	2
25=	Newcastle United	1	–	1	1
25=	Oldham Athletic	1	–	1	1
25=	Rochdale	1	–	1	1
25=	Rotherham United	1	–	1	1
25=	Southampton	1	–	1	1
25=	Sunderland	1	–	1	1
25=	Tranmere	1	–	1	1

The League Cup, brainchild of Alan Hardaker, started life in 1961 as the competition the big clubs didn't want; it wasn't until several years later that all clubs entered a team. As it approaches its half-century it is again unpopular with the 'big boys', even if it involves a Wembley appearance as opposed to the original two-legged final. It has also laboured under an inordinate number of sponsors – six at last count – which has not helped its identity. But in the pre-sponsorship days of 1969 Third Division Swindon Town enjoyed their finest hour when beating the mighty Arsenal.

1973..Norwich City
1972...Chelsea
1971 ....Aston Villa
1970 ....West Bromwich Albion
1969...Arsenal
1968...Arsenal
1967 ....West Bromwich Albion
1966 ....West Ham United
1965 ....Leicester City
1964 ....Stoke City
1963 ....Aston Villa
1962 ....Rochdale
1961 ....Rotherham United

Charity Shield Winners

The Charity Shield, now known as the Community Shield, has for most of its history been a one-off game contested annually by the league and cup winners of the previous season (though on occasion other systems have been used to determine the participants). The following is a list, arranged chronologically, of all the winners of the Charity Shield since its inception.

Community Shield

2006...Liverpool
2005..Chelsea
2004..Arsenal
2003 ....Manchester United

Charity Shield

2002..Arsenal
2001..Liverpool
2000 ....Chelsea
1999..Arsenal
1998..Arsenal
1997 ....Manchester United
1996 ....Manchester United
1995..Everton
1994 ....Manchester United
1993 ....Manchester United
1992..Leeds United
1991 ....Arsenal/Tottenham Hotspur
1990 ....Liverpool/Manchester United
1989..Liverpool
1988..Liverpool
1987...Everton
1986.............................Liverpool/Everton
1985...Everton
1984...Everton

1983 ....Manchester United
1982..Liverpool
1981...............Aston Villa/Tottenham Hotspur
1980..Liverpool
1979..Liverpool
1978....................................Nottingham Forest
1977..Liverpool
1976 ....Liverpool/Manchester United
1975..Derby County
1974..Liverpool
1973...Burnley
1972 ....Manchester City
1971 ....Leicester City
1970..Everton
1969..Leeds United
1968 ....Manchester City
1967....Manchester United/Tottenham Hotspur
1966..Liverpool
1965 ....Liverpool/Manchester United
1964 ....Liverpool/West Ham United
1963...Everton
1962..............................Tottenham Hotspur
1961 ....Tottenham Hotspur
1960 ....Burnley/Wolverhampton Wanderers
1959.....................Wolverhampton Wanderers
1958...................................Bolton Wanderers
1957 ....Manchester United
1956 ....Manchester United
1955...Chelsea
1954 ....Wolverhampton Wanderers/
..................................West Bromwich Albion
1953...Arsenal
1952 ....Manchester United
1951 ....Tottenham Hotspur
1950 ....World Cup XI *
1949 ....Portsmouth/
............................Wolverhampton Wanderers
1948...Arsenal
1947 ....World War 2
1946 ....World War 2
1945 ....World War 2
1944 ....World War 2
1943 ....World War 2
1942 ....World War 2
1941 ....World War 2
1940 ....World War 2
1939 ....World War 2
1938 ....Arsenal
1937 ....Manchester City
1936 ....Sunderland
1935 ....Sheffield Wednesday
1934 ....Arsenal

* The Charity Shield was introduced in 1908 as a successor to the Sheriff of London (Dewar) Charity Shield, which had been contested between the two sides judged to be the best professional and the best amateur sides in the country. For many years, the Charity Shield continued this tradition, and teams were often assembled specially for the event. In 1913, 1923, 1924, 1925, 1926 and 1929, the shield was contested by two such sides, one made up of Professional players, one of Amateurs, and in 1950 it was contested by a World Cup XI and a Canadian Touring XI. Between 1948 and 1992, with the exception of a brief period at the beginning the 1970s, the shield was shared between the two sides in the event of a drawn game. During that brief period, and again since 1993, a penalty shoot-out has been used to decide the match.

Queens Park Rangers take on Football League Champions Manchester United in the first ever FA Charity Shield game.

English Minor Cups

Teams in the lower tiers of English football participate in a number of cup competitions. The winners of some of the more notable of these minor cup competitions are recorded here.

Associate Members' Cup (1984–91)/ Football League Trophy (1992–present)

Johnstone's Paint Trophy
2007 ....Doncaster Rovers
2008 ....Milton Keynes Dons

The Football League Trophy
2006 ....Swansea City

LDV Vans Trophy
2005 ....Wrexham
2004..Blackpool
2003 ....Bristol City
2002...Blackpool
2001..Port Vale

Auto Windscreens Shield
2000 ....Stoke City
1999 ....Wigan Athletic
1998..Grimsby Town
1997 ....Carlisle United
1996 ....Rotherham United
1995 ....Birmingham City

Autoglass Trophy
1994 ....Swansea City
1993..Port Vale
1992..Stoke City

Leyland DAF Cup
1991 ....Birmingham City
1990 ....Tranmere Rovers

CLUB FACTS

When Crewe beat Hartlepool 8–0 in the opening round of the Auto Windscreens Trophy in 1995, eight different players scored the goals. Amongst them were Danny Murphy, Steve Macauley and Robbie Savage.

Charity Shield Success

Club	Appearances	Winners (Shared)
Liverpool	21	16 (5)
Manchester United	23	15 (4)
Arsenal	19	12 (1)
Everton	11	9 (1)
Tottenham Hotspur	9	7 (3)
Professionals	6	4
Wolverhampton Wanderers	5	4 (3)
Chelsea	6	3
Manchester City	7	3
Amateurs	6	2
Burnley	3	2 (1)
Leeds United	3	2
Sheffield Wednesday	2	2
West Bromwich Albion	4	2 (1)
Aston Villa	4	1 (1)
Blackburn Rovers	4	1
Bolton Wanderers	1	1
Brighton & Hove Albion	1	1
Cardiff City	1	1
Derby County	1	1
Huddersfield Town	1	1
Leicester City	1	1
Newcastle United	6	1
Nottingham Forest	2	1
Portsmouth	1	1 (1)
Sunderland	2	1
West Ham United	3	1 (1)
World Cup XI 1950	1	1
Ipswich Town	2	–
Queen's Park Rangers	2	–
Sunderland	2	–
Blackpool	1	–
Canadian Touring XI 1950	1	–
Corinthians	1	–
Coventry City	1	–
FA XI	1	–
Northampton Town	1	–
Preston North End	1	–
Swindon Town	1	–
Wimbledon	1	–

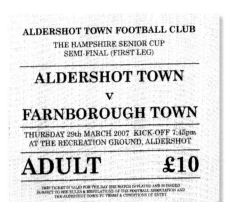

A ticket for Aldershot Town's game against Farnborough Town in the Hampshire Senior Cup of 2007. At the lower levels of English football, clubs compete for a multitude of honours, sadly too numerous to list here.

Sherpa Vans Trophy
1989...................................Bolton Wanderers
1988.....................Wolverhampton Wanderers

The Freight Rover Trophy
1987 ....Mansfield Town
1986 ....Bristol City
1985 ....Wigan Athletic

The Associate Members' Cup
1984..................................AFC Bournemouth

Texaco Cup
1975 ....Newcastle United
1974 ....Newcastle United
1973...Ipswich Town
1972 ....Derby County
1971.....................Wolverhampton Wanderers

The Football League Group Trophy
1983 ....Lincoln City
1982..Grimsby Town

The Anglo-Scottish Cup
1981 ....Chesterfield
1980 ....St Mirren
1979 ....Burnley
1978 ....Bristol City
1977 ....Nottingham Forest
1976 ....Middlesbrough

Domestic Honours
The following list, arranged alphabetically, shows domestic honours won by each English club. Clubs with no domestic honours to their name are omitted from the list, and only recognised 'major' or notable honours are included; many clubs may have enjoyed success in other, less well-known competitions which are not recorded here.

AFC Bournemouth
Division Three (Tier Three) Champions 1987
Associate Members' Cup Winners 1984

Arsenal
Premiership Champions 1998, 2002, 2004
Football League Champions 1931, 1933, 1934, 1935, 1938, 1948, 1953, 1971, 1989, 1991
FA Cup Winners 1930, 1936, 1950, 1971, 1979, 1993, 1998, 2002, 2003, 2005
League Cup (Littlewoods Cup) Winners 1987
League Cup (Coca-Cola Cup) Winners 1993
Community Shield Winners 2004
Charity Shield Winners 1930, 1931, 1933, 1934, 1938, 1948, 1953, 1991 (shared with Tottenham Hotspur), 1998, 1999, 2002

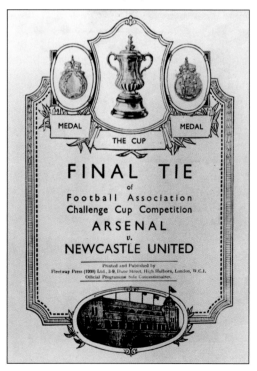

Aston Villa

Football League Champions 1894, 1896, 1897, 1899, 1900, 1910, 1981

Division Two (Tier Two) Champions 1938, 1960

Division Three (Tier Three) Champions 1972

FA Cup Winners 1887, 1895, 1897, 1905, 1913, 1920, 1957

League Cup Winners 1961, 1975, 1977

League Cup (Coca-Cola Cup) Winners 1994, 1996

Charity Shield Winners 1981 (shared with Tottenham Hotspur)

Barnsley

Division Three (North) Champions 1934, 1939, 1955

FA Cup Winners 1912

Birmingham City

Division Two (Tier Two) Champions 1893 (as Small Heath), 1921, 1948, 1955

Division Two (Tier Three) Champions 1995

League Cup Winners 1963

Associate Members' Cup (Leyland DAF Cup) Winners 1991

Football League Trophy (Autowindscreens Shield) Winners 1995

Blackburn Rovers

Premiership Champions 1995

Football League Champions 1912, 1914

Division Two (Tier Two) Champions 1939

Division Three (Tier Three) Champions 1975

FA Cup Winners 1884, 1885, 1886, 1890, 1891, 1928

League Cup (Worthington Cup) Winners 2002

Full Members' Cup (Simod Cup) Winners 1987

Charity Shield Winners 1912

Blackpool

Division Two (Tier Two) Champions 1930

FA Cup Winners 1953

Football League Trophy (LDV Vans Trophy) Winners 2002, 2004

Bolton Wanderers

Division One (Tier Two) Champions 1997

Division Two (Tier Two) Champions 1909, 1978

Division Three (Tier Three) Champions 1973

FA Cup Winners 1923, 1926, 1929, 1958

Associate Members' Cup (Sherpa Vans Trophy)
Winners 1989
Charity Shield Winners 1958

Bradford City

Division Two (Tier Two) Champions 1908
Division Three (Tier Three) Champions 1985
Division Three (North) Champions 1929
FA Cup Winners 1911

Brentford

Division Two (Tier Two) Champions 1935
Division Three (Tier Three) Champions 1992
Division Three (Tier Four) Champions 1999
Division Three (South) Champions 1933
Division Four (Tier Four) Champions 1963

Brighton & Hove Albion

Division Two (Tier Three) Champions 2002
Division Three (Tier Four) Champions 2001
Division Three (South) Champions 1958
Division Four (Tier Four) Champions 1965
Charity Shield Winners 1910

Bristol City

Division Two (Tier Two) Champions 1906
Division Three (South) Champions 1923,
1927, 1955
Anglo-Scottish Cup Winners 1978
Associate Members' Cup (The Freight Rover
Trophy) Winners 1986
Football League Trophy (LDV Vans Trophy)
Winners 2003

CLUB FACTS

In 1945, Bristol City beat Cardiff City 2–1
in a war-time cup game after a 'sudden
death' winner in the 202nd minute.

Bristol Rovers

Division Three (Tier Three) Champions 1990
Division Three (South) Champions 1953

Burnley

Football League Champions 1921, 1960
Division Two (Tier Two) Champions 1898,
1973
Division Three (Tier Three) Champions 1982
Division Four (Tier Four) Champions 1992
FA Cup Winners 1914

Anglo-Scottish Cup Winners 1979
Charity Shield Winners 1960 (shared with
Wolverhampton Wanderers), 1973

Bury

Division Two (Tier Two) Champions 1895
Division Two (Tier Three) Champions 1997
Division Three (Tier Three) Champions 1961
FA Cup Winners 1900, 1903

Cardiff City

Division Three (Tier Four) Champions 1993
Division Three (South) Champions 1947
FA Cup Winners 1927
Charity Shield Winners 1927

Carlisle United

Division Three (Tier Three) Champions 1964
Division Three (Tier Four) Champions 1995
League Two (Tier Four) Champions 2006
Football League Trophy (Autowindscreens
Shield) Winners 1997

Charlton Athletic

Division One (Tier Two) Champions 2000
Division Three (South) Champions 1929, 1935
FA Cup Winners 1947

CLUB FACTS

Charlton operate a 'Valley Express' bus
service to bring fans from outside London
to matches. The Medway Towns have been
particularly targeted, which has angered
some fans of Gillingham FC, who claim that
Charlton are stealing fans who would
otherwise attend matches at their own
Priestfield Stadium.

Chelsea

Premiership Champions 2005, 2006
Football League Champions 1955
Division Two (Tier Two) Champions 1984,
1989
FA Cup Winners 1970, 1997, 2000, 2007
League Cup Winners 1965
League Cup (Coca-Cola Cup) Winners 1998
League Cup (Carling Cup) Winners 2005, 2007
Community Shield Winners 2005
Full Members' Cup Winners 1986

Full Members' Cup (Zenith Data Systems Cup) Winners 1990
Charity Shield Winners 1955, 2000

Chesterfield
Division Three (North) Champions 1931, 1936
Division Four (Tier Four) Champions 1970, 1985
Anglo-Scottish Cup Winners 1981

CLUB FACTS
Chesterfield was the last League side to install floodlights, finally playing their first floodlit fixture on October 23rd 1967. Ironically, they might have been the joint-first to play a floodlit league game had their board not turned down Rochdale's proposal to play under the lights at Spotland sometime in 1955.

Coventry City
Division Two (Tier Two) Champions 1967
Division Three (Tier Three) Champions 1963
Division Three (South) Champions 1936
FA Cup Winners 1987

Crystal Palace
Division One (Tier Two) Champions 1994
Division Two (Tier Two) Champions 1979
Division Three (Tier Three) Champions 1921
Full Members' Cup (Zenith Data Systems Cup) Winners 1991

Darlington
Division Three (North) Champions 1925
Division Four (Tier Four) Champions 1991

Derby County
Football League Champions 1972, 1975
Division Two (Tier Two) Champions 1912, 1915, 1969, 1987
Division Three (North) Champions 1957
FA Cup Winners 1946
Texaco Cup Winners 1972
Charity Shield Winners 1975

Doncaster Rovers
Division Three (Tier Four) Champions 2004
Division Three (North) Champions 1935, 1947, 1950

Division Four (Tier Four) Champions 1966, 1969
Football League Trophy (Johnstone's Paint Trophy) Winners 2007

Everton
Football League Champions 1891, 1915, 1928, 1932, 1939, 1963, 1970, 1985, 1987
Division Two (Tier Two) Champions 1931
FA Cup Winners 1906, 1933, 1966, 1984, 1995
Charity Shield Winners 1928, 1932, 1963, 1970, 1984, 1985, 1986 (shared with Liverpool), 1987, 1995

Fulham
Division One (Tier Two) Champions 2001
Division Two (Tier Two) Champions 1949
Division Two (Tier Three) Champions 1999
Division Three (South) Champions 1932

Gillingham
Division Four (Tier Four) Champions 1964

Grimsby Town
Division Two (Tier Two) Champions 1901, 1934
Division Three (Tier Three) Champions 1980
Division Three (North) Champions 1926, 1956
Division Four (Tier Four) Champions 1972
Football League Group Trophy Winners 1982
Football League Trophy (Autowindscreens Shield) Winners 1998

Hereford United
Division Three (Tier Three) Champions 1976

Huddersfield Town
Football League Champions 1924, 1925, 1926
Division Two (Tier Two) Champions 1970
Division Four (Tier Four) Champions 1980
FA Cup Winners 1922
Charity Shield Winners 1922

Hull City
Division Three (Tier Three) Champions 1966
Division Three (North) Champions 1933, 1949

Ipswich Town
Football League Champions 1962
Division Two (Tier Two) Champions 1961,

1968, 1992
Division Three (South) Champions 1954, 1957
FA Cup Winners 1978
Texaco Cup Winners 1973

Leeds United

Football League Champions 1969, 1974, 1992
Division Two (Tier Two) Champions 1924, 1964, 1990
FA Cup Winners 1972
League Cup Winners 1968
Charity Shield Winners 1969, 1992

Leicester City

Division Two (Tier Two) Champions 1925, 1937, 1954, 1957, 1971, 1980
League Cup Winners 1964
League Cup (Coca-Cola Cup) Winners 1997
League Cup (Worthington Cup) Winners 2000
Charity Shield Winners 1971

Leyton Orient

Division Three (Tier Three) Champions 1970
Division Three (South) Champions 1956

Lincoln City

Division Three (North) Champions 1932, 1948, 1952
Division Four (Tier Four) Champions 1976
Football League Group Trophy Winners 1983

Liverpool

Football League Champions 1901, 1906, 1922, 1923, 1947, 1964, 1966, 1973, 1976, 1977, 1979, 1980, 1982, 1983, 1984, 1986, 1988, 1990
Division Two (Tier Two) Champions 1894, 1896, 1905, 1962
FA Cup Winners 1965, 1974, 1986, 1989, 1992, 2001, 2006
League Cup Winners 1981
League Cup (Milk Cup) Winners 1982, 1983, 1984
League Cup (Coca-Cola Cup) Winners 1995

League Cup (Worthington Cup) Winners 2001, 2003
Community Shield Winners 2006
Charity Shield Winners 1964 (shared with West Ham), 1965 (shared with Manchester United), 1966, 1974, 1976 (shared with Manchester United), 1977, 1979, 1980, 1982, 1986 (shared with Everton), 1988, 1989, 1990 (shared with Manchester United), 2001

Luton Town

Division Two (Tier Two) Champions 1982
Division Three (South) Champions 1937
Division Four (Tier Four) Champions 1968
League One (Tier Three) Champions 2005
League Cup (Littlewoods Cup) Winners 1988

Manchester City

Football League Champions 1937, 1968
Division One (Tier Two) Champions 2002
Division Two (Tier Two) Champions 1899, 1903, 1910, 1928, 1947, 1966
FA Cup Winners 1904, 1934, 1956, 1969
League Cup Winners 1970, 1976
Charity Shield Winners 1937, 1968, 1972

Manchester United

Premiership Champions 1993, 1994, 1996, 1997, 1999, 2000, 2001, 2003, 2007
Football League Champions 1908, 1911, 1952, 1956, 1957, 1965, 1967
Division Two (Tier Two) Champions 1936, 1975
FA Cup Winners 1909, 1948, 1963, 1977, 1983, 1985, 1990, 1994, 1996, 1999, 2004
League Cup (Rumbelows Cup) Winners 1992
League Cup (Carling Cup) Winners 2006
Community Shield Winners 2003
Charity Shield Winners 1908, 1911, 1952, 1956, 1957, 1965 (shared with Liverpool), 1967 (shared with Tottenham Hotspur), 1976 (shared with Liverpool), 1983, 1990 (shared with Liverpool), 1993, 1994, 1996, 1997

The official programme for 1974's FA Cup final proudly proclaims the previous successes of both clubs – it may surprise some to see that Liverpool had, at that stage, only a single FA Cup win to their name. Their record of success in other competitions, however, surpasses that of any other English club, and certainly that of Newcastle United!

FOOTBALL ASSOCIATION CHALLENGE CUP COMPETITION

FINAL

LIVERPOOL

F.A. CUP HONOURS

WINNERS
1965

Runners-up
1914, 1950, 1971

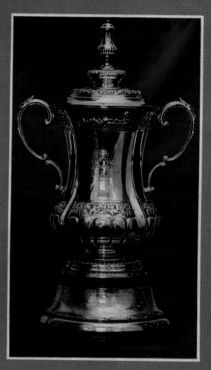

NEWCASTLE UNITED

F.A. CUP HONOURS

WINNERS
1910, 1924, 1932,
1951, 1952, 1955

Runners-up
1905, 1906, 1908,
1911

SATURDAY, 4th MAY 1974
Kick-off 3 p.m.

OFFICIAL
PROGRAMME

WEMBLEY
STADIUM

FIFTEEN
PENCE

Mansfield Town
Division Three (Tier Three) Champions 1977
Division Three (Tier Four) Champions 1975
Associate Members' Cup (The Freight Rover Trophy) Winners 1987

Middlesbrough
Division One (Tier Two) Champions 1995
Division Two (Tier Two) Champions 1927, 1929, 1974
League Cup (Carling Cup) Winners 2004
Anglo-Scottish Cup Winners 1976

Millwall
Division Two (Tier Two) Champions 1988
Division Two (Tier Three) Champions 2001
Division Three (South) Champions 1928, 1938
Division Four (Tier Four) Champions 1962

Milton Keynes Dons
Johnstone's Paint Trophy 2008

Newcastle United
Football League Champions 1905, 1907, 1909, 1927
Division One (Tier Two) Champions 1993
Division Two (Tier Two) Champions 1965
FA Cup Winners 1910, 1924, 1932, 1951, 1952, 1955
Texaco Cup Winners 1974, 1975
Charity Shield Winners 1909

Northampton Town
Division Three (Tier Three) Champions 1962
Division Four (Tier Four) Champions 1987

Norwich City
Division One (Tier Two) Champions 2004
Division Two (Tier Two) Champions 1972, 1986
Division Three (South) Champions 1934
League Cup Winners 1962
League Cup (Milk Cup) Winners 1985

Nottingham Forest
Football League Champions 1978
Division One (Tier Two) Champions 1998
Division Two (Tier Two) Champions 1907, 1922
Division Three (South) Champions 1951
FA Cup Winners 1898, 1959
League Cup Winners 1978, 1979
League Cup (Littlewoods Cup) Winners 1989, 1990
Anglo-Scottish Cup Winners 1977
Full Members' Cup (Simod Cup) Winners 1989
Full Members' Cup (Zenith Data Systems Cup) Winners 1992
Charity Shield Winners 1978

Notts County
Division Two (Tier Two) Champions 1897, 1914, 1923
Division Three (Tier Four) Champions 1998
Division Three (South) Champions 1931, 1950
Division Four (Tier Four) Champions 1971
FA Cup Winners 1894

Oldham Athletic
Division Two (Tier Two) Champions 1991
Division Three (Tier Three) Champions 1974
Division Three (North) Champions 1953

Peterborough United
Division Four (Tier Four) Champions 1961, 1974

CLUB FACTS

After the long years of World War 2, when no league football was played, players and fans couldn't wait to get started again. But both Newport County and Southampton had to wait a bit longer: their first fixtures of the 1946–47 season were postponed due to Somerton Park and The Dell suffering from waterlogged pitches.

Plymouth Argyle

Division Two (Tier Three) Champions 2004
Division Three (Tier Three) Champions 1959
Division Three (Tier Four) Champions 2002
Division Three (South) Champions 1930, 1952

Port Vale

Division Three (North) Champions 1930, 1954
Division Four (Tier Four) Champions 1959
Football League Trophy (Autoglass Trophy) Winners 1993
Football League Trophy (LDV Vans Trophy) Winners 2001

Portsmouth

Football League Champions 1949, 1950
Division One (Tier Two) Champions 2003
Division Three (Tier Three) Champions 1983
Division Three (South) Champions 1924
FA Cup Winners 1939

Preston North End

Football League Champions 1889, 1890
Division Two (Tier Two) Champions 1904, 1913, 1951
Division Two (Tier Three) Champions 2000
Division Three (Tier Three) Champions 1971
Division Three (Tier Four) Champions 1996
FA Cup Winners 1889, 1938

QPR

Division Two (Tier Two) Champions 1983
Division Three (Tier Three) Champions 1967
Division Three (South) Champions 1948
League Cup Winners 1967

Reading

Division Two (Tier Three) Champions 1994
Division Three (Tier Three) Champions 1986
Division Three (South) Champions 1926
Division Four (Tier Four) Champions 1979
The Championship (Tier Two) Champions 2006
Full Members' Cup (Simod Cup) Winners 1988

Rotherham United

Division Three (Tier Three) Champions 1981
Division Three (North) Champions 1951
Division Four (Tier Four) Champions 1989
Football League Trophy (Autowindscreens Shield) Winners 1996

Scunthorpe

Division Three (North) Champions 1958
League One (Tier Three) Champions 2007

Sheffield Utd

Football League Champions 1898
Division Two (Tier Two) Champions 1953
Division Four (Tier Four) Champions 1982
FA Cup Winners 1899, 1902, 1915, 1925

Sheffield Wednesday (The Wednesday until 1929)

Football League Champions 1903, 1904, 1929, 1930
Division Two (Tier Two) Champions 1900, 1926, 1952, 1956, 1959
FA Cup Winners 1896, 1907, 1935
League Cup (Rumbelows Cup) Winners 1991
Charity Shield Winners 1935

Shrewsbury Town

Division Three (Tier Three) Champions 1979
Division Three (Tier Four) Champions 1994

CLUB FACTS

They may have been named the Invincibles thanks to securing the Double in the Football League's first season, but Preston North End were in trophy terms one of the less successful teams in the 20th Century. Relegated to the Second Division in 1901, they were promoted three years later but only one trophy would be secured in the following 96 years – the FA Cup, won in 1938.

Southampton

Division Three (Tier Three) Champions 1960
Division Three (South) Champions 1922
FA Cup Winners 1976

Southend United

Division Four (Tier Four) Champions 1981
League One (Tier Three) Champions 2006

Stockport County

Division Three (North) Champions 1922, 1937
Division Four (Tier Four) Champions 1967

Stoke City

Division Two (Tier Two) Champions 1933, 1963
Division Two (Tier Three) Champions 1993
Division Three (North) Champions 1927
League Cup Winners 1972
Football League Trophy (Autoglass Trophy) Winners 1992
Football League Trophy (Autowindscreens Shield) Winners 2000

Sunderland

Football League Champions 1892, 1893, 1895, 1902, 1913, 1936
Division One (Tier Two) Champions 1996, 1999
Division Two (Tier Two) Champions 1976
Division Three (Tier Three) Champions 1988
The Championship (Tier Two) Champions 2005, 2007
FA Cup Winners 1937, 1973
League Cup Winners
League Cup (Rumbelows Cup) Winners
League Cup (Worthington Cup) Winners
Charity Shield Winners 1936
Swansea City (Swansea Town until 1969)
Division Three (Tier Four) Champions 2000
Division Three (South) Champions 1925, 1949
Football League Trophy (Autoglass Trophy) Winners 1994
Football League Trophy Winners 2006

Swindon Town

Division Two (Tier Three) Champions 1996
Division Four (Tier Four) Champions 1986
League Cup Winners 1969

Tottenham Hotspur

Football League Champions 1951, 1961
Division Two (Tier Two) Champions 1920, 1950
FA Cup Winners 1901, 1921, 1961, 1962, 1967, 1981, 1982, 1991
League Cup Winners 1971, 1973
League Cup (Worthington Cup) Winners 1999
Charity Shield Winners 1921, 1951, 1961, 1962, 1967 (shared with Manchester United), 1981 (shared with Aston Villa), 1991 (shared with Arsenal)

Tranmere Rovers

Division Three (North) Champions 1938
Associate Members' Cup (Leyland DAF Cup) Winners 1990

Walsall

Division Four (Tier Four) Champions 1960
League Two (Tier Four) Champions 2007

Watford

Division Two (Tier Three) Champions 1998
Division Three (Tier Three) Champions 1969
Division Four (Tier Four) Champions 1978

West Bromwich Albion

Football League Champions 1920
Division Two (Tier Two) Champions 1902, 1911
FA Cup Winners 1888, 1892, 1931, 1954, 1968
League Cup Winners 1966
Charity Shield Winners 1920, 1954 (shared with Wolverhampton Wanderers)

West Ham United

Division Two (Tier Two) Champions 1958, 1981
FA Cup Winners 1964, 1975, 1980
Charity Shield Winners 1964 (shared with Liverpool)

WILL'S CIGARETTES

G. ALSOP (WALSALL)

Wigan Athletic
Division Two (Tier Three) Champions 2003
Division Three (Tier Four) Champions 1997
Associate Members' Cup (The Freight Rover
  Trophy) Winners 1985
Football League Trophy (Autowindscreens
  Shield) Winners 1999

Wolverhampton Wanderers
Football League Champions 1954, 1958, 1959
Division Two (Tier Two) Champions 1932, 1977
Division Three (Tier Three) Champions 1989
Division Three (North) Champions 1924
Division Four (Tier Four) Champions 1988
FA Cup Winners 1893, 1908, 1949, 1960
League Cup Winners 1974, 1980
Texaco Cup Winners 1971
Associate Members' Cup (Sherpa Vans Trophy)
  Winners 1988

Charity Shield Winners 1949 (shared with
  Portsmouth), 1954 (shared with West
  Bromwich Albion), 1959, 1960 (shared with
  Burnley)

Wrexham
Division Three (Tier Three) Champions 1978
Football League Trophy (LDV Vans Trophy)
  Winners 2005

Yeovil Town
League Two (Tier Four) Champions 2005

**The following honours were won by
former Football League clubs:**

Bradford Park Avenue
Division Three (North) Champions 1928
Cambridge United
Division Three (Tier Three) Champions 1991
Division Four (Tier Four) Champions 1977

Exeter City
Division Four (Tier Four) Champions 1990

Nelson
Division Three (North) Champions 1923

Newport County
Division Three (South) Champions 1939

Oxford United
Division Two (Tier Two) Champions 1985
Division Three (Tier Three) Champions 1968,
  1984

Rushden & Diamonds
Division Three (Tier Four) Champions 2003

Southport
Division Four (Tier Four) Champions 1973

York City
Division Four (Tier Four) Champions 1984

Appendix II: Scottish Football

Scottish Football League Champions

The highest tier of the Scottish Football League has, at different times, been known as the Premier League, the Premier Division, Division One, or simply the Football League. The following list of champions, arranged chronologically, is divided into sections reflecting these changes in name, though in all instances the lists indicate status as champions of the top tier of Scottish football – i.e., Champions of the Scottish Football League itself!

Scottish Premier League Champions

2007	Celtic
2006	Celtic
2005	Rangers
2004	Celtic
2003	Rangers
2002	Celtic
2001	Celtic
2000	Rangers
1999	Rangers
1998	Celtic
1997	Rangers
1996	Rangers
1995	Rangers
1994	Rangers
1993	Rangers
1992	Rangers
1991	Rangers
1990	Rangers
1989	Rangers
1988	Celtic
1987	Rangers
1986	Celtic
1985	Aberdeen
1984	Aberdeen
1983	Dundee United
1982	Celtic
1981	Celtic
1980	Aberdeen
1979	Celtic
1978	Rangers
1977	Celtic
1976	Rangers

Scottish League Champions

1975	Rangers
1974	Celtic
1973	Celtic
1972	Celtic
1971	Celtic
1970	Celtic
1969	Celtic
1968	Celtic
1967	Celtic
1966	Celtic
1965	Kilmarnock
1964	Rangers

CLUB FACTS

Dumbarton and Rangers share the distinction of being the only two clubs ever to have held a League championship jointly. This bizarre state of affairs happened at the end of the inaugural season of the Scottish Football League, with Dumbarton and Rangers each finishing the season with 29 points from their 18 League games. Dumbarton had a much-superior goal average, but goal average was not the method that had been chosen to decide such matters – instead there would be a play-off.

The problem was, the play-off ended all-square at 2–2, and no-one had thought to devise any further way of differentiating between the two teams. In the end, an agreement was reached to share the title, the only time such a situation has occurred.

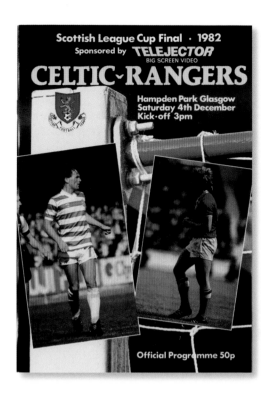

Scottish League Cup Final · 1982
Sponsored by TELEJECTOR
BIG SCREEN VIDEO

CELTIC~RANGERS

Hampden Park Glasgow
Saturday 4th December
Kick·off 3pm

Official Programme 50p

Just one of the numerous occasions on which a Scottish Cup or Scottish League Cup final has turned out to be an 'Old Firm' affair.

Year	Winner
1963	Rangers
1962	Dundee
1961	Rangers
1960	Heart of Midlothian
1959	Rangers
1958	Heart of Midlothian
1957	Rangers
1956	Rangers
1955	Aberdeen
1954	Celtic
1953	Rangers
1952	Hibernian
1951	Hibernian
1950	Rangers
1949	Rangers
1948	Hibernian
1947	Rangers
1946	World War 2
1945	World War 2
1944	World War 2
1943	World War 2
1942	World War 2
1941	World War 2
1940	World War 2
1939	Rangers
1938	Celtic
1937	Rangers
1936	Celtic
1935	Rangers
1934	Rangers
1933	Rangers
1932	Motherwell
1931	Rangers
1930	Rangers
1929	Rangers
1928	Rangers
1927	Rangers
1926	Celtic
1925	Rangers
1924	Rangers
1923	Rangers
1922	Celtic
1921	Rangers
1920	Rangers
1919	Celtic
1918	Rangers
1917	Celtic
1916	Celtic
1915	Celtic
1914	Celtic
1913	Rangers
1912	Rangers
1911	Rangers
1910	Celtic
1909	Celtic
1908	Celtic
1907	Celtic
1906	Celtic
1905	Celtic
1904	Third Lanark
1903	Hibernian
1902	Rangers
1901	Rangers
1900	Rangers
1899	Rangers
1898	Celtic
1897	Heart of Midlothian
1896	Celtic
1895	Heart of Midlothian
1894	Celtic
1893	Celtic
1892	Dumbarton
1891	League Shared – Dumbarton/Rangers

Tier Two Champions

The second tier of the Scottish Football League has, at different times, been known as Division One and (prior to the introduction of the Premiership) Division Two or Division B. The following list of champions, arranged chronologically, is divided into sections reflecting these changes in name, though in all instances the lists indicate status as champions of the second tier of Scottish football.

Scottish Division One (Tier Two) Champions

2007 ....Gretna
2006 ....St Mirren
2005 ....Falkirk
2004 ....Inverness Caledonian Thistle
2003 ....Falkirk
2002.......................................Partick Thistle
2001 ....Livingston
2000 ....St Mirren
1999..Hibernian
1998..Dundee
1997...St Johnstone
1996 ....Dunfermline Athletic
1995 ....Raith Rovers
1994 ....Falkirk
1993 ....Raith Rovers
1992..Dundee
1991 ....Falkirk
1990.......................................St Johnstone
1989 ....Dunfermline Athletic
1988 ....Hamilton Academical

1987 ....Morton
1986 ....Hamilton Academical
1985..Motherwell
1984 ....Morton
1983..St Johnstone
1982...Motherwell
1981...Hibernian
1980 ....Heart of Midlothian
1979...Dundee
1978 ....Morton
1977 ....St Mirren
1976.......................................Partick Thistle

Scottish Division Two (Tier Two) Champions

1975 ....Falkirk
1974...Airdrieonians
1973...Clyde
1972 ....Dumbarton
1971.......................................Partick Thistle
1970 ....Falkirk
1969...Motherwell
1968 ....St Mirren
1967 ....Morton
1966 ....Ayr
1965...Stirling Albion
1964 ....Morton
1963...St Johnstone
1962 ....Clyde
1961...Stirling Albion
1960...St Johnstone
1959...Ayr United
1958...Stirling Albion
1957 ....Clyde

Scottish League Championship Success

Position	Club	Division One	SPL	Total
1	Rangers*	35	16	51
2	Celtic	29	12	41
3=	Aberdeen	1	3	4
3=	Heart of Midlothian	4	–	4
3=	Hibernian	4	–	4
6	Dumbarton*	2	–	2
7=	Dundee	1	–	1
7=	Dundee United	–	1	1
7=	Kilmarnock	1	–	1
7=	Motherwell	1	–	1
7=	Third Lanark	1	–	1

* Dumbarton and Rangers were declared joint Champions in 1891.

Scottish Division B (Tier Two) Champions

1956 ....Queen's Park
1955 ....Airdrieonians
1954 ....Motherwell
1953 ....Stirling Albion
1952 ....Clyde
1951 ....Queen of the South
1950 ....Morton
1949 ....Raith Rovers
1948 ....East Fife
1947 ....Dundee

Scottish Division Two (Tier Two) Champions

1939 ....Cowdenbeath
1938 ....Raith Rovers
1937 ....Ayr United
1936 ....Falkirk
1935 ....Third Lanark
1934 ....Albion Rovers
1933 ....Hibernian
1932 ....East Stirlingshire
1931 ....Third Lanark
1930 ....Leith Athletic
1929 ....Dundee United
1928 ....Ayr United
1927 ....Bo'ness
1926 ....Dunfermline Athletic
1925 ....Dundee United
1924 ....St Johnstone
1923 ....Queen's Park
1922 ....Alloa Athletic

Scottish Division B (Tier Two) Champions

1915 ....Cowdenbeath

Scottish Division Two (Tier Two) Champions

1914 ....Cowdenbeath
1913 ....Ayr United
1912 ....Ayr United
1911 ....Dumbarton
1910 ....Leith Athletic
1909 ....Abercorn
1908 ....Raith Rovers
1907 ....St Bernard's
1906 ....Leith Athletic
1905 ....Clyde
1904 ....Hamilton Academical
1903 ....Airdrieonians

1902 ....Port Glasgow
1901 ....St Bernard's
1900 ....Partick Thistle
1899 ....Kilmarnock
1898 ....Kilmarnock
1897 ....Partick Thistle
1896 ....Abercorn
1895 ....Hibernian
1894 ....Hibernian

Tier Three Champions

The third tier of the Scottish Football League has, at different times, been known as Division Two and (prior to the introduction of the Premiership) Division Three or Division C. The following list of champions, arranged chronologically, is divided into sections reflecting these changes in name, though in all instances the lists indicate status as champions of the second tier of Scottish football.

Scottish Division Two (Tier Three) Champions

2007 ....Morton
2006 ....Gretna
2005 ....Brechin City
2004 ....Airdrie United
2003 ....Raith Rovers
2002 ....Queen of the South
2001 ....Partick Thistle
2000 ....Clyde
1999 ....Livingston
1998 ....Stranraer
1997 ....Ayr United
1996 ....Stirling Albion
1995 ....Morton
1994 ....Stranraer
1993 ....Clyde
1992 ....Dumbarton
1991 ....Stirling Albion
1990 ....Brechin City
1989 ....Albion Rovers
1988 ....Ayr United
1987 ....Meadowbank Thistle
1986 ....Dunfermline Athletic
1985 ....Montrose
1984 ....Forfar Athletic
1983 ....Brechin City
1982 ....Clyde
1981 ....Queen's Park

FF52

FOLLOW, FOLLOW
£1
The RANGERS FANZINE

SIMPLY THE BEST

Proclaimed as 'Simply the Best' by the cover of this fanzine, Rangers are indeed the most successful of the Scottish League clubs by quite some margin.

1980 ....Falkirk
1979 ....Berwick Rangers
1978..Clyde
1977.....................................Stirling Albion
1976...Clydebank

Scottish Division C (Tier Three) Champions

1949 ....Forfar Athletic
1948................................East Stirlingshire
1947.....................................Stirling Albion

Scottish Division Three (Tier Three) Champions

1926 ....Helensburgh
1925 ....Nithsdale Wanderers
1924 ....Arthurlie

Tier Four Champions

Scottish Division Three (Tier Four) Champions

2007 ....Berwick Rangers
2006 ....Cowdenbeath
2005 ....Gretna
2004 ....Stranraer
2003 ....Morton
2002 ....Brechin City
2001 ....Hamilton Academical
2000 ....Queen's Park
1999 ....Ross County
1998...Alloa Athletic
1997 ....Inverness Caledonian Thistle
1996 ....Livingston
1995 ....Forfar Athletic

FA Cup Winners

The following is a list, arranged chronologically, of the Scottish FA Cup Winners for every year since the tournament's inception.

2007..Celtic
2006 ....Heart of Midlothian
2005..Celtic
2004..Celtic
2003..Rangers
2002..Rangers
2001..Celtic
2000..Rangers
1999..Rangers
1998 ....Heart of Midlothian
1997...Kilmarnock
1996..Rangers
1995..Celtic
1994..................................Dundee United
1993..Rangers
1992..Rangers
1991...Motherwell
1990 ....Aberdeen
1989..Celtic
1988..Celtic
1987 ....St Mirren
1986 ....Aberdeen
1985..Celtic
1984 ....Aberdeen
1983 ....Aberdeen
1982 ....Aberdeen
1981..Rangers
1980..Celtic

1979	Rangers	1931	Celtic
1978	Rangers	1930	Rangers
1977	Celtic	1929	Kilmarnock
1976	Rangers	1928	Rangers
1975	Celtic	1927	Celtic
1974	Celtic	1926	St Mirren
1973	Rangers	1925	Celtic
1972	Celtic	1924	Airdrieonians
1971	Celtic	1923	Celtic
1970	Aberdeen	1922	Morton
1969	Celtic	1921	Partick Thistle
1968	Dunfermline Athletic	1920	Kilmarnock
1967	Celtic	1914	Celtic
1966	Rangers	1913	Falkirk
1965	Celtic	1912	Celtic
1964	Rangers	1911	Celtic
1963	Rangers	1910	Dundee
1962	Rangers	1909	No Winner *
1961	Dunfermline Athletic	1908	Celtic
1960	Rangers	1907	Celtic
1959	St Mirren	1906	Heart of Midlothian
1958	Clyde	1905	Third Lanark
1957	Falkirk	1904	Celtic
1956	Heart of Midlothian	1903	Rangers
1955	Clyde	1902	Hibernian
1954	Celtic	1901	Heart of Midlothian
1953	Rangers	1900	Celtic
1952	Motherwell	1899	Celtic
1951	Celtic	1898	Rangers
1950	Rangers	1897	Rangers
1949	Rangers	1896	Heart of Midlothian
1948	Rangers	1895	St Bernards
1947	Aberdeen	1894	Rangers
1939	Clyde	1893	Queen's Park
1938	East Fife	1892	Celtic
1937	Celtic	1891	Heart of Midlothian
1936	Rangers	1890	Queen's Park
1935	Rangers	1889	Third Lanark
1934	Rangers	1888	Renton
1933	Celtic	1887	Hibernian
1932	Rangers	1886	Queen's Park

CLUB FACTS

Raith Rovers hold the record for the most goals scored in any league campaign, finding the back of the net no less than 142 times in just 34 games during the 1937–38 Scottish Division Two season. They lost just two games on their way to finishing 11 points ahead of runners-up Albion Rovers. The English record is held by Peterborough United, who netted 134 times in 46 games on their way to the Division Four title in 1961, their first season as a League club. However, Bradford City and Aston Villa, both of whom have scored 128 goals in a 42-game season, can claim a better average per game.

1885	Renton
1884	Queen's Park
1883	Dumbarton
1882	Queen's Park
1881	Queen's Park
1880	Queen's Park
1879	Vale of Leven
1878	Vale of Leven
1877	Vale of Leven
1876	Queen's Park
1875	Queen's Park
1874	Queen's Park

* In 1909, the cup was withheld following a riot after two drawn matches between Rangers and Celtic.

FA Cup Runners-up

The following is a list, arranged chronologically, of the teams to finish runner-up in the Scottish FA Cup for every year since the tournament's inception.

2007	Dunfermline Athletic
2006	Gretna
2005	Dundee United
2004	Dunfermline Athletic
2003	Dundee
2002	Celtic
2001	Hibernian
2000	Aberdeen
1999	Celtic
1998	Rangers
1997	Falkirk
1996	Heart Of Midlothian
1995	Airdrieonians
1994	Rangers
1993	Aberdeen
1992	Airdrieonians
1991	Dundee United
1990	Celtic
1989	Rangers
1988	Dundee United
1987	Dundee United
1986	Heart Of Midlothian
1985	Dundee United
1984	Celtic
1983	Rangers
1982	Rangers
1981	Dundee United

1980	Rangers
1979	Hibernian
1978	Aberdeen
1977	Rangers
1976	Heart Of Midlothian
1975	Airdrieonians
1974	Dundee United
1973	Celtic
1972	Hibernian
1971	Rangers
1970	Celtic
1969	Rangers
1968	Heart Of Midlothian
1967	Aberdeen
1966	Celtic
1965	Dunfermline Athletic
1964	Dundee
1963	Celtic
1962	St Mirren
1961	Celtic
1960	Kilmarnock
1959	Aberdeen
1958	Hibernian
1957	Kilmarnock
1956	Celtic
1955	Celtic
1954	Aberdeen
1953	Aberdeen
1952	Dundee
1951	Motherwell
1950	East Fife
1949	Clyde
1948	Morton
1947	Hibernian
1946	World War 2
1945	World War 2
1944	World War 2
1943	World War 2

CLUB FACTS

Beith and Broxbourne needed no less than five games to decide their Scottish Cup first round tie in the 1909 competition, the final three replays being scheduled for consecutive days. Beith finally triumphed 4–2 on Friday, then had to play their second round game against St Mirren on the Saturday, their fourth game in as many days. No prizes for guessing that Beith went home disappointed...

Year		Year	
1942	World War 2	1890	Vale Of Leven
1941	World War 2	1889	Celtic
1940	World War 2	1888	Cambuslang
1939	Motherwell	1887	Dumbarton
1938	Kilmarnock	1886	Renton
1937	Aberdeen	1885	Vale Of Leven
1936	Third Lanark	1884	Vale Of Leven
1935	Hamilton Academicals	1883	Vale Of Leven
1934	St Mirren	1882	Dumbarton
1933	Motherwell	1881	Dumbarton
1932	Kilmarnock	1880	Thornliebank
1931	Motherwell	1879	Rangers
1930	Partick Thistle	1878	Third Lanark
1929	Rangers	1877	Rangers
1928	Celtic	1876	Third Lanark
1927	East Fife	1875	Renton
1926	Celtic	1874	Clydesdale
1925	Dundee		
1924	Hibernian		
1923	Hibernian		
1922	Rangers		
1921	Rangers		
1920	Albion Rovers		
1919	World War 1		
1918	World War 1		
1917	World War 1		
1916	World War 1		
1915	World War 1		
1914	Hibernian		
1913	Raith Rovers		
1912	Clyde		
1911	Hamilton Academicals		
1910	Clyde		
1909	Cup withheld		
1908	St Mirren		
1907	Heart Of Midlothian		
1906	Third Lanark		
1905	Rangers		
1904	Rangers		
1903	Heart Of Midlothian		
1902	Celtic		
1901	Celtic		
1900	Queen's Park		
1899	Rangers		
1898	Kilmarnock		
1897	Dumbarton		
1896	Hibernian		
1895	Renton		
1894	Celtic		
1893	Celtic		
1892	Queen's Park		
1891	Dumbarton		

Domestic Honours – Scottish Clubs

The following list, arranged alphabetically, shows domestic honours won by each Scottish club. Clubs with no domestic honours to their name are omitted from the list, and only recognised 'major' or notable honours are included; many clubs may have enjoyed success in other, less well-known competitions which are not recorded here.

Aberdeen

Scottish Premier League Champions 1980, 1984, 1985
Scottish League Champions 1955
Scottish FA Cup Winners 1947, 1970, 1982, 1983, 1984, 1986, 1990
Scottish League Cup Winners 1956, 1977, 1986, 1990, 1996

Airdrie United

Scottish Division Two (Tier Three) Champions 2004

Albion Rovers

Scottish Division B (Tier Two) Champions 1934
Scottish Division Two (Tier Three) Champions 1989

Alloa Athletic

Scottish Division Two (Tier Two) Champions 1922
Scottish Division Three (Tier Four) Champions 1998

Combined Scottish FA Cup and Scottish League Cup Final Success

Two points for winning, one point for being runners-up.
Clubs on the same number of points are ranked in order of the number of wins.

Position	Club	Total	Winners	Runners-Up	Points
1	Rangers	79	56	23	135
2	Celtic	79	48	31	127
3	Aberdeen	27	12	15	39
4	Heart of Midlothian	19	11	8	30
5	Hibernian	20	5	15	25
6	Queen's Park	12	10	2	22
7=	Dundee United	13	3	10	16
7=	Kilmarnock	13	3	10	16
9	Dundee	11	4	7	15
10	Motherwell	9	3	6	12
11	East Fife	6	4	2	10
12=	St Mirren	7	3	4	10
12=	Vale of Leven	7	3	4	10
14	Dunfermline Athletic	8	2	6	10
15	Clyde	6	3	3	9
16	Third Lanark	7	2	5	9
17	Partick Thistle	6	2	4	8
18	Renton	5	2	3	7
19	Dumbarton	6	1	5	7
20	Falkirk	4	2	2	6
21	Airdrieonians	4	1	3	5
22=	Morton	3	1	2	4
22=	Raith Rovers	3	1	2	4
24=	Livingstone	1	1	–	2
24=	St Bernard's	1	1	–	2
26=	Hamilton Academicals	2	–	2	2
26=	St Johnstone	2	–	2	2
28=	Albion Rovers	1	–	1	1
28=	Ayr United	1	–	1	1
28=	Cambuslang	1	–	1	1
28=	Clydesdale	1	–	1	1
28=	Gretna	1	–	1	1
28=	Thornliebank	1	–	1	1

Ayr United
Scottish Division Two (Tier Two) Champions
  1912, 1913, 1928, 1937, 1959, 1966
Scottish Division Two (Tier Three) Champions
  1988, 1997

Berwick Rangers
Scottish Division Two (Tier Three) Champions
  1979
Scottish Division Three (Tier Four) Champions
  2007

Brechin City
Scottish Division Two (Tier Three) Champions
  1983, 1990, 2005
Scottish Division Three (Tier Four) Champions
  2002

Celtic
Scottish Premier League Champions 1977,
  1979, 1981, 1982, 1986, 1988, 1998,
  2001, 2002, 2004, 2006, 2007
Scottish League Champions 1893, 1894,
  1896, 1898, 1905, 1906, 1907, 1908,
  1909, 1910, 1914, 1915, 1916, 1917,
  1919, 1922, 1926, 1936, 1938, 1954,
  1966, 1967, 1968, 1969, 1970, 1971,
  1972, 1973, 1974
Scottish FA Cup Winners 1892, 1899, 1900,
  1904, 1907, 1908, 1911, 1912, 1914,
  1923, 1925, 1927, 1931, 1933, 1937,
  1951, 1954, 1965, 1967, 1969, 1971,
  1972, 1974, 1975, 1977, 1980, 1985,
  1988, 1989, 1995, 2001, 2004, 2005,
  2007
Scottish League Cup Winners 1957, 1958,
  1966, 1967, 1968, 1969, 1970, 1975,
  1983, 1998, 2000, 2001, 2006

Clyde
Scottish Division Two (Tier Two) Champions
  1905, 1957, 1962, 1973
Scottish Division B (Tier Two) Champions 1952
Scottish Division Two (Tier Three) Champions
  1978, 1982, 1993, 2000
Scottish FA Cup Winners 1939, 1955, 1958

Cowdenbeath
Scottish Division Two (Tier Two) Champions
  1914, 1939
Scottish Division B (Tier Two) Champions 1915

Scottish Division Three (Tier Four) Champions
  2006

Dumbarton
Scottish League Champions 1891 (jointly with
  Rangers), 1892
Scottish Division Two (Tier Two) Champions
  1911, 1972
Scottish Division Two (Tier Three) Champions
  1992
Scottish FA Cup Winners 1883

Dundee
Scottish League Champions 1962
Scottish Division One (Tier Two) Champions
  1979, 1992, 1998
Scottish Division B (Tier Two) Champions 1947
Scottish FA Cup Winners 1910
Scottish League Cup Winners 1952, 1953,
  1974

Dundee United
Scottish Premier League Champions 1983
Scottish Division Two (Tier Two) Champions
  1925, 1929
Scottish FA Cup Winners 1994
Scottish League Cup Winners 1980, 1981

Dunfermline
Scottish Division One (Tier Two) Champions
  1989, 1996
Scottish Division Two (Tier Two) Champions
  1926
Scottish Division Two (Tier Three) Champions
  1986
Scottish FA Cup Winners 1961, 1968

East Fife
Scottish Division B (Tier Two) Champions 1948
Scottish FA Cup Winners 1938
Scottish League Cup Winners 1948, 1950,
  1954

East Stirlingshire
Scottish Division Two (Tier Two) Champions
  1932
Scottish Division C (Tier Three) Champions
  1948

Falkirk
Scottish Division One (Tier Two) Champions
  1991, 1994, 2003, 2005

Scottish Division Two (Tier Two) Champions
1936, 1970, 1975
Scottish Division Two (Tier Three) Champions
1980
Scottish FA Cup Winners 1913, 1957

Forfar Athletic

Scottish Division Two (Tier Three) Champions
1984
Scottish Division C (Tier Three) Champions
1949
Scottish Division Three (Tier Four) Champions
1995

Gretna

Scottish Division One (Tier Two) Champions
2007
Scottish Division Two (Tier Three) Champions
2006
Scottish Division Three (Tier Four) Champions
2005

Hamilton Academicals

Scottish Division One (Tier Two) Champions
1986, 1988
Scottish Division Two (Tier Two) Champions
1904
Scottish Division Three (Tier Four) Champions
2001

Heart of Midlothian

Scottish League Champions 1895, 1897,
1958, 1960
Scottish Division One (Tier Two) Champions
1980
Scottish FA Cup Winners 1891, 1896, 1901,
1906, 1956, 1998, 2006
Scottish League Cup Winners 1955, 1959,
1960, 1963

Hibernian

Scottish League Champions 1903, 1948,
1951, 1952
Scottish Division One (Tier Two) Champions
1981, 1999
Scottish Division Two (Tier Two) Champions
1894, 1895, 1933
Scottish FA Cup Winners 1887, 1902
Scottish League Cup Winners 1973, 1992,
2007

Inverness Caledonian Thistle

Scottish Division One (Tier Two) Champions
2004
Scottish Division Three (Tier Four) Champions
1997

Kilmarnock

Scottish League Champions 1965
Scottish Division Two (Tier Two) Champions
1898, 1899
Scottish FA Cup Winners 1920, 1929, 1997

Livingston

Scottish Division One (Tier Two) Champions
2001
Scottish Division Two (Tier Three) Champions
1999
Scottish Division Three (Tier Four) Champions
1996
Scottish League Cup Winners 2004

Montrose

Scottish Division Two (Tier Three) Champions
1985

Morton

Scottish Division One (Tier Two) Champions
1978, 1984, 1987
Scottish Division Two (Tier Two) Champions
1964, 1967
Scottish Division B (Tier Two) Champions
1950
Scottish Division Two (Tier Three) Champions
1995, 2007
Scottish Division Three (Tier Four) Champions
2003
Scottish FA Cup Winners 1922

Motherwell

Scottish League Champions 1932
Scottish Division One (Tier Two) Champions
1982, 1985
Scottish Division Two (Tier Two) Champions
1969
Scottish Division B (Tier Two) Champions
1954
Scottish FA Cup Winners 1952, 1991
Scottish League Cup Winners 1951

Partick Thistle

Scottish Division One (Tier Two) Champions
1976, 2002

Scottish Division Two (Tier Two) Champions
1897, 1900, 1971
Scottish Division Two (Tier Three) Champions
2001
Scottish FA Cup Winners 1921
Scottish League Cup Winners 1972

Queen of the South

Scottish Division B (Tier Two) Champions
1951
Scottish Division Two (Tier Three) Champions
2002

Queens Park

Scottish Division Two (Tier Two) Champions
1923
Scottish Division B (Tier Two) Champions
1956
Scottish Division Two (Tier Three) Champions
1981
Scottish Division C (Tier Three) Champions
2000
Scottish FA Cup Winners 1874, 1875, 1876,
1880, 1881, 1882, 1884, 1886, 1890,
1893

Raith Rovers

Scottish Division One (Tier Two) Champions
1993, 1995
Scottish Division Two (Tier Two) Champions
1908, 1938
Scottish Division B (Tier Two) Champions
1949
Scottish Division Two (Tier Three) Champions
2003
Scottish League Cup Winners 1995

Rangers

Scottish Premier League Champions 1976,
1978, 1987, 1989, 1990, 1991, 1992,
1993, 1994, 1995, 1996, 1997, 1999,
2000, 2003, 2005
Scottish League Champions 1891 (jointly with
Dumbarton), 1899, 1900, 1901, 1902,
1911, 1912, 1913, 1918, 1920, 1921,
1923, 1924, 1925, 1927, 1928, 1929,
1930, 1931, 1933, 1934, 1935, 1937,
1939, 1947, 1949, 1950, 1953, 1956,
1957, 1959, 1961, 1963, 1964, 1975
Scottish FA Cup Winners 1894, 1897, 1898,
1903, 1928, 1930, 1932, 1934, 1935,
1936, 1948, 1949, 1950, 1953, 1960,

1962, 1963, 1964, 1966, 1973, 1976,
1978, 1979, 1981, 1992, 1993, 1996,
1999, 2000, 2002, 2003
Scottish League Cup Winners 1947, 1949,
1961, 1962, 1964, 1965, 1971, 1976,
1978, 1979, 1982, 1984, 1985, 1987,
1988, 1989, 1991, 1993, 1994, 1997,
1999, 2002, 2003, 2005

Ross County

Scottish Division Three (Tier Four) Champions
1999

St Johnstone

Scottish Division One (Tier Two) Champions
1983, 1990, 1997
Scottish Division Two (Tier Two) Champions
1924, 1960, 1963

St Mirren

Scottish Division One (Tier Two) Champions
1977, 2000, 2006
Scottish Division Two (Tier Two) Champions
1968
Scottish FA Cup Winners 1926, 1959, 1987

Stirling Albion

Scottish Division Two (Tier Two) Champions
1958, 1961, 1965
Scottish Division B (Tier Two) Champions
1953
Scottish Division Two (Tier Three) Champions
1977, 1991, 1996
Scottish Division Three (Tier Three) Champions
Scottish Division C (Tier Three) Champions
1947
Scottish Division Three (Tier Four) Champions

Stranraer

Scottish Division Two (Tier Three) Champions
1994, 1998
Scottish Division Three (Tier Four) Champions
2004

**The following honours were won by former
Scottish Football League clubs:**

Abercorn

Scottish Division Two (Tier Two) Champions
1896, 1909

Airdrieonians

Scottish Division Two (Tier Two) Champions
1903, 1974
Scottish Division B (Tier Two) Champions 1955
Scottish FA Cup Winners 1924

Arthurlie

Scottish Division Three (Tier Three) Champions
1924

Bo'Ness

Scottish Division Two (Tier Two) Champions
1927

Clydebank

Scottish Division Two (Tier Three) Champions
1976

Helensburgh

Scottish Division Three (Tier Three) Champions
1926

Leith Athletic

Scottish Division Two (Tier Two) Champions
1906, 1910, 1930
Scottish Division B (Tier Two) Champions
1955
Scottish FA Cup Winners 1924

Meadowbank Thistle

Scottish Division Two (Tier Three) Champions
1987

Nithsdale Wanderers

Scottish Division Three (Tier Three) Champions
1925

Port Glasgow

Scottish Division Two (Tier Two) Champions
1902

Renton

Scottish FA Cup Winners 1885, 1888

St Bernard's

Scottish Division Two (Tier Two) Champions
1901, 1907
Scottish FA Cup 1895

Third Lanark

Scottish League Champions 1904
Scottish Division Two (Tier Two) Champions
1931, 1935
Scottish FA Cup Winners 1889, 1905

Vale of Leven

Scottish FA Cup Winners 1877, 1878, 1879

CLUB FACTS

Third Lanark are the only Scottish title
winners to have gone out of business.
Champions in 1903–04, they folded
in 1967.

Appendix III: European Competition

European Cup Winners

The following list, arranged chronologically, records the winners of the European Cup (now the Champions League) since the competition's inception. Clubs from the English or Scottish Leagues to have triumphed are indicated in bold.

Champions League

2007	AC Milan
2006	FC Barcelona
2005	**Liverpool**
2004	FC Porto
2003	AC Milan
2002	Real Madrid
2001	Bayern Munich
2000	Real Madrid
1999	**Manchester United**
1998	Real Madrid
1997	B Dortmund
1996	Juventus
1995	Ajax
1994	AC Milan
1993	Marseilles
1992	Barcelona

European Cup

1991	RS Belgrade
1990	AC Milan
1989	AC Milan
1988	PSV Eindhoven
1987	FC Porto
1986	Steaua Bucharest
1985	Juventus
1984	**Liverpool**
1983	SV Hamburg
1982	**Aston Villa**
1981	**Liverpool**
1980	**Nottingham Forest**
1979	**Nottingham Forest**
1978	**Liverpool**
1977	**Liverpool**

1976	Bayern Munich
1975	Bayern Munich
1974	Bayern Munich
1973	Ajax
1972	Ajax
1971	Ajax
1970	Feyenoord
1969	AC Milan
1968	**Manchester United**
1967	**Celtic**
1966	Real Madrid
1965	Inter Milan
1964	Inter Milan
1963	AC Milan
1962	Benfica
1961	Benfica
1960	Real Madrid
1959	Real Madrid
1958	Real Madrid
1957	Real Madrid
1956	Real Madrid

CLUB FACTS

Nottingham Forest are the only team to have won the European Cup more times than their own domestic league.

UEFA Cup Winners

The following list, arranged chronologically, records the winners of the UEFA Cup (formerly known as the Fairs Cup) since the competition's inception. Clubs from the English or Scottish Leagues to have triumphed are indicated in bold.

UEFA Cup

2007	FC Sevilla
2006	FC Sevilla
2005	CSKA Moscow
2004	Valencia CF
2003	FC Porto

Year	Winner
2002	Feyenoord
2001	**Liverpool**
2000	Galatasaray
1999	Parma
1998	Inter Milan
1997	Schalke
1996	Bayern Munich
1995	Parma
1994	Inter Milan
1993	Juventus
1992	Ajax
1991	Inter Milan
1990	Juventus
1989	Napoli
1988	B Leverkusen
1987	IFK Gothenberg
1986	Real Madrid
1985	Real Madrid
1984	**Tottenham Hotspur**
1983	Anderlecht
1982	IFK Gothenberg
1981	**Ipswich Town**
1980	Eintracht Frankfurt
1979	B Monchengladbach
1978	PSV Eindoven
1977	Juventus
1976	**Liverpool**
1975	B Monchengladbach
1974	Feyenoord
1973	**Liverpool**
1972	**Tottenham**

(Inter Cities) Fairs Cup

Year	Winner
1971	**Leeds United**
1970	**Arsenal**
1969	**Newcastle United**
1968	**Leeds United**
1967	Dynamo Zagreb
1966	Barcelona
1965	Ferencvaros
1964	Real Zaragoza
1963	Valencia CF
1962	Valencia CF
1961	AS Roma
1960	Barcelona
1959	Barcelona

Ruud Gullit, who won the European Cup with AC Milan in both 1989 and 1990. Gullit would later manage, amongst others, Newcastle and Chelsea.

European Cup Winners' Cup Winners

The following list, arranged chronologically, records the winners of the European Cup Winners' Cup from the competition's inception until its discontinuation in 1999. Clubs from the English or Scottish Leagues to have triumphed are indicated in bold.

UEFA Cup Winners' Cup

1999	Lazio
1998	**Chelsea**
1997	Barcelona
1996	Paris St.Germain
1995	Real Zaragoza

European Cup Winners' Cup

1994	**Arsenal**
1993	Parma
1992	Werder Bremen
1991	**Manchester United**
1990	Sampdoria
1989	Barcelona
1988	KV Mechelen
1987	Ajax
1986	Dynamo Kiev
1985	**Everton**
1984	Juventus
1983	**Aberdeen**
1982	Barcelona
1981	Dynamo Tbilisi
1980	Valencia
1979	Barcelona
1978	Anderlecht
1977	SV Hamburg
1976	Anderlecht
1975	Dynamo Kiev
1974	FC Magdeburg
1973	AC Milan
1972	**Rangers**
1971	**Chelsea**
1970	**Manchester City**
1969	Slovan Bratislava
1968	AC Milan
1967	Bayern Munich
1966	B Dortmund
1965	**West Ham United**
1964	Sporting Lisbon
1963	**Tottenham Hotspur**
1962	Athletico Madrid
1961	Fiorentina

European Super Cup Winners

The European Super Cup has, for most of its history, been contested annually by the Winners of the European Cup and the European Cup Winner's Cup, lately with the winners of the UEFA Cup replacing the latter. The following list, arranged chronologically, records the winners of the European Super Cup since the competition's inception. Clubs from the English or Scottish Leagues to have triumphed are indicated in bold.

2006	FC Sevilla
2005	**Liverpool**
2004	Valencia CF
2003	AC Milan
2002	Real Madrid
2001	**Liverpool**
2000	Galatasaray
1999	Lazio
1998	**Chelsea**
1997	Barcelona
1996	Juventus
1995	Ajax
1994	AC Milan
1993	Parma
1992	Barcelona
1991	**Manchester United**
1990	AC Milan
1989	AC Milan
1988	KV Mechelen
1987	FC Porto
1986	Steaua Bucharest
1985	Not Contested
1984	Juventus
1983	**Aberdeen**
1982	**Aston Villa**
1981	Not Contested
1980	Valencia
1979	**Notts Forest**
1978	RSC Anderlecht
1977	**Liverpool**
1976	RSC Anderlecht
1975	Dynamo Kiev
1974	Not Contested
1973	Ajax
1972	Ajax

Website List

Useful sites for any football fan with an enquiring mind or a passion for trivia.

www.historicalkits.co.uk

To quote the site, 'This site will be the most comprehensive archive of kits worn by English and Scottish clubs available anywhere.' It's exactly that, with constant updates where there are gaps and a welcoming encouragement for visitors to contribute.

www.footballcrests.com

A unique website that looks at the meaning and history of logos, badges and crests of soccer clubs around the world. The number of clubs is growing, so this one is always worth returning to. The thorny problem for this site is gaining permission from the clubs to display their particular crest.

www.bl.uk/collections/football.html

Shows the select catalogue of British football periodicals held by the British Library Newspaper Library in London.

www.footballgroundguide.co.uk

Comprehensive guide to all 92 League club grounds. Includes location, ground plans, prices, photographs, links to official sites and a whole lot more.

www.givemefootball.com

Official site of the Professional Footballers' Association carrying stacks of information on the player's union including the aims, values and purpose of the PFA plus historical features.

www.nationalfootballmuseum.com

Useful for those considering a visit to the museum located at Preston's Deepdale ground. Includes virtual tour and directions on how to get there.

www.scottishfootballmuseum.org.uk

Indicates what can be found at the Hampden Park museum.

CLUB FACTS

The first British representatives in Europe were Hibernian, who reached the semi-final of the 1955–56 European Cup. They made the cut despite finishing only fifth in their domestic league the previous season. They played their away leg of their tie with Sweden's Djurgardens at Partick's Firhill ground as snow prevented a Scandinavian trip.

www.fchd.btinternet.co.uk/fchd.info

The Football Club History Database offers a statistical breakdown of all football clubs in England and Wales. There is a year-by-year coverage of league performances and major cup results.

www.supporters-direct.org

The government-backed Supporters Direct was set up to assist supporters in the act of seeking ownership of their club. This tells how to do it.

http://www.footballderbies.com

Covers the whole world's derby matches, from Turkey to East Anglia and all points in between.